SharePoint® 2016

for dummies®
A Wiley Brand

by Rosemarie Withee
and Ken Withee

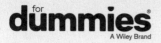

SharePoint® 2016 For Dummies®

Published by: **John Wiley & Sons, Inc.,** 111 River Street, Hoboken, NJ 07030-5774, www.wiley.com

Copyright © 2016 by John Wiley & Sons, Inc., Hoboken, New Jersey

Media and software compilation copyright © 2016 by John Wiley & Sons, Inc. All rights reserved.

Published simultaneously in Canada

For general information on our other products and services, please contact our Customer Care Department within the U.S. at 877-762-2974, outside the U.S. at 317-572-3993, or fax 317-572-4002. For technical support, please visit https://hub.wiley.com/community/support/dummies.

Wiley publishes in a variety of print and electronic formats and by print-on-demand. Some material included with standard print versions of this book may not be included in e-books or in print-on-demand. If this book refers to media such as a CD or DVD that is not included in the version you purchased, you may download this material at http://booksupport.wiley.com. For more information about Wiley products, visit www.wiley.com.

Library of Congress Control Number: 2016943715

ISBN 978-1-119-18170-5 (pbk); ISBN 978-1-119-18173-6 (ebk); ISBN 978-1-119-18172-9 (ebk)

Manufactured in the United States of America

10 9 8 7 6 5 4 3 2 1

Contents at a Glance

Table of Contents

Introduction

A centralized web portal has become a necessity in organizations both small and large. An integrated portal provides efficiencies and advantages not seen since the adoption of computers and networks. The value of getting everyone in the organization on the same page and working in unison is instrumental to success. Modern organizations have had to adapt, and the people within them have had to adapt as well. As technology giants fought to get their web portal products to market, one platform has emerged a clear winner: Microsoft SharePoint.

We wish we could say that we foresaw the success of SharePoint back when we first started working with it as consultants. The fact is that when we were new consultants, we simply worked on whatever projects were selling. Nearly a decade ago, Ken stumbled into a small SharePoint project, pulled Rosemarie into SharePoint, and we still haven't emerged from the SharePoint world.

SharePoint 2016 is the latest version of the product and has more fanfare attached to it than any previous version. Microsoft products tend to get better over time. (Some of our friends won't buy a Microsoft product until it's the third version or later.) SharePoint 2016 won't disappoint; it's a very mature and polished product.

TIP

The release of SharePoint 2016 ushers in the evolved strategy for SharePoint Online. No longer do you need to wait a couple of years to use the latest version of SharePoint in the Microsoft cloud. SharePoint Online uses SharePoint 2016, and everything you read about in this book directly relates to SharePoint Online. In fact, if you use SharePoint Online, then you will likely have already used some of the new features of SharePoint 2016. Microsoft now rolls out features to SharePoint Online as they are ready and then packages all of those features into a grand release for those who want to install SharePoint themselves. The latest release being SharePoint 2016.

If you're already familiar with SharePoint, then this latest version of the product will be familiar, and many of the annoying and painful bugs and interfaces of previous versions have finally been worked out. You no longer need a highly paid consultant to walk you through each aspect of every feature. In a nutshell, things are finally starting to get intuitive. (Although, if you need a consultant, we can recommend some good ones.)

Whether you need to create a new website for your team, a new app to store content, or a page to approve and publish critical information, SharePoint 2016 has a solution. SharePoint 2016 is intended to be a self-service environment, and this book helps you get the most out of the platform.

We're not saying that SharePoint is always easy; in fact, like any enterprise software system, you can expect some frustration. However, if your organization uses SharePoint 2016 or SharePoint Online, you have a wealth of solutions to solve your particular needs.

About This Book

This book is intended for anyone who encounters SharePoint or is curious about using the product. SharePoint is a vast product with many nooks and crannies, and no single book can cover all the pieces. This book is designed to provide an introduction and overview of the platform. It shows you how to get the most out of the product, whether you have never used it before or are deeply familiar with specific aspects it.

Others who may benefit from this book include

>> **Developers:** This isn't a development book, but the best SharePoint developers are those who understand the product. The exciting aspect of SharePoint development is that you don't need to write programming code to develop business solutions in SharePoint. If you can work with a web browser to develop a web presence in a site like Facebook or LinkedIn, then you can develop and administer your own SharePoint site.

>> **IT professionals:** This isn't a book that explains how to set up a SharePoint server farm. However, this book helps you understand what features your end users may want to see in a SharePoint farm that you architect or support.

>> **Managers:** If you manage a department or business unit, you need to understand how to get the most out of SharePoint. If your company has made significant investments in SharePoint deployment, it'd be a shame if you didn't know how to leverage that investment.

Foolish Assumptions

Because SharePoint is such a huge topic, we have to make some assumptions about your configuration and starting knowledge, such as

» **You have access to some version of SharePoint 2016.** If you don't have access to SharePoint, then sign up for SharePoint Online. After the free trial period, it costs as little as $5 a month. If you want to see all the specific things that come with the On-Premises version of the product, then there is a trial license available for 30 days. Just download it from the Microsoft download center and get started.

» **You're a contributor or administrator.** Of course, many of the scenarios in this book require only that you be a contributor. So long as you know who your administrator is, you can ask that person for elevated permissions. And if you want to be master of your own SharePoint universe as an administrator, you can sign up for SharePoint Online and control all aspects of your SharePoint environment in a fairly intuitive interface.

» **Ideally, you have a sandbox or test environment where you can try different scenarios.** It isn't the best strategy to lock down security on your Human Resources site only to find out nobody in your entire organization can get to their pay stub. You need a test environment or test site where you can play around with SharePoint, and then take that knowledge to your department site. Luckily, if you have access to SharePoint, you have your own personal My Site that you can explore. Another alternative is to use SharePoint Online (yes, you can buy a single license).

» **Many of the scenarios in this book assume your implementation includes My Site.** Unfortunately, many companies try to avoid using this feature. In SharePoint 2016, My Site is an integral component for many features. We strongly advise utilizing My Site for everyone in your organization.

Icons Used in This Book

You find a handful of icons in this book, and here's what they mean:

Tips point out a handy shortcut, or they help you understand something important to SharePoint.

REMEMBER

This icon marks something to remember, such as how you handle a particularly tricky part of SharePoint configuration.

TECHNICAL STUFF

This icon is our chance to share with you details about the inner workings of SharePoint. Most of the information you find here pertains to some aspect of SharePoint that requires configuration at the server. That means you can point out the stuff beside this icon to IT and ask IT to make SharePoint do that.

WARNING

Although the Warning icon appears rarely, when you need to be wary of a problem or common pitfall, this icon lets you know.

Beyond the Book

In addition to what you're reading right now, this product also comes with a free access-anywhere Cheat Sheet that describes some common SharePoint site templates, apps, and Web Parts, among other things. To get this Cheat Sheet, simply go to `www.dummies.com` and enter **SharePoint 2016 For Dummies Cheat Sheet** in the Search box.

Where to Go from Here

All right, you're all set and ready to jump into this book. You can jump in anywhere you like — the book was written to allow you to do just that. But if you want to get the full story from the beginning, jump to Chapter 1 — that's where all the action starts. (If you are already familiar with SharePoint, you might want to flip ahead to Chapter 2, where you can get your hands dirty with creating a site and developing it to fit your needs.)

1

Getting Started with SharePoint 2016

Get familiar with SharePoint as a product and platform. SharePoint is a complicated beast, and most people use only a smidgen of its functionality.

Dive into a quick intro into what makes up the SharePoint Online product and get a handle on the buzzwords around SharePoint.

Figure out what it means to develop a SharePoint site and how SharePoint works at a fundamental level.

Get your head around the vastness of SharePoint by exploring some of its functionality at a high level.

Chapter 1

Getting to Know SharePoint 2016

When we first heard about SharePoint, we just didn't get it. What the heck was this new thing called SharePoint? We knew it was a Microsoft product that was supposed to do lots of things, but we just couldn't figure out exactly what it was or how to get started working with it.

Well, after years of working with SharePoint, we have finally figured a few things out. SharePoint is indeed a Microsoft product and it is definitely capable of doing lots of things. In fact, SharePoint can do more things than you could ever imagine. And therein lies the problem. If you ask ten people what SharePoint does, you're very likely to get ten different answers. SharePoint has such a depth to it that it's hard to get your head around it.

In this chapter, we help you see the SharePoint big picture. You discover how SharePoint works and gain understanding on exactly what the term *SharePoint* means. This chapter peels away the mystery and shows you SharePoint at a basic level. After all, you need to understand SharePoint at a basic level before you can dive into its advanced functionality.

Wrapping Your Head around SharePoint

At a basic level, SharePoint is a *web-based software platform*, meaning that Share-Point is software designed for you to interact with using a web browser.

TIP

In past versions of SharePoint, you really needed to use Microsoft's web browser to work with SharePoint. Times have changed though, and you can now use most any web browser to work with SharePoint.

No, really, what is SharePoint?

Maybe you're a whiz at Word or a spreadsheet jockey with Excel. Going forward, you're going to have to be just as good at SharePoint to get the most out of your desktop Office client applications. Microsoft continues to integrate functionality that used to be locked up in client applications, or not available at all, with Share-Point. For example, using SharePoint 2016 with Office 2016, you can create an online gallery of PowerPoint slides, display interactive spreadsheets in web pages, or reuse information from your company's databases in Word documents. You can even use Visio 2016 to automate your business processes using SharePoint.

Officially, Microsoft represents SharePoint 2016 as a "business collaboration plat-form for the enterprise and web." *SharePoint* is a platform from Microsoft that allows businesses to meet their diverse needs in the following domains:

>> **Collaboration:** Use SharePoint's collaboration sites for activities, such as managing projects or coordinating a request for proposal.

>> **Social networking:** If you work in a large company, you can use SharePoint as a social network for the Enterprise experience to help you track coworkers and locate people in expertise networks.

>> **Information portals and internal websites:** With SharePoint's web content management features, you can create useful self-service internal portals and intranets.

>> **Enterprise content management:** SharePoint offers excellent document- and record-management capabilities, including extensive support for metadata and customized search experiences.

>> **Business intelligence:** SharePoint is an ideal platform for providing entrée into your organization's business analysis assets. You can use insightful dashboards that allow users to get the big picture at a glance and then drill down to get more detail.

>> **Business applications:** Use SharePoint to host sophisticated business applications, integrate business processes' backend databases and your SharePoint content, or simply use SharePoint as the means to present access to your applications.

The functionality we discuss in the preceding list is delivered by an On-Premises version of the product and an online cloud service:

>> **SharePoint Server 2016** is a set of applications that deliver all the functionality mentioned in the previous bulleted list. When SharePoint is installed locally and managed by your IT department, then you're using SharePoint in what is known as an on-premises environment because it is hosted on your local premises.

>> **SharePoint Online** is a cloud-based service offered by Microsoft that allows you to create much the same SharePoint experience as you can with SharePoint installed on a local server, but you don't have to install and maintain it. It can come bundled with an Office 365 monthly subscription, giving you access to hosted email, calendaring, and conferencing with Exchange and Skype for Business, or you can buy a SharePoint Online monthly subscription on its own.

TIP

SharePoint Server 2016 has been designed to work with SharePoint Online. Some organizations prefer to keep sensitive content under their own control but still leverage the ease of use and other benefits of SharePoint Online. For this reason, Microsoft designed SharePoint Server 2016 to integrate with SharePoint Online. This scenario is called a *hybrid environment* because part of SharePoint is on your local premises and part is hosted up in the Microsoft cloud.

You can approach SharePoint with the following model in mind:

>> **Product:** SharePoint is a product with a lot of features. Explore how SharePoint works without any customization when you're deciding how to approach a solution, and then decide if you want to customize it for your specific needs.

>> **Platform:** SharePoint provides everything you need to deliver a robust business solution. It provides the infrastructure (the "plumbing") required to deliver web-based solutions.

>> **Toolkit:** Finally, SharePoint is a set of components and controls that you can mix and match to provide a solution. You can create sites, pages, and apps, all without leaving the comfort of your web browser.

A Microsoft product

SharePoint is a software product that Microsoft develops and sells to customers. As you see in Chapter 2, SharePoint can be purchased in a couple of different ways. Regardless of how you purchase and use SharePoint, you can be rest assured that your organization is paying Microsoft a licensing fee. In other words, SharePoint isn't free.

In the past, SharePoint had a very large cost for an organization wishing to adopt it. In addition to buying all of the licenses for your organization, you also need an IT team to install and manage SharePoint. For this reason, SharePoint used to be considered enterprise-class software because only large organizations could afford it. This is all changing though, and Microsoft now offers SharePoint Online for as little as $5 per user per month.

TIP

Microsoft also offers SharePoint Online as a bundle of other products. The branding for the bundle of products is called Office 365. To find out more about Office 365, check out *Office 365 For Dummies* 2nd Edition by Rosemarie Withee (Wiley).

Many different SharePoint definitions

SharePoint has many different types of users, and depending on where your role fits in, you might have a very different experience from a fellow SharePoint user. For example, you might be assigned to create and administer a SharePoint website for your team. In this case, you might see first-hand the vast functionality of SharePoint websites. On the other hand, you might be a user of a SharePoint site. In this case, your SharePoint world might be only the site that someone has already created for you. To confuse matters even further, many organizations will roll out SharePoint and give it a spiffy internal name; for example, "Connect." So even though the cool new web tool called Connect is actually SharePoint, most users don't even realize it!

On the more technical side, if you're an infrastructure administrator, you see SharePoint as a platform capable of offloading the difficult job of website administration. If you're a software developer, you see SharePoint as a web platform for developing programs for users.

The vastness of SharePoint creates areas of specialization. The result is that a person's view of SharePoint is greatly affected by how that person uses the product. It's important to keep this in mind when talking with people about SharePoint. If you ask ten people to define SharePoint, you're likely to get ten different answers, as illustrated in Figure 1-1.

FIGURE 1-1:
There are many different ways to define SharePoint.

TIP

SharePoint has many different administration levels, and each requires a different level of technical ability. For example, if you're comfortable working with software like Microsoft Word and Excel, then you won't have any problem administering a SharePoint site. At a deeper level, there are also SharePoint infrastructure administrators. To administer SharePoint at the infrastructure level is a role that falls squarely into the realm of the IT geeks.

SharePoint is a platform, so the user roles an organization defines depend on the organization itself. Here are some examples of the possible roles of users in SharePoint:

>> **Anonymous visitor:** A person that browses to a website that just happens to be using the SharePoint platform. An anonymous visitor just sees SharePoint as a website and nothing else.

>> **SharePoint visitor:** A person that browses to the site and authenticates so that SharePoint knows who they are. The visitor might still just see a SharePoint site as any other website, except he notices his name in the top-right corner of the screen and knows he must log in to reach the site. Visitors might not use any of the features of SharePoint, however, and just browse the information posted to the website.

>> **SharePoint casual user:** A person that knows all the company documents are posted to SharePoint and knows she can upload her own documents to

her personal SharePoint site. A casual user might realize that she is using SharePoint, or she might just think of the platform as the name the organization has given to SharePoint. For example, I have seen organizations give their web platform tool names such as Source or Smart or Knowledge Center. SharePoint is the name of the web platform product from Microsoft, which is often unknown by users of a tool built on the SharePoint platform.

» **SharePoint user:** A person that is familiar with SharePoint and its main features. A SharePoint user often performs various administrator functions even if he doesn't realize it. For example, he might be responsible for an app that stores all the company policies and procedures. He is thus an app administrator. A user might also be responsible for a site for a small team, in which case he is a site administrator. As you can see, a user can play many different roles.

» **SharePoint power user:** A power user is not only familiar with the main SharePoint features and functionality but also dives deeper. A power user might be familiar with the functionality differences of different features, routing documents using workflows, and building site hierarchies. A power user might also be a site collection administrator and thus is responsible for a collection of sites.

» **SharePoint technical administrator:** A technical administrator is someone from the IT department who is responsible for SharePoint. A technical administrator is less concerned with using SharePoint for business and more concerned about making sure the platform is available and responsive. An administrator might play many different roles. For example, farm administrators are responsible for all the servers that make up SharePoint, such as web front end servers, applications servers, and database servers. Specialized database administrators focus just on the database components. There are even administrative roles for specific services, such as the search service or user profile service. Depending on the size of the SharePoint implementation, these technical administrator roles might be filled by a single overworked individual or a team with highly specialized skills.

More than a website

SharePoint is called a *web platform*, as opposed to just a website, because of the sheer amount of functionality and capabilities it includes. In fact, if you already administer a SharePoint website, you can easily create a new website right within the existing website. You can also develop websites with an extraordinary amount of functionality without writing a single line of code. The result is a platform for websites instead of just a single website. The multitude of features and the complexity of the product are what lead to confusion.

TIP

The terms *SharePoint website* and *SharePoint site* can be used interchangeably. Both terms mean a website that is powered by SharePoint. Because this book is all about SharePoint, we sometimes abbreviate these terms to just *site*.

One thing that makes SharePoint so special is that you don't need to be a computer genius or even a power user to be a website developer and administrator in SharePoint. You just need to be comfortable using a computer.

TIP

The terms *website* and *web application* are often used interchangeably. In the deep, dark technical world of SharePoint administration, the term *web application* has a very specific meaning. A web application is a technical construct, and each web application has its own databases associated with it. If you create two SharePoint web applications, they store their content and configuration information in different databases. As with technology these days, a simple word can have different meanings, depending on the context of the conversation.

Getting Familiar with SharePoint Building Blocks

In order to obtain a perspective on SharePoint, it is important to understand how SharePoint is put together. As mentioned previously, SharePoint is a web-based platform. A number of technologies are required in order to make the platform available. Each technology builds on the one below it. In this manner, it is common to call the whole ball of wax a *technology stack*.

The SharePoint technology stack begins with server computers running the Microsoft Windows Server operating system. On top of Windows Server are some additional technologies required by SharePoint. In particular, SharePoint needs a database and a web server — Microsoft SQL Server and Microsoft Internet Information Services (IIS), respectively. In addition, SharePoint also needs Active Directory, which manages the servers in the domain. Only when this entire stack of technology is available can you install SharePoint, as shown in Figure 1-2.

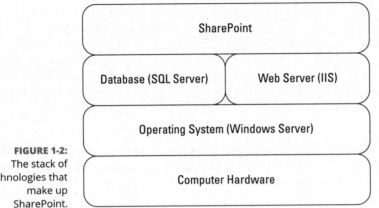

FIGURE 1-2:
The stack of technologies that make up SharePoint.

WARNING

SharePoint will only work with the Microsoft stack of supporting technologies. For example, you cannot swap in an Oracle database or the open source Apache web server. SharePoint would simply refuse to install and might ask you what the heck you are trying to do using a non-Microsoft product to install SharePoint.

Taking a Peek at a SharePoint Site

The primary purpose of SharePoint is to provide websites. When you create a website, you select which type of template you want to use to create the site. The dialog box shown in Figure 1-3 shows the different templates available. Creating a site is explored in detail in Chapter 4.

TIP

The templates you have available depend on where you are creating your SharePoint site and what features have been activated for your SharePoint environment. For example, in SharePoint Online, a tab for Duet Enterprise and Publishing only shows up if the feature is activated.

The template tells SharePoint which features and functionality should be included on the site. Keep in mind that you can always add more features and add and remove features as you decide to make your site more specific for your needs.

FIGURE 1-3:
The dialog box
used to select a
website template
when creating a
SharePoint site.

Template Selection

Select a template:

Collaboration | Enterprise | Publishing

Team Site
Blog
Project Site
Community Site

A place to work together with a group of people.

One of the most common SharePoint site templates is called the Team Site template. The Team Site website template includes features such as a discussion board, library to store documents, and a calendar. In fact, many books simply talk about the Team Site template and call that SharePoint. As you will learn in this book, the Team Site is very important, but it is just another SharePoint website template. Part 2 explores building a site based on the Team Site template.

A SharePoint website created using the Team Site template is shown in Figure 1-4. This team site has been customized a bit to show the latest team morale event for Portal Integrators along with some additional navigational items.

FIGURE 1-4:
A standard
SharePoint
website created
using the Team
Site template.

Getting Familiar with SharePoint Terminology

You should add a number of terms to your SharePoint vocabulary. Some terms are made up by Microsoft marketing, some are industry standards, and others are buzzwords that have grown to have various meanings depending on the context of the conversation. In the following sections, I describe the various components of SharePoint, how the terms that define functionality fit together, and what they mean.

Branding

The term *branding* refers to the way a SharePoint site looks and behaves to users. Branding includes things like the colors, fonts, images, logos, and layout of the various components on a site. Branding your SharePoint 2016 site will be covered in Chapter 13.

The term branding is not specific to SharePoint and refers to the way something looks and behaves. The term is borrowed from the marketing industry in which an organization will brand its product. For example, Coca-Cola has a very strong brand. In the software world, branding refers to the look and feel of a piece of software or website.

Business Connectivity Services

Business Connectivity Services (BCS) is a specific feature of SharePoint Server. BCS enables you to connect SharePoint with external systems. For example, say you have a customer relationship system and you need SharePoint to interact with the data in that system. You could use BCS to make it happen.

TIP

BCS can be a fairly in-depth piece of SharePoint and also often requires the skill-set of a developer.

Business intelligence

The term *business intelligence* is definitely not new. An article was published in the October 1958 edition of the *IBM Journal* by H. P. Luhn called "A Business Intelligence System." The article describes how an organization can process documents in order to make business decisions. Business intelligence has continued to evolve over the years and has morphed into something of a catch-all phrase for using data to drive business.

In the Microsoft realm, business intelligence consists of a number of different technologies. In fact, I wrote an entire sister book on the subject — *Microsoft Business Intelligence For Dummies* by Ken Withee (Wiley). As SharePoint has become a central and nearly ubiquitous application, it has also become a prime place to show the data that decision makers need to make decisions. In other words,

SharePoint is a perfect display case for all those fancy charts, graphs, performance indicators, and other data.

Unfortunately, business intelligence has a fairly steep learning curve in Share-Point. Tools such as Report Builder, Dashboard Designer, and PowerPivot unleash endless possibilities, but figuring out how to use them all takes time. One thing you will find with business intelligence in SharePoint is that there are often many ways to achieve the same result. And therein lies the learning curve.

At the basic level, if you can create a chart in Excel, you can plunk it into a Share-Point library and embed it on a page using a Web Part. Ta-da! You just achieved business intelligence in SharePoint. The consumers of the data might never even know how easy it was to put that data in Excel and embed it in a SharePoint web page. And that is the point. These things shouldn't be difficult to get started.

At the other end of the spectrum, however, you might need to create a data cube (a specialized database in the big data world) with millions or billions of records, and then use a specialized tool such as Dashboard Designer to create an interactive graph with clickthrough capabilities. Whew! That sounds complicated, and trust me, it is.

You need serious expertise when diving into the depths of business intelligence, but that doesn't mean you can't understand it at a high level. Many different tools and features make up business intelligence in SharePoint 2016, and Part 5 walks you through them at a high level and provides you with insights into quick techniques you can use to get started right away.

eDiscovery

The term *eDiscovery* relates to the legal world of business. In particular, the word derives from *electronic discovery* in litigation. If you have ever watched *Law & Order*, you understand that critical evidence can make or break a case. In the high-tech world of digital information, it's a rather tricky endeavor to discover and hold electronic documents.

SharePoint 2016 has a number of features specifically designed for eDiscovery. This is great news if you're a decision maker looking to comply with legal requirements, or you're a lawyer. If neither applies to you, then just knowing SharePoint 2016 handles eDiscovery is good enough.

Identity management

Frankly, modern technology can often be a real pain. It seems that there are gazillions of systems in any organization, and each requires its own username and password.

I have so many usernames and passwords on various websites across the Internet that my mind just tries to block it out. Of course, then I forget my password and have to go through the tiring process of resetting it each time I want to log in to a particular system. On the other side, when a user logs in to a system, that system also needs to know what the user can access.

TIP

Identity management refers to the functionality of a software system that manages users and what they can access. Identity management isn't specific to SharePoint and is used by any system that requires you to enter a username and password.

SharePoint 2016 has made great strides in simplifying identity management. SharePoint 2016 uses claims-based authentication in conjunction with an open authentication standard called Open Authorization (OAuth for short) in order to play nicely with other systems. What this means for you is that you shouldn't have to remember yet another username and password when working with SharePoint 2016. If only the rest of the Internet could be so thoughtful!

Mobile

It's amazing how quickly mobile computing has taken over our lives. Not that long ago, the flip phone was a technological marvel. Not any longer! The trend towards using your smartphone or tablet to get things done is accelerating rapidly.

Previous versions of SharePoint had the capability to access a site from a smartphone, but the experience was less than stellar. SharePoint 2016 support for smartphone devices has come a long way. When paired with the new Windows 10, you might even say accessing your Word, Excel, OneNote, and PowerPoint is enjoyable on your smartphone or tablet. Well, as enjoyable as information work can be.

Here's a great example: When viewing a SharePoint 2016 site on your phone, the site contents appear as a list; however, if you prefer the regular experience, you can select the option to switch to PC view.

Working with SharePoint from your smartphone or tablet is covered in Chapter 17.

Records management and compliance

In the world of information work, you often hear about *records management* and *compliance*. Depending on how much of a rebel you are, you might think of these terms as keeping people and processes in line or as an invitation to break some rules.

Every organization has a different set of rules around managing records and keeping processes compliant with company policy. This line of thinking is not specific to SharePoint, and, depending on your organization and industry, could be buttoned-up strict, as in the banking industry, or open to the world and free loving, as in many technology startup companies.

In SharePoint 2016, a number of features are specifically designed to keep records organized and easily managed. In addition, SharePoint has compliance features that even the stodgiest of stodgy big banks will adore. And as someone who has done consulting work for the banking industry, let me tell you, there are some really strict compliance rules out there. (Considering that they're keeping track of our money, that's a good thing.) Chapter 20 covers records management and compliance features in SharePoint.

Search

If you have ever used Google, Bing, or Ask.com, then you're familiar with search engines. These search engines for the Internet are amazingly powerful and eerily comprehensive. SharePoint does a bang-up job of managing content, and the next logical step in managing content is finding content when you need it. As an organization grows, the need for search grows too.

Microsoft acquired a top-notch search company based in Oslo, Norway. The company was called FAST, and Microsoft moved quickly to integrate FAST search with SharePoint. The result now is that you have a very powerful and seamless search experience right out of the box.

TIP

Search is one of those topics that spans from simple to mind-numbingly complex. At a base level, you have search capabilities for every SharePoint site right out of the box. The tech geeks can go deeper and optimize search for your organization. For example, your search query can be aware of your role in the organization and display results specifically for you. So, for example, if you're in sales and searching for a product, your search results will be sales materials. If you're an engineer and searching for a product, your results will include specifications. SharePoint search can make this happen, but configuring it is best left to the IT department.

Social

In recent years, computers and the Internet have been connecting people like never before. This new way of interacting through computers is called social computing. The biggest public social network of all is Facebook. Not every organization wants to be in such a public space though.

SharePoint is designed for organizations, and the social aspects of SharePoint share a common goal with Facebook — connecting people. The difference is that SharePoint connections are limited to people in a particular organization. The social aspects of SharePoint are covered in Chapter 16.

Web content management

Content is a fairly simple concept. When you create a Word document or an Excel spreadsheet, you generate content. If you develop a web page for your colleagues to admire, you generate content. Even if you just pull out a pencil and paper and start writing, that's content. If you scanned that paper, you could then let SharePoint work its content management wonders on the scanned image file.

SharePoint 2016 is especially powerful in handling content, as described in Chapter 18. One particularly tricky piece of content, however, is the content you develop for websites. You know, all of those web pages that contain policies and procedures and documentation and all of that? If the content is created for a web page, then it's web content and it holds a special place in the heart of SharePoint. The web content management features of SharePoint are legendary, and many organizations first started using SharePoint for just this reason.

TIP

Content management often goes by the name Enterprise Content Management (ECM). Don't be fooled by the terminology though. The *Enterprise* portion of ECM just means the system manages content at a large scale, as found in a large company or enterprise.

SharePoint and web content have a special relationship that all comes down to delegation and control. SharePoint provides the ability for many people to generate content and for a few people to approve content. This maintains order because a select group of people control what goes out to the world. SharePoint streamlines this process by allowing approved content to be published automatically.

You might be wondering what makes the relationship between SharePoint and web content so special. Well, it all comes down to delegation and control. SharePoint provides the ability for many people to generate content and for a few to approve content. After it's approved, content can be published automatically to be consumed by the world or those in your organization.

IN THIS CHAPTER

Exploring SharePoint Online

Determining why SharePoint Online has become so popular

Figuring out the difference between SharePoint Online and SharePoint On-Premises

Understanding some of the benefits to a cloud-based offering

Chapter 2

Introducing SharePoint Online

Just a handful of years ago, it wasn't easy to adopt SharePoint. SharePoint fell squarely into the realm of enterprise-class software. *Enterprise-class software* is powerful but expensive and resource-intensive, so in order to adopt SharePoint, you needed to be a large organization with big bucks and a large IT support team.

The rapid rise of super-fast and ubiquitous Internet connectivity caused a paradigm shift in the software world. Microsoft and other companies quickly came out with new applications that offered enterprise-class software, including SharePoint, over the Internet. Microsoft branded its SharePoint offering as SharePoint Online and packaged it with products such as Exchange (email), Skype for Business (instant communication), and Office (productivity). The combined package of services (SharePoint, Exchange, Skype for Business, and Office) is called Office 365. To find out how the technologies in Office 365 fit together, check out *Office 365 For Dummies* 2nd Edition by Rosemarie Withee (Wiley).

In this chapter, you see how SharePoint Online has changed the game and what it means to use a cloud-based solution. You read about the differences between SharePoint Online and SharePoint On-Premises and find out which you should use and when. Finally, you explore some of the benefits of using SharePoint Online.

Getting Familiar with SharePoint Online

Microsoft offers SharePoint over the Internet in a product called SharePoint Online. With SharePoint Online, Microsoft takes care of all the heavy lifting. To get SharePoint going, someone has to procure and set up the servers, and install the operating system, databases, web server, and SharePoint server. This all has to be done in a special climate-controlled room called a data center. The data center has to be secure and redundant. After all, what if a disaster happened and the data center computers in the data center — or worse, the data center itself — were destroyed? Finally, the whole setup must be scalable so that as more users begin using SharePoint for mission-critical business processes, the servers and sites can keep up with the added load. And that isn't the end — after everything is up and running, someone still needs to manage all the updates and keep the servers humming smoothly. Whew! What a lot of work.

With a hosted solution, you or your organization are paying someone else to do all this for you, and you simply use the final product, SharePoint. With SharePoint Online, Microsoft sells its SharePoint platform as a service, so the actual servers and software run in its data centers, managed and maintained by its employees. You, being a customer of Microsoft, connect to this managed version of Share-Point over a secure channel of the Internet and use it to develop business solutions on the SharePoint platform. (Maybe a better name would be "SharePoint Infra-structure Hosted and Managed by Microsoft," though it's too cumbersome for marketing.) Figure 2-1 illustrates the point.

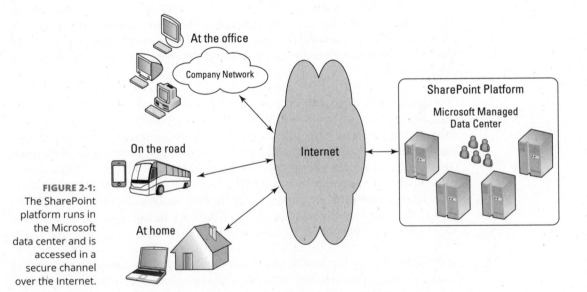

FIGURE 2-1:
The SharePoint platform runs in the Microsoft data center and is accessed in a secure channel over the Internet.

Microsoft is not the only company that offers SharePoint over the Internet. Other companies, such as Fpweb.net (www.fpweb.net) and Rackspace (www.rackspace.com), also offer SharePoint over the Internet. SharePoint Online is the brand name for Microsoft's offering.

SharePoint Online is when Microsoft manages SharePoint in its data centers and you access it over the Internet. SharePoint On-Premises is when your local IT gurus manage SharePoint in your company data center.

Understanding Why SharePoint Online Has Become So Popular

Putting a complex computer platform in place is difficult. Organizations discovered this when they implemented Enterprise Resource Planning software in the 1990s and 2000s, and it still holds true today. Putting the SharePoint platform in place is not an easy endeavor. Larger organizations usually require a more complex implementation. As the complexity of the implementation increases, so do the costs, time, and risk.

The current best practice is to use an experienced consulting firm with expertise in implementing a SharePoint platform. As in dealing with any services company, sometimes you pick a winner, and sometimes it's a complete disaster.

SharePoint Online takes the implementation of the infrastructure out of the equation with a known variable in cost and resources. This is music to a bean counter's ears! Predictability! The predictability of cost and time to implement are why SharePoint Online and other cloud solutions are becoming so popular. They reduce complexity and provide a fixed and certain cost on a SharePoint platform that is guaranteed to follow best practices.

Having a known variable in place for the infrastructure frees up resources to focus on the actual business problems. Which, by the way, are your main reasons for implementing SharePoint in the first place, right?

Microsoft has introduced the SharePoint Online offering to cater to everyone from small businesses to large multinationals. In fact, you can even purchase just one license if you're a solo entrepreneur. Because Microsoft has already built out the offering, it's just as easy to offer the same reliability and security to small companies as it is to large companies. It is, after all, the same product — the only difference is the scale.

Differences between SharePoint Online and SharePoint On-Premises

In the past, there have been some major differences between SharePoint Online and SharePoint On-Premises. For one, SharePoint Online used to trail the version of SharePoint that was available On-Premises. For example, when SharePoint 2013 came out, it took SharePoint Online a painfully long time before it became SharePoint 2013.

REMEMBER

The current version is SharePoint 2016. The previous version was SharePoint 2013, and the version before that was SharePoint 2010. SharePoint Online doesn't have a version number.

Times have changed, and Microsoft has said that going forward SharePoint Online will be where they release new features. Later they will bundle all those new features that have been rolled out over the past few years into an On-Premises release. Maybe SharePoint 2019? Who knows! One thing is certain, though: If you want the latest and greatest features, then SharePoint Online is your best bet. If you want a tried and true and stable release for your local premises, on the other hand, then On-Premises is the version for you.

TIP

One of the major development areas with SharePoint Server 2016 is its integration with SharePoint Online. This is to accommodate organizations that want to keep some of their data on their local premises and in their own control but want to leverage some of the benefits of having Microsoft manage their SharePoint for them. This concept of using some SharePoint Online and some SharePoint On-Premises is called a *hybrid approach*.

With that said, there are still integration points with other local server products and advanced functionality that are only available with SharePoint On-Premises. This is an ever-changing landscape, so the best way to stay on top of the available features is on the frequently updated SharePoint Online feature matrix located on Microsoft's TechNet website at `http://technet.microsoft.com/en-us/library/jj819267.aspx`.

REMEMBER

SharePoint Online is when Microsoft manages SharePoint in their data centers and you access it over the Internet. SharePoint On-Premises is when your local IT gurus manage SharePoint in your company data center.

GETTING TO THE BOTTOM OF THE CLOUD

Network diagrams often show a network as a cloud, as shown in the following figure, because it would be too complex to diagram all the components that make up the network (such as routers, switches, hubs, and cables).

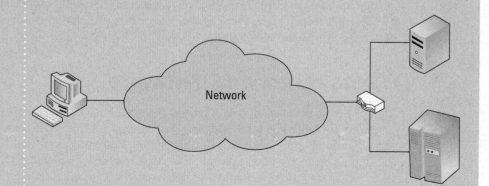

The biggest network, and cloud, of all is the Internet. When a diagram shows communication over the Internet, a big cloud is used because it would be impossible to try to show all the network hardware that might be encountered between two computers communicating via the Internet. The cloud simply becomes an abstraction for a network with the assumption that communication can occur over that cloud.

If a company sells access to software that lives in their data centers and that is connected to by customers over the Internet, that solution is said to live "in the cloud." The term comes from the perspective of the customer, who may have no idea where the actual servers that serve up the software are located. From the customers' perspective, they just access the software using an Internet domain name. This cloud concept and technology is nothing new. Whenever you surf the web, you use a service in the cloud. You just know that when you type in the web address, the site appears in your web browser. This concept is catching on with business applications; you hear more and more about cloud solutions.

Exploring the Benefits of SharePoint Online

If you use SharePoint in your day-to-day operations, then the good news is that it doesn't really matter whether you are using SharePoint On-Premises or SharePoint Online. They are both SharePoint, and you can focus on your job. With that said, it's nice to at least have a high-level understanding of some of the infrastructure benefits to SharePoint Online. If nothing else, you can impress your IT friends.

Using SharePoint Online instead of trying to build and manage the platform with your own organization's resources gives you a number of benefits. You simply sign up, pay a monthly licensing fee, and access SharePoint over the Internet. The following sections take a look at some of the things that Microsoft does behind the scenes with SharePoint Online.

Data center and hardware

If you have ever toured a data center, then you have some idea of the amount of effort and resources it takes to keep everything running. Data centers have rows and rows of computers with flashing lights, humming fans, and coils of cables running ceiling to floor. Control rooms that resemble something NASA would use to run space missions monitor all these servers. The control rooms contain computers and monitors that report on everything in the data center, from temperature and humidity to individual fans in particular servers and everything in between. These control rooms are often called a Network Operation Center (NOC) and are the nerve center for a modern data center.

Most organizations that have the need for servers find a data center that can be used to host their gear. Hosting your computers in a data center can cost a fortune, but paying to host your own gear in an inferior environment can cost even more in the long run.

Microsoft invested a tremendous amount of money in building its own state-of-the-art data centers that house the servers that make up SharePoint Online. The nice thing about SharePoint Online is that you don't have to worry about the various costs of hosting and managing your own gear. The price you pay for SharePoint Online covers everything, including the data center.

The servers that run SharePoint Online are state of the art and come from the leading industry manufacturers. In fact, Microsoft has modularized the setup, and the computers come in massive containers that look very similar to the containers you see on cargo ships. These container pods are sealed by the manufacturer and never opened at the data center. This is a security mechanism to keep humans away from the computers. When a single piece of hardware fails, the workload of that server is simply shifted automatically to other servers (possibly in other pods). When enough servers fail, the pod is taken offline and the workload of that pod is shifted to another pod without service interruption. A new pod with the latest hardware is then shipped to replace it, and the old pod is decommissioned, with the data being wiped to security standards, and sent back to the manufacturer.

Microsoft has developed this system of data centers and pods throughout the country with built-in redundancy. If a data center goes down, the workload is shifted to another data center. If a pod goes down, the workload of that pod is shifted to another pod. If a server within a pod goes down, the workload of that server is shifted to another server. This system of redundancy is included in the price of SharePoint Online. You might care about how it works or you might just care that Microsoft has guaranteed uptime of 99.9 percent. In the end, you're free to focus on your business and solving business problems using the SharePoint platform without having to worry about what it takes to make that platform consistently available.

Software platform

The physical computers required to run the SharePoint platform are one thing, but you also have to take into account the operating systems and associated software such as the web servers, databases, and SharePoint itself that run on the server computers. The Microsoft platform uses the Windows Server operating system, the Internet Information Service (IIS) web server, and the SQL Server database, as described in Chapter 1. All these software systems are just the supporting actors for the SharePoint software itself. The amount of time and resources it takes to get all these software components installed, updated, and configured can be daunting. Administrators are valuable resources, and their time is often better spent dealing with the desktop computers of the users.

When you sign up for SharePoint Online, you don't have to worry about installing and managing the software components that make up the SharePoint platform. Microsoft takes care of all of that for you, and it's all included in the price. In addition, when new versions of the software stack are released, Microsoft upgrades everything automatically without additional cost for the service. Microsoft also monitors the servers and logs 24 hours a day in order to make sure nothing goes awry. The monitoring takes place in Network Operation Centers described in the previous section.

Backup, redundancy, and security

You might think that with the hardware and software in place, the rest would be easy. However, the SharePoint platform itself needs to have a backup and disaster recovery plan, in addition to being available, redundant, and secure. With SharePoint Online, the Microsoft teams take care of all this for you, and it's guaranteed in the contract.

With the hardware, software, and plans in place, you as a customer are free to focus on developing business solutions on the platform instead of working through the process of setting everything up yourself.

IN THIS CHAPTER

Understanding the functionality that makes up SharePoint

Finding out how SharePoint components fit together

Discovering which functionality is most important to you

Chapter 3

Wrangling SharePoint Functionality

The reason SharePoint is so difficult to define is that it's a product that has a tremendous amount of functionality. SharePoint has functionality for administrators, business users, report developers, analysts, programmers, and just about anyone else in any organization. You name it, and SharePoint provides functionality designed for that particular user. Coming to terms with the vastness of SharePoint is a key concept in learning about the product.

In this chapter, you discover some of the main functionality that makes up SharePoint. You find out about SharePoint templates and how they're used to create websites. You discover the importance of the Team Site, but find out it isn't the only game in town. You explore apps and see that almost everything in SharePoint 2016 is an app. Finally, you take a high-level fly-over of some of the most common functionality in SharePoint. The whole smorgasbord of functionality is really the definition of SharePoint, and you get a bird's-eye view in this chapter.

Coming to Terms with Website Templates

If you haven't experienced SharePoint before, you might think that creating a new website is difficult. Before SharePoint, you would need to gather up the right files and write HTML code to create a website. Tweaking the code and building the website was a burdensome task. To make matters worse, you had to fiddle with the web server and the security and get everything just right. In short, you needed an advanced level of technical expertise. Some would have argued you needed an advanced degree in computer science! Making changes to the website after it was completed required the same advanced skillset. One of the main reasons SharePoint took off was that it allowed people to create and manage websites with advanced functionality, such as content management and workflow, without needing an advanced technical skillset.

Creating a SharePoint website is as easy as a few clicks of the mouse (assuming you have the right permissions). The primary decision you need to make when you create a SharePoint site is which template to use. Choosing a template is accomplished on the New Site Creation screen, shown in Figure 3-1. Instructions for creating a new site are outlined in Chapter 4.

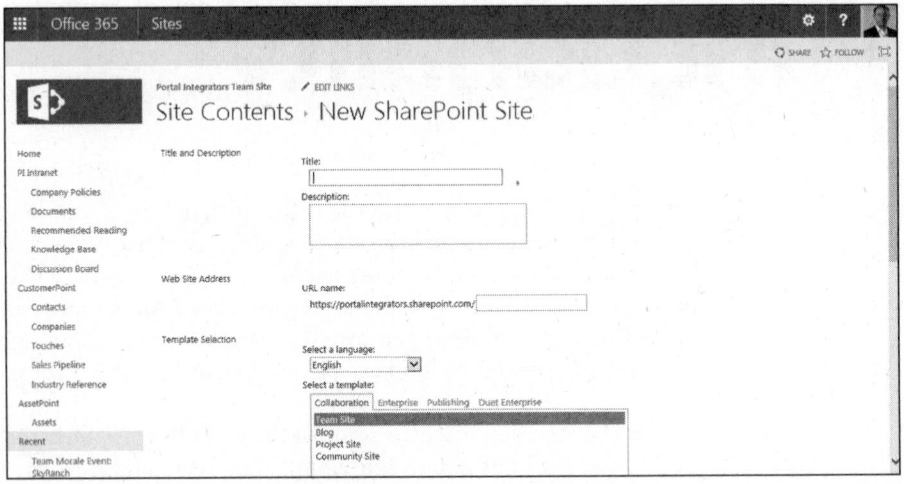

FIGURE 3-1:
Choosing a template on the New Site Creation screen.

A SharePoint site template outlines what functionality the site will include after it's created. You can always add or remove functionality as you see fit. Keep in mind that the templates you see depend on a number of factors including the edition of SharePoint you are using, whether you are using SharePoint Online or SharePoint On-Premises, and which features are activated.

The most popular SharePoint site template is called Team Site. The Team Site template is so popular that many books forget to mention that there are other templates available as well. Working with a SharePoint site built using the Team Site template is covered in Chapters 4 through 9.

Show Me the Apps

SharePoint 2016 extends the way you think about adding functionality to a site. In previous versions of SharePoint, all containers were considered a type of list. What a list meant was fairly generic. You might have a list that provides calendar functionality, or you might have a list that provides discussion board functionality. The concept of a special list with some functionality was one of the hardest things to get our minds around when we started working with SharePoint. SharePoint 2016 removes the confusion by calling everything an app. Instead of a specialized calendar list, you now have a Calendar app. Need a discussion board? You now add the Discussion Board app.

Microsoft has also expanded the ability to develop custom developed solutions for SharePoint called *add-ins*. The result is that third parties or in-house developers can create add-ins for any purpose you can conceive. Imagine that you're in Accounts Payable and you use SharePoint 2016 to manage your invoice documents. You might request an add-in from your IT department to route documents through the various approvals before finally being submitted to the payment system.

If you use SharePoint Online, you can browse, purchase, and install apps and add-ins from the SharePoint Store without leaving SharePoint. It's similar to using the App Store on an iPhone or Google Market on an Android phone to buy and download an app.

Many SharePoint power users are comfortable with the concept of a data container called a list. You can still start with a blank list and add functionality as required. Nothing has changed in this ability. You are now just creating your own custom app by starting with the Custom List app. After you give your new app a name, it appears alongside all the other apps.

SharePoint apps are covered in Chapter 7.

Working with Web Pages

A SharePoint site wouldn't be very interesting without content. A SharePoint site is a container for pages. Pages in turn are a container for actual content; developing pages allows you to add content to your SharePoint sites.

The three primary types of pages that can be created and developed from the browser in SharePoint 2016 are

>> Wiki page

>> Web Part page

>> Publishing page

Wiki page

A *wiki page,* also known as a content page, is the Swiss Army knife of pages and allows for easy development and customization using a rich text editor built right into the browser. A wiki page is easy to develop and is an extremely powerful and intuitive collaboration, data capture, and documentation tool. This is the default page that is created when you select Add a Page from the Site Settings gear icon.

Web Part page

A *Web Part page* provides Web Part zones where you can drag and drop various Web Parts from the gallery. A *Web Part* is a reusable piece of functionality that can be dragged and dropped right onto your pages. A number of Web Parts are available right out of the box, and Web Parts can also be custom developed to meet your specific needs. Imagine a Web Part developed specifically for your organization. After the Web Part is deployed, you could add that custom Web Part to any page you work with on any site in your organization.

Publishing page

The *publishing page* is designed to separate the functionality between managing content and managing the look and feel of the page. A publishing page is only available when certain features are turned on by site administrators. All publishing pages live in a special library called Pages. The Pages library is created automatically when the publishing features are turned on for the site. These pages use a special library because the Pages library already has preconfigured functionality such as versioning and workflow that is designed for the management and distribution of content, or in other words, publishing content.

TIP

The publishing page is only available when the Publishing feature has been activated at the site collection and site level.

Chapter 5 covers creating and developing pages.

Understanding Web Parts

A Web Part is one of those fairly rare things in technology that has a descriptive name: A Web Part is a part of a web page. You can think of a Web Part as a bundled piece of web functionality that can be added to a SharePoint page.

SharePoint 2016 has a number of Web Parts available that you can add to your pages. You add a Web Part using the Web Part Gallery, shown in Figure 3-2.

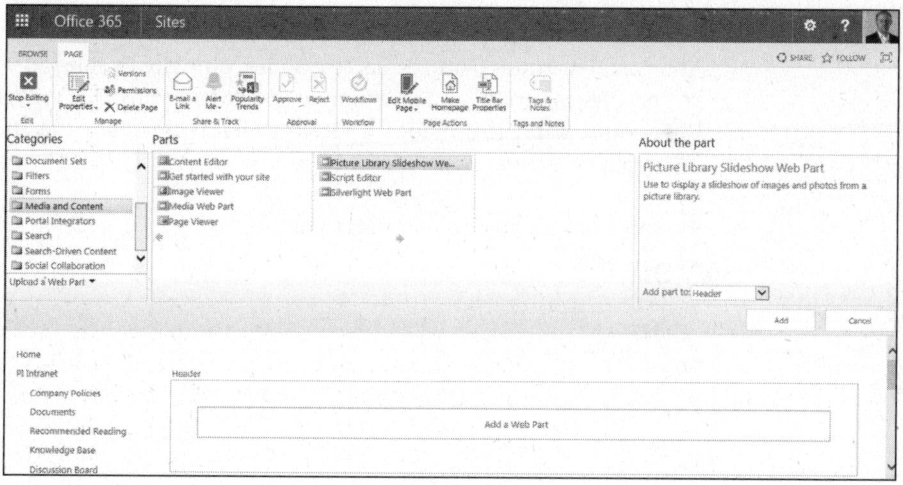

FIGURE 3-2:
The Web Part Gallery in SharePoint 2016.

TIP

The Web Parts that are available out of the box depend on how your SharePoint implementation was set up and which features are activated.

In addition to the Web Parts that ship with SharePoint, you can also add custom Web Parts to the Web Part Gallery. A number of third-party developers create Web Parts that can be purchased; Web Parts can also be developed by in-house SharePoint developers.

Web Parts are covered in Chapter 6.

Digging into SharePoint Features

Terminology is often a central point of confusion in most technology. SharePoint is no different. For example, the term *feature* means some sort of functionality or grouping of functionality. In SharePoint, the word *feature* has a very technical meaning: a collection of SharePoint functionality that can be activated and deactivated. When SharePoint programmers hear the term feature, they immediately think of a particular technical part of SharePoint. SharePoint programmers can bundle together a grouping of functionality they have developed for SharePoint into a single feature. Programmers might develop a bundle of functionality and package the entire thing into a single feature that users can activate or deactivate. For example, if you work in financial services, you might need a number of workflows, pages, images, and custom Web Parts on your SharePoint site. A programmer could build all of this functionality for you and package it all into a feature. When you're ready to use the functionality, you activate the financial services feature.

Microsoft developed a number of features that ship with the SharePoint product. You can view these features on any SharePoint site as long as you're an administrator. (See Figure 3-3.) For example, the Mobile Browser View feature ships with SharePoint 2016; it provides a view of SharePoint data specifically designed for smartphone browsers.

Features are covered in detail in Chapter 12.

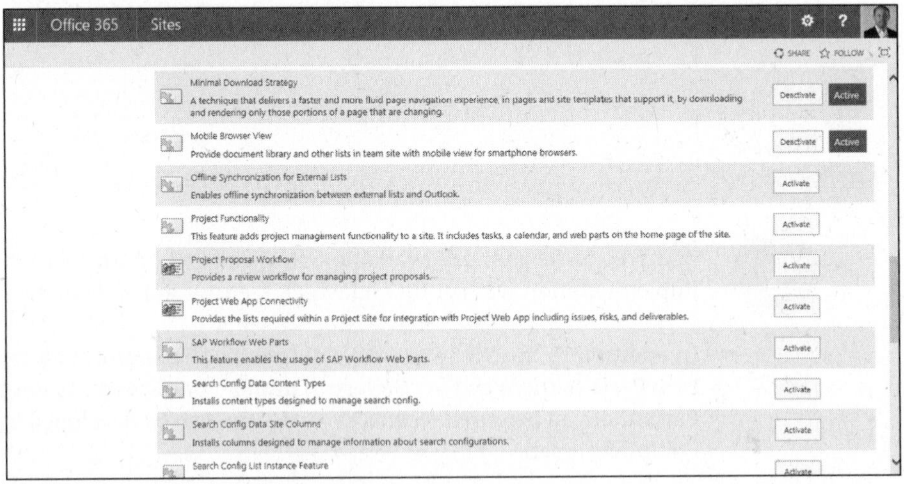

FIGURE 3-3:
The Mobile
Browser View
feature in
SharePoint 2016.

SharePoint Tools

You use a number of tools in SharePoint. For example, the SharePoint Designer tool is used to build a workflow for integrated business processes. Another tool called Report Builder can be used to develop reports in SharePoint. The Dashboard Designer tool helps users build Business Intelligence dashboards. Working with these tools warrants a book unto itself, but at the very least, you should know these tools and what they are used for.

Integrating with Office 2016

One aspect of SharePoint that fails to get as much attention as it deserves is the integration with Microsoft Office. If you use Office products such as Word, Excel, PowerPoint, OneNote, and Outlook, then you're already primed to leverage SharePoint. In fact, you might be working with SharePoint from within Office and not even realize it!

Working with SharePoint from Microsoft Office products is covered in Chapter 18.

2

Diving Headfirst into SharePoint 2016

Chapter 4

Getting to Know the Team Site

As you can read in Chapter 3, you create a SharePoint site using a template. You choose the template when you create the site. The most popular site template is the Team Site. A site created using the Team Site template contains a broad set of features designed for team interaction and collaboration.

In this chapter, you walk through creating or requesting a SharePoint site based on the Team Site template. You then find out how to access your Team Site and discover the available functionality.

Creating a SharePoint Site

If you have used SharePoint before, you know that there are often multiple ways to do the same thing. This sounds good in theory, but it led to a lot of confusion by users. Microsoft recently made some significant changes to reduce confusion and streamline the product. Creating a new site is a perfect example. Where you could create a site multiple ways in the past, there is now one way in SharePoint 2016. This might be frustrating at first if you're familiar with previous versions, but it's a good thing. At long last, all content that describes how to create a Share-Point site has come together and is the same.

You create a new site in SharePoint by doing the following:

1. **Click the Settings gear icon and select Site Contents, as shown in Figure 4-1.**

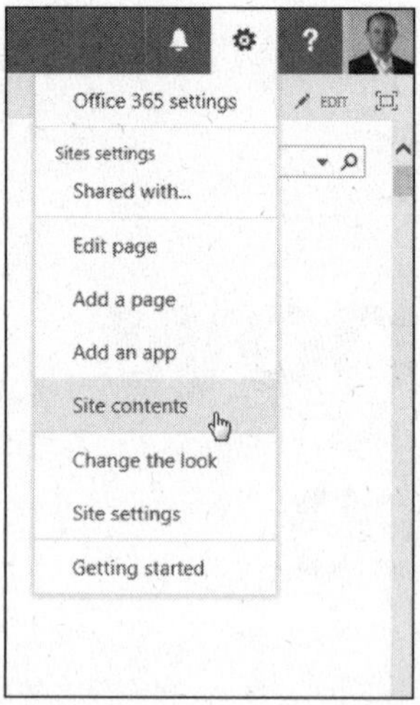

FIGURE 4-1:
Selecting Site
Contents from
the Settings
menu.

2. **Scroll down to the bottom of the page and click the New Subsite link, shown in Figure 4-2, to open the New SharePoint Site form.**

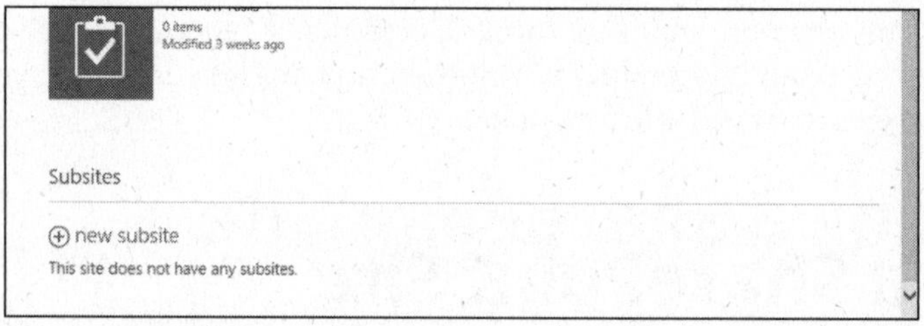

FIGURE 4-2:
Creating a new
SharePoint 2016
site based on the
Team Site
template.

3. **In the Title and Description text boxes, type a name and description for the new site.**

4. **Enter a unique site name that will be used in the URL in the URL Name text box.**

5. **Select the Team Site template for the site by clicking the Team Site template on the Collaboration tab to select it.**

   Notice that Team Site is not the only template option. You can choose other templates. Regardless of the template you start with, you can then develop the site to add SharePoint functionality as you see fit.

6. **Choose whether to use the same permissions as the parent site or use unique permissions by selecting the appropriate radio button.**

7. **Choose whether you want to display this site on the top link navigation of the parent site or not by selecting the Yes or No radio button.**

   The top link navigation is the menu across the top of the site.

8. **Click Create to create the site.**

   The new site is displayed in the browser.

TIP

A SharePoint site created using the Team Site template is often referred to as simply a team site, as in, "Check out my team site." If you really want to impress and astound your audience, you could say, "Check out my SharePoint site based on the Team Site template," but that's a mouthful.

TECHNICAL STUFF

Every SharePoint site is contained within another SharePoint site in a hierarchy. At the top of the hierarchy is a special type of site called a Site Collection. Creating and administering a Site Collection takes special permissions. Every site within the Site Collection is called a Subsite. Both types of websites are often just referred to as a website or site. The site you just created is a Subsite of whatever site you were in when you created it. There are really no differences between using a site that is a Site Collection and a site that is a Subsite. To users, both types of sites look and act the same. The differences lie in the navigation, security settings, and features. (The differences between administering a Subsite and a Site Collection are discussed in Chapter 10.)

Requesting a SharePoint Site

If you aren't a site administrator, then you won't have permissions to create a new SharePoint site. In this case, you need to request it. Most organizations have a process for requesting a team site. For example, you might send an email request to the SharePoint administrator or fill out a form.

Whatever you have to do to get your SharePoint 2016 team site, get one. At a minimum, you need to provide your SharePoint administrator with this information to get a team site:

>> **The site name:** The friendly caption that appears in the header of your site and in any site directory where your site may be listed.

>> **The site template:** The template determines what kind of site SharePoint makes for you. SharePoint includes dozens of predefined site templates. Your company may even create its custom site templates. Tell your administrator you want a team site, which is the most popular of all the SharePoint 2016 site templates.

>> **The web address or URL:** The unique location where your team site is hosted. In most organizations, all team sites are located off the same root web address. Some examples I've seen include

```
http://intranet.company.com/sites
http://portal/projectsites
http://sharepoint/sites
```

Your organization may also ask who has permission to access the site. By default, all SharePoint team sites have three basic kinds of users, which are called SharePoint groups:

>> **Visitors** have Read Only permission. They can view your site without making any contributions.

>> **Members** can participate in your team site by uploading and editing documents or adding tasks or other items.

>> **Owners** have Full Control permission to customize the site. As the person requesting the team site, the SharePoint administrator likely assumes that you're the proud owner unless you specifically tell him or her who owns the site.

You need to decide which users fit into these three SharePoint groups. SharePoint offers more than just these three groups, and you can create your own groups to meet your needs. (SharePoint groups are discussed further in Chapter 14.)

Your site's users must be connected physically to your network or have permission from your network administrator to access your network remotely. Some companies set up a special kind of deployment for SharePoint, called an *extranet*, that provides a secure way for non-employees to log in to their SharePoint team sites without actually being on the internal company network.

Setting up SharePoint in an extranet environment can be done in lots of ways. Configuring a SharePoint extranet in your company's network can be complex and is outside the scope of this book. However, the good news is that SharePoint Online, which is part of the Office 365 suite, eliminates many of the technical barriers to creating an extranet. In Chapter 23, we walk you through the steps to use SharePoint Online to create an extranet for collaborating with clients.

Viewing Your Team Site in the Browser

To access your team site, you use a web browser, such as Microsoft Edge, Google Chrome, Mozilla Firefox, or Apple Safari. You need the web address or URL of your team site, which you can get from your primary SharePoint administrator or IT department. You also need a network user account with permissions to access the team site.

In our case, the web address for our team site is

```
http://portalintegrators.sharepoint.com
```

To access your team site:

1. **Open your web browser.**
2. **Type the web address for your team site in the address bar and press Enter.**

CHOOSING AMONG EDGE, CHROME, FIREFOX, AND SAFARI

Which browser should you use with SharePoint? Firefox, Chrome, Edge, and Safari browsers have some differences; for instance, some pages look better in Firefox or Chrome than in Edge. Because Chrome and Firefox were designed to be OS-agnostic, they support Mac and Linux users as well as Windows users. Microsoft has worked hard to make the SharePoint experience the same in all mainstream browsers; however, you might find a scenario where something doesn't work as expected in all browsers. The bottom line is that if you think something should work and it isn't currently working, try the same thing in a different browser, then choose the one that works the best and is speedy.

REMEMBER
Depending on whether you are using SharePoint Online or SharePoint On-Premises your login experience will be slightly different.

Figure 4-3 shows the home page for a SharePoint team site. In this case, it is the Portal Integrators team site.

FIGURE 4-3:
A SharePoint team site home page.

All SharePoint team sites have the same features. If you're using a new team site, your site should be similar to the one in Figure 4-3. If your site has been customized, it may look slightly different. Never fear: All the same features are still there. You may just have to hunt a little bit to find them.

The SharePoint page has the following major sections:

» **Header:** The header spans the entire top of the page. The header in a SharePoint page acts much like the menu in a traditional Windows application, such as Microsoft Word. SharePoint 2016 even features the Ribbon in the page header, similar to how the Ribbon appears in the top of many Office applications. You expand it by clicking one of the tabs such as Files or Library. After you click a tab, the Ribbon expands in a way that looks very similar to the rest of the Office products.

» **Left navigation pane:** The navigation pane provides quick access to the site's document libraries, lists, and discussion boards. You can even add links to content you create, such as documents and web pages.

» **Page content:** The content displays in the body of the page.

Generally speaking, the header and left navigation pane stay fairly consistent, whereas the body of the page changes to display the content for the web page. This is very similar to how most websites work. In our example, the Portal Integrators team has uploaded pictures from their team morale event so they can relive the fun every time they log into the site. To see a brand spanking new team site, check out Figure 4-6.

Microsoft has spent a lot of money on usability research to determine how best to lay out the pages in SharePoint. We highly encourage you to use the layouts provided by Microsoft instead of creating your own custom layouts for team sites.

Accessing Team Sites in Office 365

Accessing a site that is hosted in SharePoint Online, part of Office 365, may be a little different than sites that are hosted on your network. You may access your site through the main SharePoint Online portal URL, which is `http://Part.sharepoint.com`.

Depending on how your company has configured its connection with Office 365, you may not be prompted to log in to Office 365. However, in our experience, most small to medium companies don't bother integrating their logins, so you will probably have to use your Office 365 username and password, which will be different from your account for your internal network.

Single sign-on is the name of the technology that enables your internal network login to be integrated with Office 365. As the name implies, you only have to sign in to the network once to access all network services, regardless of where those services live.

Figure 4-4 shows an example of the login screen for Office 365. You may want to select the Keep Me Signed In check boxes so you aren't prompted continuously to log in to Office 365. You still get prompted occasionally to change your password or verify your password.

You can set up dual authentication for Office 365 for added security. *Dual authentication* means you enter your username and password (the first type of authentication) and then you must enter a second type of authentication, which can be a code sent to your phone in a text message, a code on an associated app on your phone, or even a phone call from Microsoft that asks you to enter a PIN. The second form of authentication is configurable in Office 365.

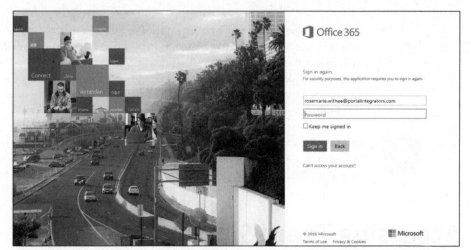

FIGURE 4-4:
Logging in to
Office 365.

Figure 4-5 shows the Office 365 main portal page for a user who has access to all the features of Office 365. In addition to SharePoint Online, it includes Exchange Online, Skype for Business Online, and Microsoft Office 2016. If your subscription only covers SharePoint Online, you don't see these other options.

FIGURE 4-5:
The main Office
365 portal home
page.

You can click the waffle icon in the upper-left corner of the page and then click Sites to reach your company's default team site.

Alternatively, your administrator may give you the direct link to your team site. In that case, you would bypass the screen shown in Figure 4-5. However, you still have to log in to Office 365 if your company doesn't have the logins integrated. If you are viewing your site on a mobile device, the appearance is optimized for a mobile experience and will look different than the one in the figure. However, there is an option to switch to PC view if you don't mind squinting at your phone to see the full site as you would on your full size computer.

Introducing the SharePoint Team Site

Although you can choose from many different site templates when you create a SharePoint website, the most popular is the Team Site template. A website created using the Team Site template is designed with a number of useful features for teams. (Hence the template name, Team Site.)

When you first open your new team site, you can do a number of things right out of the gate. You can store your digital documents in the prebuilt Document Library app, and you can get up and running with other apps using the fancy Pop-Up app.

As you hover the mouse over each tile in the Pop-Up app, a description pops up, as shown in Figure 4-6. When you click the tile, you can perform the operation described.

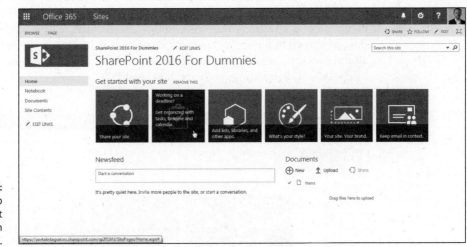

FIGURE 4-6:
The fancy Pop-Up helper app to get you started with your site.

The pop-up guidance allows you to

» Share your site with others

» Get organized with tasks, a calendar, a timeline, and a place to store your digital documents

» Add lists, libraries, and other apps

» Change the style and brand of your site

» Share email on your site and connect documents to Outlook

Simply clicking a tile walks you through a particular task. This is a common theme in SharePoint. SharePoint often tries to be helpful and do things for you automatically. That often makes things very simple but can also lead to confusion by making you wonder, "What just happened?" In order to get familiar with SharePoint, it's a good practice to understand what SharePoint is doing for you. When you know what it is doing, it's very easy to take the next step and extend default behavior to meet your specific needs.

Uploading documents

On a default team site (see Figure 4-6), you see a section in the lower-right part of the page called Documents. This seemingly innocuous little thing is actually SharePoint at its finest.

In a nutshell, Documents is a digital repository to store your documents. Under the covers, however, Documents is a combination of pages, apps, and Web Parts. (You discover how it all comes together in the next few chapters.) Adding a document, such as an Office Word file, to Documents is as simple as clicking the New link, as shown in Figure 4-7. After a document is located in SharePoint, you have all the content management functionality right at your fingertips, such as check-in/check-out, versioning, security, and workflow.

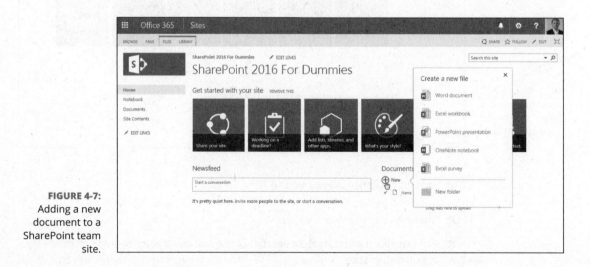

FIGURE 4-7: Adding a new document to a SharePoint team site.

Sharing your site

A site without any users is a bit pointless. You can share your site in a number of different ways. For a Team Site, the easiest way is to click the Share Your Site tile on the Pop-Up app on the main page. You can also share your site by clicking the Share button at the top of the screen.

If you don't have permission to share access to the site, then you won't see the Share button. SharePoint automatically removes it. In general with SharePoint, if you read about something and it doesn't match what you see on your site, then it is probably one of two issues: First, you might not have the right permissions for that particular feature; or second, the feature might not be activated or configured for your site. For example, if email is not configured for your SharePoint instance, then you won't see the Share button.

To find out more about activating and deactivating features, check out Chapter 12. And of course, you must also have the right permissions to activate the feature you're looking for.

If you use SharePoint Online, you have the ability to share a site with people outside your organization. This ability can be turned on and off by your administrator. If your site has the ability, you can just click the Share button (in the upper-right area of the screen), and then enter the email address of the person with which you want to share to send that person an invitation link.

Getting organized

The Working on a Deadline tile walks you through adding organizational apps to your Team Site. The pop-up tile lets you create the Task and Calendar apps and adds a Timeline to the top of your Team Site homepage, as shown in Figure 4-8.

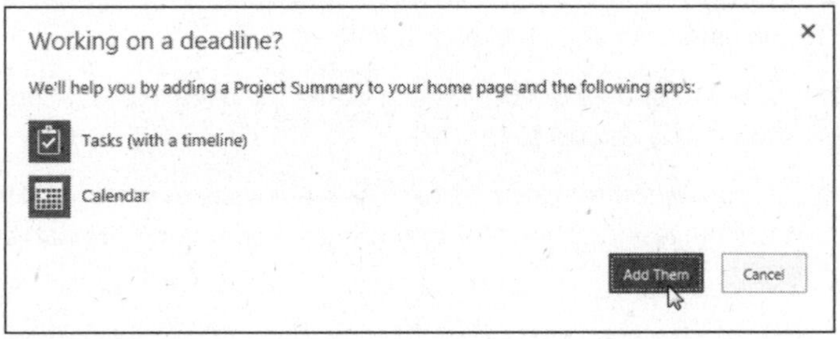

Working on a deadline?   ✕

We'll help you by adding a Project Summary to your home page and the following apps:

    Tasks (with a timeline)

    Calendar

                                          Add Them   Cancel

FIGURE 4-8: Adding task and calendar apps by the Working on a Deadline pop-up tile.

Just after the Working on a Deadline tile is the Add Lists, Libraries, and Other Apps tile. This pop-up tile takes you to the Your Apps page. This is the same result as clicking the Settings gear icon in the top right of the page and selecting Add an App. (Chapter 7 explores apps in detail.)

Changing the style and brand of your site

The What's Your Style pop-up tile enables you to change the look and feel of your site. The tile takes you to the Change the Look page of your site, where you can choose a look. This is the same as navigating to the page by clicking the Settings gear icon, selecting Site Settings, and then clicking the Change the Look link in the Look and Feel section. (Changing the look and feel of your site is covered in Chapter 13.)

The next tile on the screen is called Your Site, Your Brand. This tile takes you to the Title, Description, and Logo page, where you can add a description and logo to your site. You can also access this page on the Site Settings page by clicking the Title, Description, and Logo link in the Look and Feel section.

The last tile on the site, Keep Email in Context, walks you through sharing email on your site and connecting your documents to Outlook. You can also set up a site mailbox in Office 365 but you need to be part of the SharePoint Owners group. A *site mailbox* is just a special email address that goes directly to your SharePoint site.

REMEMBER

The pop-up tiles are designed to get you up and going quickly. You can achieve the same result using the Settings gear icon and the Site Contents page.

Staying in sync and collaborating

Many kinds of teams can use a SharePoint team site to collaborate. For example:

» Department members can use document libraries to upload document files and enter meetings in a team calendar.

» Project members can use a team site home page to post announcements and track issues and risks.

» Corporate communications can use a team site to store the documents and track the tasks required for preparing the company's annual report.

Chapter 5

Working with Web Pages

How many times have you heard, "We need the team to get on the same page?" Well, no problem if you're using SharePoint. If you're a facilitator, communicator, and/or have a creative streak, you need this chapter. Although SharePoint gives you a lot of helpful tools to work with content, the ability to communicate effectively with your team, starting with a customizable home page, pulls everything together.

Web pages and Web Parts let you arrange and present information in a collaboration site. Pages can display freeform text, tables, hyperlinks, and images, as well as Web Parts showing app content from your site (or other sites!) arranged as you want. Web Parts can be closed temporarily or moved. You can modify the Web Parts to show only the data you want from an app. You can inform, organize, and focus your team with your pages, something that otherwise would take a lot of effort with emails and network shares.

In this chapter, we show you how to work with web pages. In Chapter 6, we go into more detail about working with Web Parts.

Introducing the Ribbon

In order to edit the contents of a SharePoint 2016 page, you need to access the Ribbon. The Ribbon is tucked away in the header of the SharePoint 2016 team site and is accessed by clicking the Page tab. When you click the Page tab, the header automatically switches to the Ribbon, and you can begin editing your SharePoint page. To flip back to the standard header, click the Browse tab. The Ribbon was introduced in Microsoft Office and is a convenient way to display many menu items in a small amount of screen space.

The Ribbon in SharePoint 2016 features menu items that are relevant to the kind of page you're viewing, arranged in tabs. For example, the home page of a team site displays two tabs: Browse and Page. You find most of the menu commands you need to use on the Ribbon, and some Ribbon buttons contain drop-down lists. Figure 5-1 shows the Ribbon with the Page tab active.

FIGURE 5-1:
Use the Ribbon to access menu commands.

![Ribbon screenshot showing Office 365 Sites with Page tab commands]

TIP

An app displays commands on the Ribbon that provide additional configuration options. These commands are *contextual* because the commands that appear depend on the context of where you are in the site. For example, the Document Library app adds a Files and Library tab to the Ribbon, in addition to the standard Browse tab.

In past versions of SharePoint, all data containers were a list or library. The list and library are still there, but in SharePoint 2016 they are called apps.

Understanding SharePoint Web Pages

Your team site is really just a collection of web pages. You have two different types of web pages for displaying your content — *Wiki Content pages* and *Web Part pages*.

TIP

There is also an advanced type of page known as a publishing page. Publishing pages are explored in Chapter 18.

If you're already familiar with SharePoint team sites, you've probably worked with Web Part pages. In SharePoint 2016, Wiki Content pages are now the default web page type. They are stored in a wiki page library called *Site Pages*.

Choosing a wiki page

A wiki page is designed to be intuitive and easy to get up and running with Share-Point pages. A *wiki page* is similar to an Office Word document. You place the page in Edit mode and start adding content. Just like a Word document, you have the Ribbon at the top to format text and insert items. And when you want to get advanced and modify the HTML, all you need to do is click a button to edit the source code.

Only members of your team site's default Members group have permission to modify wiki pages. If you want some people to be able to read your wiki pages but not edit them, add those users to your site's default Visitors group. See Chapter 14 for more details on managing site access.

A Wiki Content page consists of a very editable region where you place your content. In this editable region, you can place almost any kind of content imaginable — freeform text, tables, hyperlinks, images, even Web Parts. A Wiki Content page combines the best aspects of a typical wiki page with a Web Part page.

You can create new Wiki Content pages for your site by clicking the Settings gear icon and choosing Add a Page. (The Settings gear icon is found in the upper-right corner of the page.) These new Wiki Content pages are also stored in the Site Pages library.

As with most things in SharePoint, there are multiple ways to achieve the same outcome. For example, you can also create a wiki page by opening the New Document drop-down menu and selecting Wiki Page.

TIP

You can create additional wiki page libraries if you want to manage a specific wiki topic in your site.

Choosing a Web Part page

A Web Part page contains various Web Part zones in which you can place Web Parts; it doesn't have the same editing experience as the Wiki Content page. The Web Part page, however, provides for a consistent layout of Web Parts in order to create ordered pages with Web Part functionality. For example, you can drag and drop Web Parts between zones without reconfiguring the Web Parts. A Wiki Content page, on the other hand, is more freeform. You could insert a table on a Wiki

Content page and then insert Web Parts into different cells of the table, but that's a lot of work. With a Web Part page, you choose the Web Part zone layout when you create the page and add Web Parts to the available zones.

Web Part pages live in a library just like a Wiki Content page. You can create a new Web Part page in your Site Pages library by clicking the Files tab in the Ribbon and then selecting Web Part Page from the New Document drop-down list, as shown in Figure 5-2.

FIGURE 5-2:
Creating a new
Web Part page in
the Site Pages
library.

Choosing a Wiki Content page over a Web Part page or vice versa

For some who have lived through different versions of SharePoint over the years, it may simply be familiarity that keeps you using a Web Part page. Converting previous sites to the new version may be a factor as well. However, the need for creating rich content pages in a collaboration site is now better served by the Wiki Content page.

The following list helps you decide which type of page to create, based on your needs:

>> **Web Part page:** Use when you need mostly Web Parts with little text content. Examples include pages with multiple List View Web Parts, Office application Web Parts, custom search and site directories, and pages that use connected Web Parts. Web Part pages are simple to create without the editor needing skills in rich content editing. Although versioning may be turned on in the

library you store your Web Part pages in, the Web Parts themselves don't retain history.

>> **Wiki Content page:** Use when you have mostly a need for rich text content, for example, text, tables, links, and images. You can still insert Web Parts or use no Web Parts at all. The HTML content in wiki pages is also subject to versioning if versioning is turned on in the library.

TIP

There is also a special type of site called a publishing site. Publishing sites contain a special type of page called a publishing page. You can lock down a publishing page and allow people to enter or edit content but not change the look and feel or the location of the content. This is important for broadly consumed websites in order to maintain a consistent look and feel of content throughout the site. Publishing sites are a very advanced topic and require significant resources to implement and manage and are beyond the scope of this book. However, if you are a large organization and want to control at a very granular level how content is published to your SharePoint website pages, then dig further with publishing sites.

Creating a New Wiki Content Page

If you want additional pages in your site that look and function like the home page, create a new Wiki Content page. Creating a new page of this type is slightly different than creating other content. You can create a new page in multiple ways, including clicking the Settings gear icon and choosing Add a Page, creating a Forward link in a wiki page, and selecting the New Document command in the wiki library.

To create a new Wiki Content page using the New Page option, follow these steps:

1. **Click the Settings gear icon and choose Add a Page.**

This creates a Wiki Content page only, not a Web Part page.

A dialog box appears, asking for the name of your new page and informing you where you can find it. If you look at the location, you see that the page will be created in the Site Pages library.

2. **Type the name for your page in the New Page Name text box and click the Create button.**

I suggest typing a single word that's a meaningful name, and use the text editors to type any title or other text in the page to communicate its purpose. As you type the name of the page, you see how the URL will look as the location preview is automatically updated.

Your new page is created and placed in Edit mode. You see other recently modified pages in this wiki library via links on the lower-left corner of the Quick Launch pane.

By default, the page is a single column, but you can change the page's layout to include more columns by clicking the Text Layout button on the Format Text tab of the Ribbon, as shown in Figure 5-3.

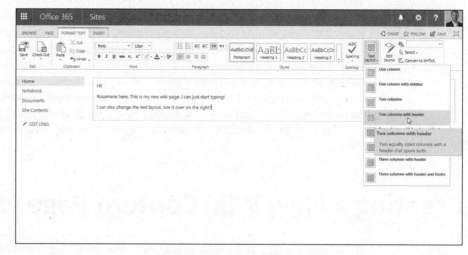

FIGURE 5-3:
Change the layout of your wiki page.

TIP

Every wiki library is created with a How to Use This Library page. After you have experience working with wiki libraries, you can choose to delete this page; however, it contains many helpful instructions and tips on working with the wiki functionality. You can access the How to Use This Library page by clicking the View All Pages button in the Ribbon of your new Wiki Content page. The View All Pages button takes you to the library that holds the page you're currently editing.

Your wiki pages are stored in the Site Pages library. You can browse to the Site Pages library using the left navigation pane or by clicking the Settings gear icon and choosing Site Contents ➪ Site Pages. You can also click the View All Pages button in the Ribbon when editing any page that resides in the Site Pages library.

Adding media

Of course, you can add much more to a wiki page than just text. The Insert tab of the Ribbon provides menus for adding tables, media, links, reusable content, App Parts, and Web Parts. One advantage to using wiki pages over Web Part pages is that you can upload your media file and display it in your page without leaving the page. You don't have to upload your media files first and then link to them.

Inserting a video (or embedding a YouTube video)

To display media in your wiki page, such as a YouTube video, follow these steps:

1. **Create a new wiki page or browse to an existing page.**

2. **On the Page tab of the Ribbon, click the Edit button to place the page in Edit mode.**

3. **Click inside the layout area where you want to display the media (in this example, a YouTube video).**

4. **On the Ribbon, click the Insert tab.**

5. **Click the Video and Audio drop-down list and select From Computer.**

   The Upload Media dialog box appears.

6. **Click Browse and choose the media you want to upload.**

   You can also embed a YouTube or other video site video. On YouTube, find the video you want to place on your page and click the Share link. Click the Embed link, and copy the code. To insert this code in your wiki page, click the Embed Code button on the Ribbon and paste the code into the page. Your YouTube video displays right in your SharePoint wiki page.

7. **Accept the default setting to upload the file to the Site Assets library and click OK.**

   SharePoint uploads the file to the Images document library.

8. **Select the Web Part and then click Edit Web Part. A property window appears so you can enter metadata about the video file. Enter any metadata you want and click Save.**

   If you wish to include a preview image, you can upload one to the Images folder and then provide the link in the metadata field called Preview Image URL.

   You don't need a preview image, but it makes your page look more polished.

9. **Hover over the Media Web Part and click the Play button. The video starts to play.**

Pretty cool, huh? You can upload a video and display it in a page during one editing session.

Inserting a Note Board

Want to allow your team to add comments about the wiki page? Follow these steps to insert a Note Board Web Part to capture social comments:

1. **Create a new wiki page or browse to an existing page.**

2. **On the Page tab of the Ribbon, click the Edit button to place the page in Edit mode.**

3. **Click inside the layout area where you want to display the media (in this example, a Note Board Web Part).**

TIP

The Note Board Web Part isn't available in all editions of SharePoint when it is installed on your local premises. The features and functionality available in the different Office 365 plans and on-premises editions of SharePoint can be complicated. Microsoft provides a nice matrix on their TechNet website to help make sense of it all at http://technet.microsoft.com/en-us/library/ jj819267.aspx. The top of the matrix includes the feature matrix for SharePoint Online. If you scroll to the bottom, you see the feature matrix for SharePoint On-Premises.

4. **On the Ribbon, click the Insert tab.**

5. **Click Web Part to display the Web Part gallery.**

6. **In the Categories list, click Social Collaboration.**

7. **In the Parts list, select Note Board, as shown in Figure 5-4.**

8. **Click Add to add the Note Board Web Part to the page.**

   The Web Part is added to the page.

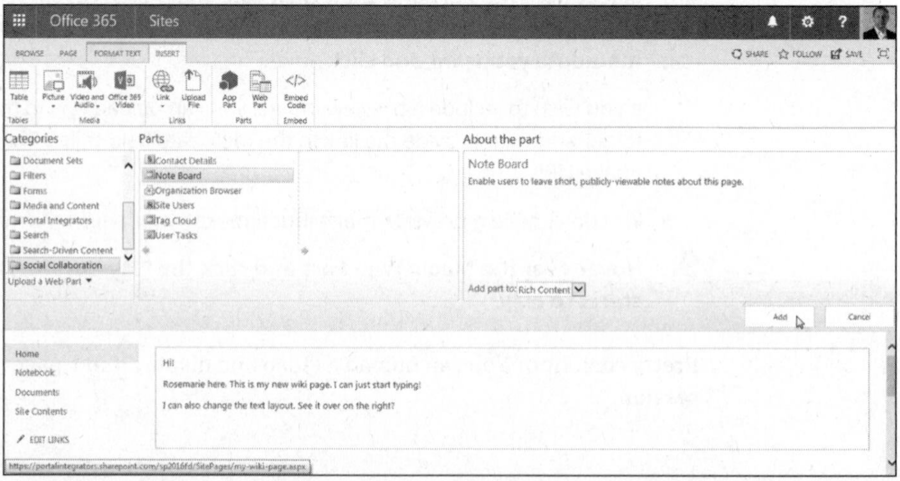

FIGURE 5-4: Upload and display media without leaving the page.

Managing wiki pages

Wiki Content pages have commands on the Page tab of the Ribbon that are useful for managing pages. Some of the commands you will probably use (as shown in Figure 5-5) include

>> Page History allows you to easily see all the edits made to the current page.

>> Page Permissions lets you set unique permissions on the page.

>> Make Homepage sets the current page as the home page for the team site.

>> Incoming Links shows all the pages that link to the current page.

>> View All Pages takes you to the wiki library where the page is saved.

FIGURE 5-5:
Manage wiki
pages with the
Page tab of the
Ribbon.

After you are in the wiki library, you can use all the standard document library functions to manage the library's settings.

Categorizing your wiki pages

Wikis often include a way to categorize pages, and SharePoint wikis are no different. By default, the wiki library includes an Enterprise Keywords field that allows you to enter freeform keywords or tags on your wiki page. These tags can be displayed in a *tag cloud,* a visual representation of tags that indicates how often they occur in relation to each other and can help users find content they are interested in.

To add a tag to your wiki page:

1. **Activate the Enterprise Keywords column for the Site Pages library by clicking Library Settings on the Library tab and then clicking Enterprise Metadata and Keywords Settings.**

   The Enterprise Metadata and Keywords functionality is not available in all editions of SharePoint.

2. **Select the Add an Enterprise Keywords Column to This List and Enable Keyword Synchronization check box.**

TIP

If you are using SharePoint 2016 On-Premises, then you will see an option for social tags; however, if you are using SharePoint Online, you won't see this additional option. This is an example of the slight variations that appear depending on the way your SharePoint environment is set up.

3. **Click OK to save the change.**

4. **Browse to your wiki page, click the Page tab on the Ribbon, and click the Edit Properties button.**

   The Edit form appears.

5. **Type tags in the Enterprise Keywords field.**

6. **Click the Save button.**

   The web page has your keywords associated with it.

If you aren't sure of the difference between Enterprise Keywords and social tags, be sure to check out Chapter 16 for insights on how to use these important tagging mechanisms.

TECHNICAL STUFF

If you can't save the properties of a page, then it's likely that some services are not running for your SharePoint farm. Ask your farm administrator to check to make sure the Search Host Controller Service and the Search Query and Site Settings services are running. This is done in Central Administration on the Services on Server page.

TIP

If you need your wiki page to have a consistent layout that displays the Enterprise Keywords field on every page, you should probably use an Enterprise Wiki site template.

Creating a New Web Part Page

We outline reasons earlier in this chapter on why you may need a Web Part or multiple Web Part pages in your collaboration site. A Web Part page can also be set as the home page. You can use links to connect your Wiki Content pages and Web Part pages.

To create a new Web Part page:

1. **Click the Settings gear icon and choose Site Contents.**

2. **Click the Site Pages library or whichever library you want to hold your new Web Part page.**

3. **Click the Files tab of the Ribbon.**

   The Files tab appears.

4. **Click the New Document drop-down list on the left of the Ribbon and select Web Part Page (refer to Figure 5-2).**

5. **Enter a name for the new page in the Name text box, and then select a Layout by clicking a layout in the Choose a Layout Template box.**

   Click different options in the list box to see a thumbnail of the layout options.

   Layouts for Web Part pages can't be changed after the fact. You don't need to use every zone that appears on your layout, but you do want to select a layout that supports the desired design of your page.

6. **Select the document library that will contain this page by selecting an option from the Document Library drop-down list.**

   Web Part pages are stored in libraries, so a default library, such as the Site Assets library, is selected for you. You can also choose a different library, such as Site Pages, or even create a new library to store your Web Part pages if you want to be different.

7. **Click the Create button.**

   Your new Web Part page opens in Edit mode, ready for you to start adding Web Parts.

TIP

You can change the home page of your site to any Wiki Content page or Web Part page. Simply click the Make Homepage button in the Page Actions area of the Edit tab on the Ribbon while editing the preferred page.

Chapter 6

Working with Web Parts

*W*eb Parts are reusable components that display content on web pages in SharePoint. Just as the name implies, a Web Part is a part of a web page that is all packaged together nicely and easy to work with. Web Parts are a fundamental part of the team site experience, so make it a point to get comfortable with them and know what your options are.

REMEMBER

The Team Site template is just one option when creating a new SharePoint website. There are other templates you can choose to create a new website, and Web Parts are critical to all of them in SharePoint.

In this chapter, we introduce you to Web Parts and show you how to use them on your web pages.

Adding a Web Part to Your Page

A *Web Part* is an individual component of content that can be placed on a Share-Point page, in either a zone in a Web Part page or in Rich Content areas of the Wiki Content page. Web Parts can be moved, added, and deleted, framed by borders and titles, and closed and reopened, depending on your need. In other words, they are a little piece of web functionality all wrapped up in a nice package for you.

In a team site, you may place Web Parts on your home page for your users to read and access items from your apps, such as announcements, documents, links, calendars, and contacts. You can add text for additional instructions and images to enhance the collaboration experience.

The Web Parts used to show your List and Library apps are called *List View Web Parts.* Over the versions of SharePoint, the number and complexity of Web Parts have grown considerably. Some of these Web Parts can be used only if certain functionality is enabled in your site, such as Business Data Sources to use the Business Data Web Parts. Other categories of Web Parts, such as Content Rollup Web Parts, provide the ability to feed data from lower-level sites to a site higher in the hierarchy, such as the home page of an intranet.

SharePoint 2016 has a familiar interface for selecting and inserting Web Parts. The interface is called the Web Part Gallery, and you see it whenever you click to insert a Web Part. The Web Part Gallery first shows a list of Web Part categories, and when you click a category, you see all the parts contained in that category. When the Web Part name is highlighted, you can see a description as well as an example of each in the About the Web Part section before inserting it.

Follow these steps to insert a Web Part:

1. **Make sure you're in Edit mode of either the Wiki Content page or the Web Part page (click the Page tab and click Edit Page).**

   In a Wiki Content page, insert Web Parts into one of the Rich Content containers in the layout. In a Web Part page, insert Web Parts into one of the zones on the page.

2. **In a Web Part page, click in a zone. In a Wiki Content page, click in a Rich Content zone, and then click Web Part on the Insert tab.**

   The Web Part Gallery appears.

   Because a Web Part page can contain only Web Parts, the Insert tab buttons for text and images actually insert a Content Editor Web Part or an Image View Web Part, respectively, for those selections.

3. **After you decide on a Web Part, you can add it to the page.**

   Either select the area from the drop-down list and then click the Add button (as shown in Figure 6-1) or drag the Web Part name into the zone or Rich Content area you want to place it in.

You can also use the Add button under the About the Web Part section to insert the Web Part into the zone or Rich Content section your cursor is in.

In a Web Part page, the About the Web Part section contains a drop-down list containing the names of all the zones on the page. You can select the zone and then click the Add button. In any case, the Web Part is placed on the page.

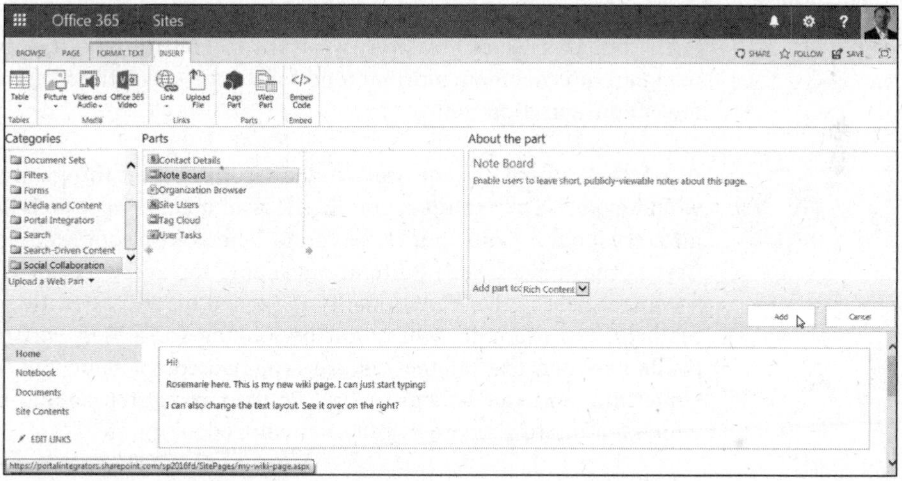

FIGURE 6-1:
Inserting a Web Part on a Web Part page.

4. **Modify the Web Part properties by clicking the Edit drop-down list (in the far right of the Web Part title) and choosing Edit Web Part.**

   By clicking on the Web Part, additional configuration options may appear in the Ribbon. (Skip ahead to the "Changing Web Part Properties" section, later in this chapter, for more about configuring Web Parts.)

TIP

Web Parts can be moved in a Web Part page or a Wiki Content page simply by dragging them from one zone or area to another.

Choosing the Right Web Part

The SharePoint 2016 gallery contains more than 80 Web Parts, as well as List View Web Parts created for any Library or List–based apps that you've made. In addition, your company may create custom Web Parts or purchase them from third–party vendors.

REMEMBER

Your company may purchase or create additional Web Parts. Conversely, your company may choose not to supply every Web Part that we describe in the upcoming list. Companies may also modify some Web Parts, such as the Content Editor Web Part, to disallow certain styles or JavaScript content.

With so many choices, how do you decide which Web Part to use? If you're like us, we're sure you'll find your favorites. We think about Web Parts as being either specialized or generalized in what they do. We tend to use the more general Web Parts, but in a lot of websites, we want to control how it appears. When we're using an internal team site, we tend to use the specialized Web Parts that contain fewer configuration items.

TIP

A constant source of confusion in SharePoint is that things aren't always as you would expect. For example, you might read about a cool Web Part, but when you go to try it out, it's nowhere to be found. There are a couple of reasons for this. The first is that not all Web Parts are available for every edition of SharePoint. The second reason is that functionality is turned on and off with specific SharePoint features. For example, you might be looking for a Web Part that only becomes available when the related feature is activated for your site. If you read about something and can't seem to find it, your next step should be in figuring out which feature to activate to get what you're looking for.

When you insert a Web Part onto your page, you're presented with the Web Part Gallery. The Web Part Gallery organizes Web Parts into categories, as shown in Figure 6-2. The top category in the list is always Apps. These are all of the apps you have added to your site. It also includes custom apps you have developed, such as a custom List or Library app.

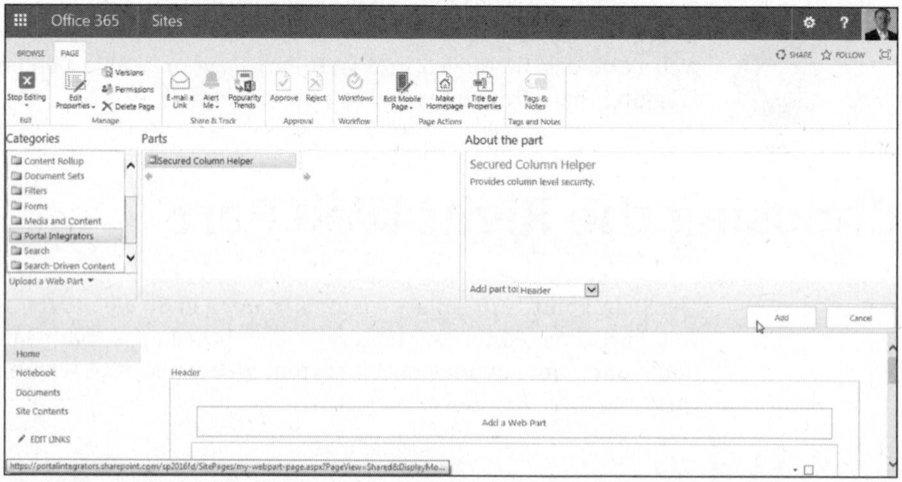

FIGURE 6-2:
Web Part categories can contain third-party Web Parts.

The Web Part categories include the following:

- **Apps:** These Web Parts display items from the List and Library apps on your site. You can use Views to filter, sort, and group the information presented in the Web Part.

- **Blog:** This category includes Web Parts for working with blogs. For example, you can add Web Parts that provide links to older blogs, show blog notifications, or even provide tools for blog owners and administrators.

- **Business Data:** The Business Data Web Parts allow you to display data from external data sources. This category includes Web Parts for displaying Excel and Visio documents in your web page.

- **Community:** These Web Parts are designed for Community sites and include functionality for providing information about the community, joining the community, community membership details, and what's happening information. In addition, there is a Tools Web Part for community owners and administrators.

- **Content Rollup:** This category includes Web Parts for rolling up content from multiple sources. For example, there are Web Parts to aggregate sites, query content, and search for content. In addition, this category contains Web Parts to view RSS and XML feeds. Because more and more content is available in RSS and XML formats, these Web Parts are especially useful. You use an XSL template to tell the Web Part how to display the RSS or XML content on your web page.

- **Document Sets:** These Web Parts display the content and properties of a Document Set. A *Document Set* is a grouping of documents in a Library app.

- **Filters:** The filter Web Parts provide numerous ways to filter the information displayed on the page. For example, you can add the Choice filter to a page and then connect it to a List View Web Part so that the list is filtered by the value selected by the user. Your filter options include filtering by the current user who's visiting the page, date, good old-fashioned text values, or a query string. A *query string* is a value that you pass into the page by using a question mark, such as `mypage.aspx?filter=somevalue`. Another example would be adding a SharePoint List Filter Web Part to your page to only show certain items from a list. The actual list might include every product in your company, but you could add the Web Part to a department page and only show the products for that particular department.

- **Forms:** There are two Web Parts for displaying forms: the HTML Form Web Part and the InfoPath Form Web Part. An HTML form uses basic HTML code to show a form. InfoPath is a retired Office product that was used to build forms. InfoPath is no longer included with Office 2016.

>> **Media and Content:** These Web Parts work well when your content needs are simple. Use the Media Web Part to display Windows Media Player on your web page. The Image Viewer Web Part lets you link to an image and display it on your page. If your company has Silverlight applications, they can be played using the Silverlight Web Part. The Content Editor Web Part is a perennial favorite because it allows you to enter almost any HTML, CSS, or JavaScript you want on your page.

WARNING

Some of these Web Parts, especially the Content Editor Web Part, can really make it difficult to manage a site's content long-term. Imagine you have a team site with ten web pages. On each web page, you've placed three Content Editor Web Parts. That's 30 individual components you have to touch every time you need to change content. Rather than add all this custom HTML and CSS code into a Content Editor Web Part, it would be better to have a developer create a custom Web Part to solve your specific need and to add the custom Web Part to the SharePoint gallery.

>> **PerformancePoint:** PerformancePoint is a Business Intelligence platform designed for such specialties as Dashboards, Key Performance Indicators, and Scorecards. These Web Parts let you display PerformancePoint information in your web pages. The PerformancePoint Services Site Collection feature must be enabled before the PerformancePoint category appears in the Web Parts gallery.

>> **Search:** Although these Web Parts may seem specialized, they are actually quite powerful. You can use the Search Web Parts to create a custom search results page that is scoped to the content you want to filter.

>> **Search-Driven Content:** These Web Parts take search to a whole new level. Using these Web Parts, you can build a web page based on search results. This creates a very dynamic page that is constantly updated as content is added and removed from the site. You can use Web Parts for searching and displaying pages, pictures, popular items, tagged items, recently changed items, recommended items, videos, web pages, and wiki pages.

>> **Social Collaboration:** These Web Parts are designed for displaying social functionality on your web pages. You can add a number of social features to your pages such as contact details, Note Boards, site users, tag clouds, and user tasks. The Note Board Web Part is a particularly cool collaboration function. Dropping this Web Part on your page adds a Social Commenting box so that folks can add comments right inside your web page. Social commenting is part of SharePoint's new social networking features, which we discuss in Chapters 15 through 17.

TIP

In addition to the standard categories, you might also see custom or third-party categories. For example, Portal Integrators is a company that develops Web Parts for SharePoint. If your IT team has installed Portal Integrators Web Parts, then they will show up in a category called Portal Integrators (refer to Figure 6-2).

WARNING

Any configuration or content that you put inside a Web Part isn't version-controlled. In other words, each time you change the Web Part, you write over any previous configuration or content. That's another reason we caution against using the Content Editor Web Parts. Store your content in lists and libraries where the content is subject to version control and retention policies, rather than placing it directly in the web page. You can export your Web Part's configuration using the Export on the Web Part's menu.

TIP

Content that you place inside a Rich Content control on a wiki page is version-controlled if versioning is enabled in your library.

Changing Web Part Properties

After you select and insert a Web Part into your page, you may want to modify its properties to fit your needs. The number and type of properties you can modify are based on the type of Web Part you use.

Reviewing Web Part properties

When you select the Edit Web Part command by clicking the Web Part menu (in the far right of the Web Part title), SharePoint opens the Web Part tool pane. In some Web Parts, SharePoint creates a link to this tool pane as part of the place-holder text. Following is a list of properties in the tool pane common to List View Web Parts:

REMEMBER

» **Selected View:** The options in the Selected View drop-down list are dependent on the type of library or list and/or other views you may have created.

The Current View is simply what's showing currently. You change view properties on-the-fly using the Edit the Current View link in the tool pane. Your changes are now part of the current view. If you use the Edit in Current View link, you can't revert to a past view.

The Edit the Current View options are, for the most part, identical to what you see when you create a view in the Library or List app. Make sure you look at Styles and Item limits when creating a view for a Web Part because these options are frequently overlooked.

If the changes you need to make to the view are simple and few, the Edit the Current View link is handy. If you need to consistently apply the same view selections for this Web Part, create a view in the Library or List app so that you can apply the view and don't lose the options you chose.

>> **Toolbar Type:** Depending on the Library or List app, this drop-down list allows you the options of Full Toolbar, Summary Toolbar, No Toolbar, or Show Toolbar. For example, in a Document Library app, choosing Full Toolbar enables users to upload the document, check it out, and so forth.

>> **Appearance:** The Appearance section allows you to title the Web Part, fix the height and width as necessary, and determine the chrome type. *Chrome* is another word for the Web Part surround; for example, title and border options.

>> **Layout:** In the Layout section, you can change the zone location of the Web Part, as well as hide it without closing it.

>> **Advanced:** This section contains many of the options you use to allow users with permissions to modify Web Parts, such as Allow Minimize or Allow Close.

>> **AJAX Options:** This section gives the owner/admin the choice of enabling *asynchronous behaviors.* This means that the data in the Web Part is sent to the page without causing the web page to refresh.

>> **Miscellaneous:** Miscellaneous options including sample data, XSL link, and some caching properties.

TIP

In addition to these common categories, a third-party Web Part might have additional categories that are specific to the Web Part. For example, the Portal Integrators Web Parts include configuration categories specific to the purpose of the Web Part.

Editing Web Part properties

Editing Web Part properties is pretty straightforward. Again, experimenting is the key. The most commonly used sections are located at the top of the tool pane: Selected View, Toolbar, and Appearance. Many users don't realize how much they can enhance the user experience with the Web Part by using the options available.

To open the Web Part tool pane and modify Web Part properties, follow these steps:

1. **Click the Web Part menu on the Web Part and choose Edit Web Part.**

   The tool pane opens. You see several of the categories of properties that we describe in the preceding list. You may need to click the plus sign to open certain sections.

TIP

   You need to be in page Edit mode before the drop-down list to select Edit Web Part appears.

2. **Adjust properties as desired (see Figure 6-3).**

   Make your selections based on the categories and options that we describe in the preceding list or other options available per the specific Web Part.

3. **Click the Apply button to apply your current changes before modifying others, or click OK to finish modifying.**

   Your changes are visible in the Web Part.

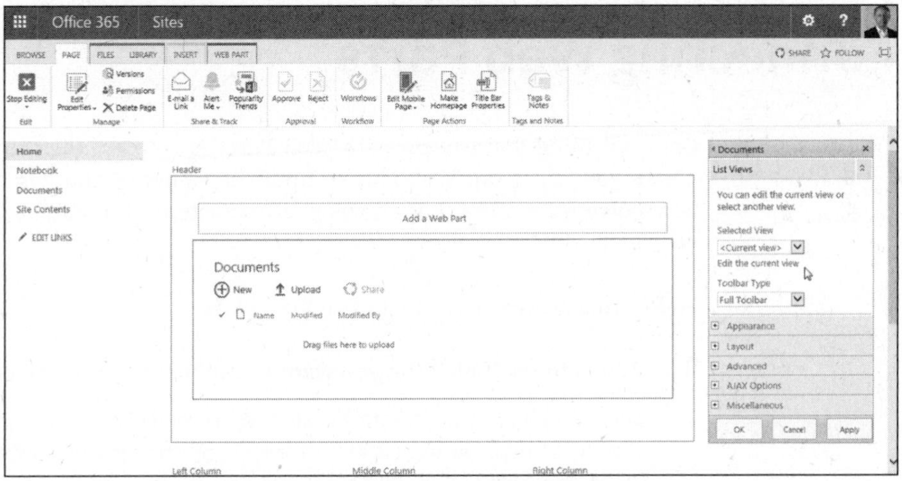

FIGURE 6-3: Change your Web Part's configuration.

Minimizing or deleting Web Parts

You have two options for removing a Web Part from your page — minimizing a Web Part or deleting it. Minimizing a Web Part leaves the Web Part on the page so you can restore it again for future use. Deleting the Web Part removes the Web Part from your page (but doesn't delete it from SharePoint).

To minimize or delete a Web Part from your page, click the Web Part menu, as we describe in the preceding list, and choose Minimize or Delete.

To Restore a Web Part that was previously minimized, open the page in Edit mode, click the drop-down for the Web Part, and choose Restore.

TIP

In previous versions of SharePoint you could also "close" a Web Part. (SharePoint Online may still display this option.) Closing a Web Part saves it to a special category in the SharePoint Web Part Gallery. When you want to add a closed Web Part back to the page, you find a category in the Web Part Gallery called Closed Parts. Clicking the Closed Parts category reveals all the Web Parts on the page that have been closed. On the other hand, if you delete a Web Part, it will be gone forever.

If you spend time configuring a Web Part and want to remove it, it's better to minimize it so that you don't lose all your configuration changes. Keep in mind that having a minimized Web Part on a page causes the same performance impact as if they were open. So you don't want a ton of minimized Web Parts if you don't need them.

Connecting Web Parts

One cool thing you can do with Web Parts is connect them to each other. This allows you to use one Web Part to filter the values of another Web Part. This is a very powerful feature that allows you to create useful, data-driven web pages in your team site.

Follow this process to connect two Web Parts:

1. Add both the Web Parts you want to connect to your web page.

For example, you can create a custom app called Customers based on the Custom List app. Assume the Customers app contains a column for customer name and a column for customer city. You can then add the associated Customers Web Part to the page along with a SharePoint List Filter Web Part. You must first select the SharePoint List Filter Web Part to which you want to associate the list by selecting the list on the Web Part property window along with the identifying column that needs to be filtered. You must set and save this selection before the Send Filter Values To choice in the Connections menu will be enabled.

TIP

Creating a custom list app is covered in Chapter 7.

2. Click the drop-down arrow on the SharePoint List Filter Web Part, choose Connections ⇨ Send Filter Values To, and then choose the name of the Customers Web Part you want to filter, as shown in Figure 6-4.

The Choose Connection dialog box appears. The Choose Connection tab displays the connection type that you selected in this step.

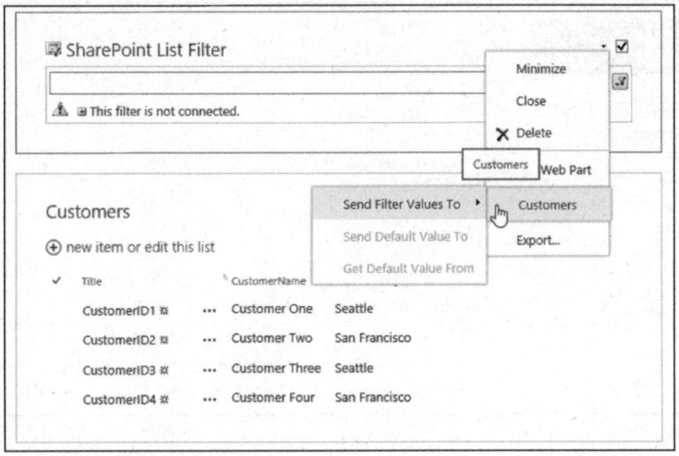

FIGURE 6-4:
Choosing which
Web Part to filter.

SharePoint List Filter

⚠ ⊞ This filter is not connected.

Minimize

Close

✖ Delete

Customers   Web Part

Send Filter Values To ▸ Customers

Send Default Value To   Export...

Get Default Value From

Customers

⊕ new item or edit this list

✓	Title		CustomerName	
	CustomerID1 ⚙	...	Customer One	Seattle
	CustomerID2 ⚙	...	Customer Two	San Francisco
	CustomerID3 ⚙	...	Customer Three	Seattle
	CustomerID4 ⚙	...	Customer Four	San Francisco

TIP

If you don't see this dialog box, make sure your web browser is allowing pop-ups from the site.

3. **Click the Connection Type drop-down list, choose Get Filter Values From, and click the Configure button.**

This is the field that has the set of values you want to match from your filtering Web Part. To filter a Customers list Web Part with a City column, we chose the City field as the Consumer Field Name, as shown in Figure 6-5.

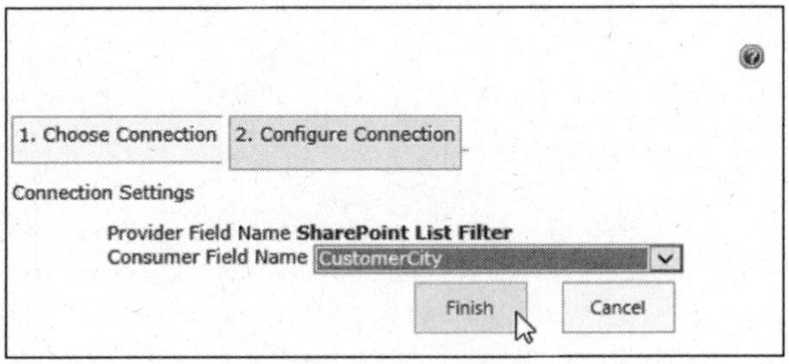

FIGURE 6-5:
Select the field
that contains
your filter values.

1. Choose Connection   2. Configure Connection

Connection Settings

Provider Field Name **SharePoint List Filter**
Consumer Field Name CustomerCity ▾

Finish   Cancel

4. **Click the Finish button.**

The connection is established.

5. **On the Page tab of the Ribbon, click Stop Editing.**

The page exits Edit mode. As you select values in the filter Web Part, the connected Web Part is filtered accordingly, as shown in Figure 6-6.

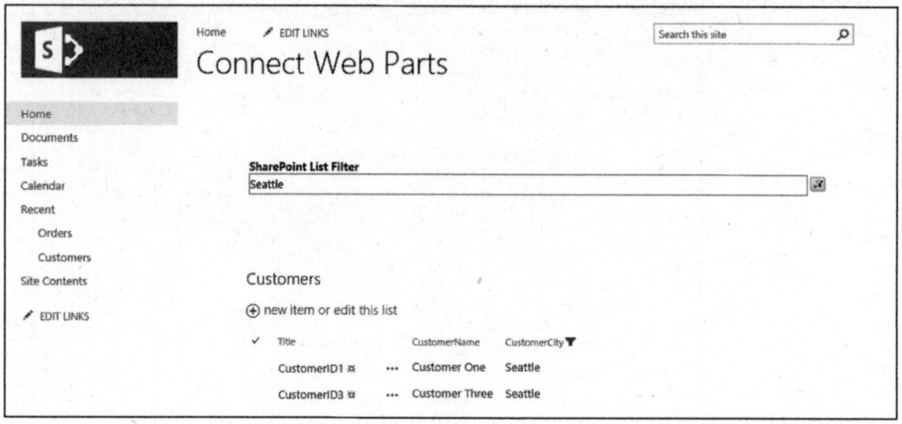

FIGURE 6-6: A filtered Web Part.

Chapter 7

Getting Familiar with Apps

The concept of an app is relatively new in SharePoint. An *app* is Microsoft's attempt to help stem confusion because getting your head around lists and libraries is difficult, especially when you start customizing them. For example, say you start with a custom list and then add columns to make it specific to customers. Is it still just a custom list or is it a Customers list or what? Microsoft posed this question to a number of focus groups and found that people were more comfortable with the concept of an app than a list or library. The result is that every list and library is now called an app.

Apps don't end at lists and libraries, though. Web developers can create apps that do all sorts of cool things. Because SharePoint 2016 is built using HTML standards, a web developer can take any web functionality and roll it into a SharePoint app. Third parties can put up their apps for sale on the online SharePoint App Store, which you access from within SharePoint.

In this chapter, you delve into apps. You find out how to add apps to your site and how to configure apps. You find out that most apps are based on lists. And finally, you see how to configure these list-based apps.

Introducing SharePoint Apps

The concept of an app in general is nothing new. If you use a smartphone, you're surely familiar with apps. Each type of smartphone has thousands and thousands of apps available. SharePoint has jumped on the app bandwagon and embraced the concept of an app. An app can be simple or complex. For example, you might create an app by customizing the Custom List app. On the other hand, you might hire a web developer to build a complete accounting system as a SharePoint app.

TIP

An app displays commands on the Ribbon that provide additional configuration options. These commands are *contextual* because the commands that appear depend on the context of where you are in the site. For example, the Document Library app contains a Files and Library tab in addition to the Browse tab.

Adding Apps to Your Site

When you create a new SharePoint site you choose a template. Depending on the template you choose, your site already has a number of apps by default. You can add more apps to your site, however. For example, you might want to add a Survey app to your site.

You can add an app (for example, the Survey app) to your site by following these steps:

1. **Click the Settings gear icon and choose Add an App.**

   The Your Apps page appears, showing all the apps you can add to your site. (See Figure 7-1.) There is a Noteworthy section at the top for the most common apps.

2. **Scroll down and click the Survey app.**

   The Adding Survey dialog box appears.

3. **Provide a name for your Survey app.**

   You can also click Advanced Options to set app specific options. In this case, you can choose to show usernames in the survey and also choose whether you want the Survey app to allow multiple responses.

4. **Click Create to create the app and add it to your site.**

   The Site Contents page is displayed, which shows all of the apps on your site. A green New! label is displayed next to any new apps. Notice you now have a new Survey app with the title you provided in Step 3. Figure 7-2 shows the app on the Site Contents page.

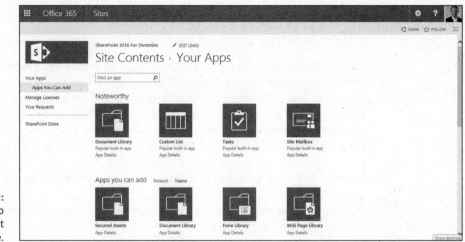

FIGURE 7-1:
Add a new app to
your SharePoint
2016 team site.

FIGURE 7-2:
A Survey app
on the Site
Contents page.

You can access an app by clicking on it in the Site Contents page. If you click an app you just created, it will display on the screen.

TIP

The apps that are available on the Your Apps page depend on which SharePoint features are activated. To find out more about SharePoint features, check out Chapter 10.

Accessing App Settings

Most apps are based on a list or library. A list or library has a settings page where you can configure your app. To view or change the configuration settings of your Library or List app, use the Library Settings or List Settings page. This page is the hub where you can find all the options for configuring and customizing your List or Library app to meet your business requirements. You can find shortcuts to many of these options on the Ribbon.

Follow these steps to access the Library Settings or List Settings page:

1. **Navigate to your library or list by clicking the name of the library or list on the Site Contents page.**

   You can access the Site Contents page from the Settings gear icon.

2. **On the Ribbon, click the Library or List tab.**

   Locate the Settings section, which is on the far right.

3. **Click the Library (or List) Settings button, as shown in Figure 7-3.**

   The Library Settings or List Settings page appears. (You may have already accessed this page when completing the steps in other chapters in this book.)

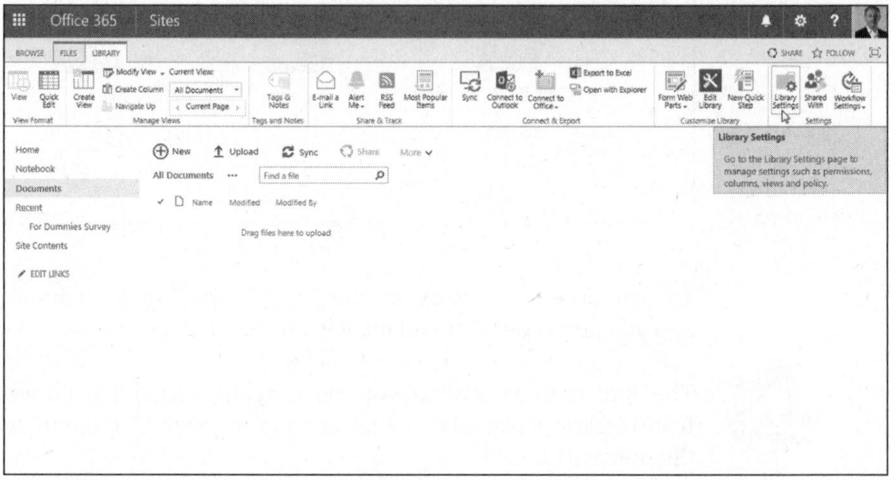

FIGURE 7-3:
Click the Library Settings button to change your library's configuration.

The Library (or List) Settings page is divided into several sections. Each section contains many configuration choices, as shown in Figure 7-4. We suggest you spend some time browsing this page. Some of the sections you see include

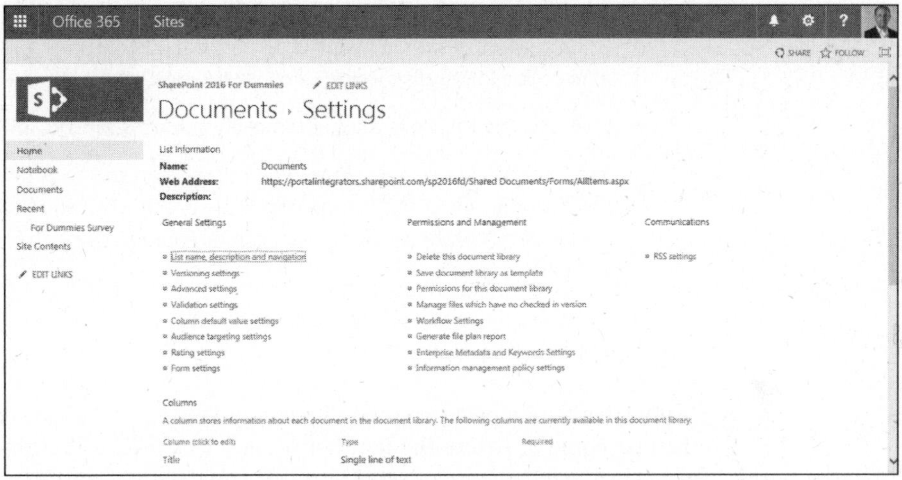

FIGURE 7-4:
The Library
Settings or List
Settings page.

- *List Information:* Displays the library (or list) name, web address, and description.

  You can change the list's name and description by clicking the List Name, Description, and Navigation link in the General Settings column.

  The web address is set to the list's default view. Change the default view by scrolling down to the Views section of the Library (or List) Settings page.

  When you link to a list or library, use the root of the web address. That way, you can change the default view any time you want without needing to change any links that target the list. For example, to create a link to the Shared Documents library, you would use the following:

  ```
  http://intranet.portalintegrators.com/Shared Documents
  ```

- *General Settings:* Includes list name and description as well as settings for Versioning, Advanced, Validation, Column Default Value, Rating, Audience Targeting, and Form. See Table 7-1 for a complete list of General Settings.

- *Permissions and Management:* Includes saving the library or list as a template as well as settings for Permissions, File Management, Workflow, Information Management Policy, and Enterprise Metadata and Keywords. You can also generate a file plan report from this section. (See Chapter 14 for more about security settings.)

- *Communications:* Configure RSS and incoming email settings for the library or list.

- *Content Types:* If you have configured your library or list to allow for content types, a Content Types section appears. Use this section to associate content types with your list or library. With content types, you can reuse columns across sites, as well as across lists and libraries. (See Chapter 8 for a more thorough discussion of content types.)

- *Columns:* Create, view, add, and modify columns for the library or list.

  See Chapter 8 to review column types. You can create your own column for this list only, add a site column from the preconfigured SharePoint site columns, or create a new site column of your choosing that can be added to multiple lists.

- *Views:* Display and modify the library or list views. You can also create new views.

Many site owners never change the default settings options; some simply change the List name or delete the list. For others, this level of optional setting detail is what they want to know first! Microsoft supplies descriptions on the how and/or why to use the settings on each of the individual settings pages; however, this chapter may become one of the most dog-eared chapters in the book because there are so many options to remember!

Configuring the General Settings

The General Settings area of the Library or List app has recently been expanded to include multiple new settings, including Validation, Column Default Value (for libraries), Rating, Audience Targeting, and Form. See Table 7-1 for an overview to see what you can do with each of these options.

TABLE 7-1   **General Settings Configuration Options**

Setting Name	What You Can Accomplish
List Name, Description, and Navigation	Just like it sounds! (See the section, "Changing the title, description, and navigation," later in this chapter.)
Versioning	Configure item approval, versioning (major and minor), and require check-out.
Advanced	A plethora of options, including allowing for the management of content types, search visibility, allowing for folders, or datasheet view.
Validation	Allows you to create formulas that compare two or more columns in your library or list.
Column Default Value	Add or edit default values for columns indicated in the library or list Validation settings.
Rating	A Yes or No option that allows items in the library or list to be rated.

Setting Name	What You Can Accomplish
Audience Targeting	A Yes or No option that allows the library or list to use audience targeting. Enabling audience targeting creates a Targeting column for this list. Some Web Parts can use this data to filter list contents based on whether the user is in the audience.
Form	Available for lists only. You need InfoPath to utilize these settings. However, because Microsoft stopped shipping InfoPath in Office 2016, your only option is to use an older version of InfoPath. Because InfoPath is on its way out, be prepared for this option to disappear in future versions of SharePoint.

Changing the title, description, and navigation

The General Settings page is a simple, self-descriptive settings page. Most of these options are what you configure when you first create the Library or List app, including whether the app appears on the Quick Launch navigation.

WARNING

Changing the title does *not* change the web address (URL) of the app. If having the title match the URL is important, or less confusing to your team, consider re-creating a new app with the desired title and deleting the old one. Of course, this works better early in the process, before you upload documents or create apps!

TIP

If you already have many items in your app, you can copy documents from one Library app to another, or export an existing List app to Excel and re-import into a new one. However, this shouldn't be taken lightly. Some column configuration settings, such as a Choice column, need to be re-created along with all the app settings we discuss in this chapter. If you're unsure what you want to name an app when you create it, take some time to consider your terminology before creating the app.

Versioning settings

The Versioning Settings area contains some of the most sought-after settings in any app. Versioning settings cover most of the document management or content management choices. So your new document/content management mantra is *approval, versioning,* and *check out.* You can say it in your sleep. By default, Approval, Versioning, or Check Out Requirement settings are *not* turned on in a team site.

The reason versioning is turned off by default is that it takes up a large amount of space in the database. Each time a new version is created, the database grows. However, versioning is important for any real work, so we recommend you turn it on.

TIP

If you want to have these options enabled when your sites are configured, consider using a publishing site instead.

Before selecting these options, make sure you know the business processes of your team. If documents are thoroughly vetted and approved outside the Share-Point process, you may not want or need Approval settings or Check Out enforced. If your documents are images, you may or may not want to apply versioning if the versions don't matter to you and you would not need to revert to an older version.

TIP

Consider using multiple Document Library apps and apply different settings based on need. For example, if you have 100 documents in a Library app and really only need versioning and approval on 5 of those documents, perhaps they can be placed in a Library app with extra configuration.

Versioning can be one of the most misunderstood features of SharePoint document management. Versioning is a helpful protection mechanism because you can revert to a previous version of the document if necessary. *Versions* in SharePoint are copies of the same document at different intervals during editing.

TIP

We suggest adding the Versions column to your views so that users can quickly see the version of the document. Otherwise, you end up with users appending versioning information to the document's name or title, such as Employee Handbook v1.0, Employee Handbook v2.0, or my favorite, Client_Proposal_Final_v3.0_ FINAL_KW-edited_RW-reviewed_FINAL-DO-NOT-REVISE_02-06-2017_ ROSEMARIE-SIGNED-OFF-FINAL_FINAL.

Follow these steps to apply or modify Versioning settings:

1. **Click the Versioning Settings link in the Library Settings or List Settings page.**

   The sections of the Versioning Settings page include Content Approval, Document Version History, Draft Item Security, and Require Check Out (Library apps only).

2. **Next you need to choose whether you want to require content approval for submitted items. You make this selection by choosing the Yes or No radio button on the Versioning Settings page (accessed in Step 1).**

   If you selected Yes in answer to Require Content Approval for Submitted Items?, individuals with the Approve Items permissions can always see draft items.

   Items that aren't approved yet (meaning they are draft versions) aren't visible to site members or visitors. You can designate who you want to view drafts in the Draft Item Security section. See Chapter 18 for details on content approval.

3. **In the Document Version History section, select a radio button to indicate whether to use No Versioning, Create Major Versions, Create Major and Minor (Draft) Versions, or (optional) specify the Number of Versions to keep by entering a number.**

   The default for a List or Library app is No Versioning. You can select Major Versions (1.0, 2.0., 3.0, and so on) or Major and Minor Versions (1.0, 1.2., 1.3, 2.0, and so on). Selecting either of the last two options enables you to designate a limit for the number of versions of each type by entering a number up to 10,000.

4. **Choose who can see draft items by selecting a Draft Item Security radio button in the Draft Item Security section.**

   This section is disabled unless you allow for minor (draft) versions or require content approval of your documents or list items. Here are the three options for who can see draft items — Any User Who Can Read Items, Only Users Who Can Edit Items, or Only Users Who Can Approve (and the Author).

5. **Determine whether to require check out for users editing documents by selecting the Yes or No radio button.**

   Although it can sometimes be a hassle (We often forget we have checked out a document, sometimes months ago!), requiring check out is another good safety mechanism that makes sure the other users don't see a document in mid-modification or have multiple users editing at the same time (last save wins).

TIP
   Consider adding the Checked Out To column to your views so that users can quickly see who has an item checked out.

6. **Click OK or Cancel.**

   If you click OK, your Versioning settings are applied. Go try them out!

When viewing documents in a Library app, you can click the ellipsis to see a contextual menu, as shown in Figure 7-5. This menu allows a document's editor to check out/check in the document, approve, set off a workflow, and so forth. Because the menu is contextual, if approval isn't set on the library or list, for example, Approve doesn't appear on the menu. If a document is checked out, the option to Discard Check Out appears.

TIP
In most cases, team members navigate to the site using a browser to work with list apps. However, think about how your team interacts with documents. They may be navigating to an app using the browser, but they may also be linking from a bookmark or opening the document directly from the editing application (such as Word, Excel, or PowerPoint). Although current versions of Office support and interact with SharePoint Library app settings, users may not know where to find these commands.

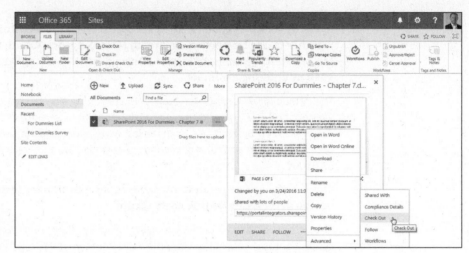

FIGURE 7-5:
A document's
context menu.

REMEMBER

Avoid frustration by taking a little time to review the settings and options with your team. Training on these document management options is one of my number one recommendations for SharePoint collaboration success, especially for teams with many members or contributors.

Advanced settings

Advanced settings include many powerful configuration options for Library and List apps:

>> **Content Types:** Allows you to add and remove content types associated with the app. See Chapter 18 for details on creating your own content types.

>> **Document Template (Library app only):** Allows you to specify the default template, such as a Word, Excel, or PowerPoint template, that is used when someone clicks the New button to create a new document.

TIP

You can also associate document templates with content types, so you can use multiple content types with a library to associate multiple document templates. Sounds confusing, but in a nutshell, having multiple document types and templates enables you to have multiple options for creating a document when you click the New button. For example, you might have a Word template for expenses and a Word template for vacation requests. These can both show up in the New drop-down list (located in the Ribbon on the Files tab) using content types.

>> **Opening Documents in the Browser (Library app only):** Enables you to determine the behavior of the browser when someone clicks on a document to open it. If you don't want to use the Office Web apps, disable the opening

of documents in the browser. This also allows users to send direct links to the documents if necessary.

>> **Custom Send to Destination (Library app only):** This is a great option that lets you add your own web address to the Send To menu on a document's Edit menu. Your SharePoint administrator can also add global addresses that appear in the Send To menu in every document library. The Send To command sends a copy of your file to another location, such as another team site where you want to share the document.

>> **Folders:** Indicates whether users can create new folders in the Library app. We like to turn off this option so people don't go folder crazy. You can always turn on the option so you can create folders when necessary and then turn it back off.

>> **Search:** Specifies whether items in the app should appear in search results.

>> **Indexing:** Options for indexing non-default views and re-indexing the document library. Indexing provides extra data for searches so that searching the library is faster. There is some overhead with indexing, though, so SharePoint makes available some options to control it.

>> **Offline Client Availability:** Allows you to specify whether users of desktop client software, such as Outlook, can download content for offline viewing.

>> **Site Assets Library (Library app only):** Allows you to designate the Library app as a Site Assets library, which makes it easier for users to browse to the Library app to find multimedia files.

>> **Quick Edit:** Lets you specify whether Quick Edit can be used on this library. Quick Edit lets users open the view in a grid and make edits to metadata on the fly. This is much like editing the metadata (data about the documents in the library) on the fly in an Excel type interface.

>> **Dialogs:** By default, list and library forms launch in a dialog box. This option lets you specify that forms should open in the browser window as a page instead of a dialog box.

In addition, List app advanced settings include item-level permissions and attachments.

Follow these steps to apply or modify Advanced settings:

1. **Click the Advanced Settings link in the Library Settings or List Settings page.**

   The Advanced Settings page appears, as shown in Figure 7-6.

2. **Choose whether to enable management of content types by selecting the Yes or No radio button.**

   If you select Yes, after applying, your Library Settings or List App Settings page will contain a new section for Content Types. The default is No.

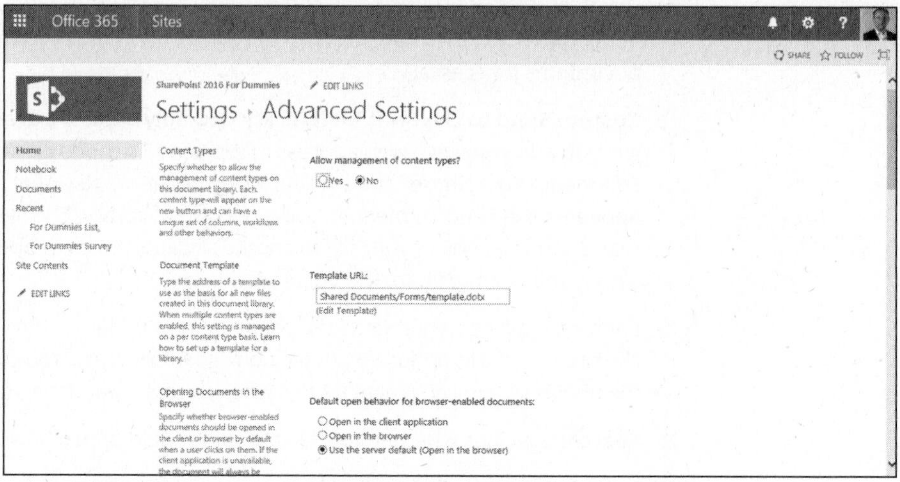

FIGURE 7-6:
Configuring
Advanced
Settings.

3. Change the document template (Library app only) by specifying a template URL in the Template URL text box.

Library apps have a default template for new documents. Remember, you can create a new document in a Library app, as well as upload documents that have been created previously. For example, the document template for a Document Library app is the default Word template. You could change this to an Excel or PowerPoint template. You could also change it to a custom template you created in one of these applications.

If you're working with content types, you can enable a different template for each document type. For example, your library may house contracts and have three content types for different contracts, all with a different template available on the New button.

If you opt for a different document template, upload the template to the Forms folder in Document Library app and change the Template URL in the Document Template section of the Advanced Settings page.

REMEMBER

4. Choose when to open documents in the browser (Library app only), the client application, or as the server default by selecting a radio button option in the Opening Documents in the Browser section.

If the client application is unavailable, the document opens in the browser.

5. Add a Custom Send to Destination (Library app only) by entering the name that should display on the Send To menu and the URL destination.

Similar to Windows commands (for example, Send to Desktop), you can create an option to appear on the Edit menu for documents in this Library app to be sent to another SharePoint destination. Supply a short name to appear on the contextual menu and a URL for the destination in the Destination Name and URL text boxes.

6. **Select whether folders can be created in this app by selecting the Yes or No radio button in the Folders section.**

   Selecting Yes or No determines whether the New Folder command is available on the New menu. The default is Yes.

   We usually disable folders unless we have a good reason to use them. In our opinion, the only good reason to use folders is when you have a set of documents that require unique permissions but must remain in the same app. If you leave folders enabled, people will use them.

   TIP

7. **Determine the search visibility for this app by selecting the Yes or No radio button in the Search section.**

   Selecting No for the Search option can keep the items in the app from being presented in search results, even if the site or app is included in Search settings. The default is Yes.

8. **Enable offline client availability by selecting the Yes or No radio button in the Offline Client Availability section.**

   The Offline Client Availability option determines whether items in the app can be downloaded to offline client applications, such as Outlook. The default is Yes.

9. **Add app location to the Site Assets Library (Library app only) by selecting the Yes or No radio button in the Site Assets Library section.**

   This new Site Assets Library option specifies whether this Library app appears as a default location when uploading images or other files to a wiki page. This can be especially beneficial for Document Library apps that contain images or a Picture Library app. This keeps wiki editors from searching all over for the images they should be using. The default is No.

10. **Determine whether the app can be edited using Quick Edit by selecting the Yes or No radio button in the Quick Edit section.**

    This option determines whether Quick Edit can be used to bulk-edit data on this app. The default is Yes.

11. **Indicate whether forms should launch in a modal dialog box by selecting the Yes or No radio button in the Dialogs section.**

    Modal dialog boxes get old pretty quickly, so we suggest you select the No option on this section quite often.

12. **Click OK or Cancel.**

    If you click OK, your selections are applied.

Other advanced configuration settings available in a List app (not Library app) include a Yes/No option for allowing attachments for a list item (default is Yes) and item-level permissions. The default for item-level permissions in a List app is for all members (contributors) to be able to read and modify all items. You can adjust these settings for users to either read only their own items and/or edit only their own items.

Validation settings

Validation is a formula or statement that must evaluate to TRUE before the data can be saved. SharePoint has two different types of validation: column-level and app-level validation. The difference between column and app validation is that column validation compares only the data in that single column to some test, such as whether a discount is less than or equal to 50%.

```
= [Discount] < = .50
```

On the other hand, validation settings in the app level compare two or more columns to evaluate to TRUE. You can set a rule that [Discount] < [Cost] so customers don't get an item for free (or get money back!) because they buy an item with a discount.

To use validation settings, follow these steps:

1. **Click the Validation Settings link in the Library Settings or List Settings page.**

   The Validation Settings page has two sections, Formula and User Message. The Formula section is the test your comparison of the columns must pass for the item to be valid. The User Message section is what the user receives if the test fails. Users can then adjust the values until the test passes.

2. **Create a formula for the validation by entering it in the Formula field.**

   The formula needs to compare (or validate) one or more columns in your app. The App Settings page provides an example and a link to learning more about the proper syntax.

   A selection list of columns in your app is available for use in your formula.

3. **In the User Message text box, enter a message to be shown to users who enter an invalid item.**

4. **Click OK or Cancel.**

   If you click OK, your validation is applied to your list.

Validations aren't retroactive. They apply only to new and modified entries on the specified columns.

Rating settings

Rating settings is a simple Yes/No option to allow the items in the app to be rated by users. The Rating feature is a much requested feature. When enabled on your app, a Rating field appears, as shown in Figure 7-7. The Rating field allows users to select a star rating.

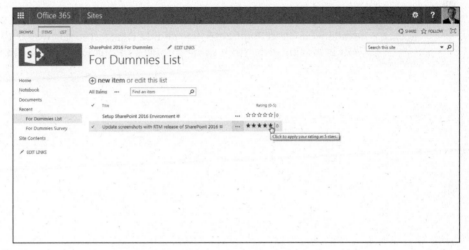

FIGURE 7-7:
Rating a
document.

In addition to rating items with a star rating, you can also approve of items by using a simple Like button. If you are familiar with social-networking sites like Facebook, then you'll know how the Like button works. Changing from a star rating to a Like button is accomplished on the Rating Settings page when you enable ratings.

Audience Targeting settings

The Audience Targeting setting includes one section with a Yes/No option to enable Audience Targeting for the app. Selecting Yes creates a column called Target Audiences in the list or library app. Certain Web Parts, such as the Content Query Web Part, can use this column to filter list contents based on the user's inclusion in a specific audience.

Audience Targeting isn't the same thing as permissions. A user can still access content even if he or she isn't included in an audience. Audience targeting is simply a way to filter the presentation of content to certain groups of people.

Form settings

The Form Settings option is available only for List apps. If InfoPath is installed on your machine, you can opt to allow customization of the list form using InfoPath by selecting the Customize the Current Form Using Microsoft InfoPath radio button.

Microsoft didn't ship InfoPath with Office 2016 and even though this option is still available in SharePoint 2016, you should expect it to go away in the future. Microsoft is moving away from using InfoPath for managing forms in SharePoint.

Chapter 8

Creating a Custom App

SharePoint ships with a number of very useful apps, including apps for calendars, tasks, pictures, links, announcements, contacts, discussions, issues, surveys, assets, and even reports, just to name a few. These apps are useful, but there comes a time when you need to create your own app for very specific data. To create a custom app based on a list, use the Custom List app.

Creating your very own SharePoint app may sound a little daunting. The good news is that creating and customizing an app couldn't be easier. The easiest way to create your own app is to start with a Custom List app and then customize it for your particular need.

In this chapter, you find out how to create your own app. You see how to add columns to store data, create views into the data, validate data, and import data into your app. Finally, you explore the SharePoint Store, where you can search for and purchase third-party apps, and discover that your own organization can even have its own private SharePoint Store.

Planning Your Custom App

Capturing information is nothing new. Ancient civilizations (millennia ago) used stone or clay tablets, pre-computer organizations (decades ago) used typewriters, and many organizations still use Excel. Often, the problem with data is not in collecting it but in sharing and aggregating it.

Excel does a great job with data aggregation but not such a great job with sharing. SharePoint is all about sharing (hence the name). A SharePoint app is a centralized container of data that is easy to manage and maintain. In addition, by the very nature of a centralized web portal, the data is easily shared and viewed by anyone in the organization with access.

Creating an app specifically for your data needs is important. You need to determine the columns of data you will capture and how the data will relate to each other. In addition, you need to determine which data will be valid and which should be rejected.

Planning a custom list is similar to starting a new spreadsheet in Excel or a table in Access. In all cases, a little up-front planning saves time in the long run. Plan ahead so you know what order you want the columns to be in and what options you want in drop-down lists.

TIP

Already have a spreadsheet that you think would make a good list in SharePoint? Make sure you check out the section "Importing a Spreadsheet as an App," later in this chapter. That section can help you create a custom app in no time.

REMEMBER

Columns can also be called *fields* (for those used to database terminology). When these columns are used to describe files (usually documents in a Document Library app), they're also referred to as *metadata* or *properties (of the file)*.

TIP

One of the neat features about SharePoint is the ability to add columns to the predefined apps. The process for adding columns is the same in Library and List apps. However, in a Library app, your columns capture information about a *file*, such as its category or author. List apps generally are all data columns and are used for tracking and communication.

Creating a Custom App

You create a custom app using the Custom List app. The Custom List app creates a very basic list app that you can then customize for your particular scenario.

Follow these steps to create a custom app:

1. **Click the Settings gear icon and select Add an App.**

    The Your Apps page is displayed.

2. **Click the Custom List app on the Your Apps page, as shown in Figure 8-1.**

    The Adding Custom List dialog box appears.

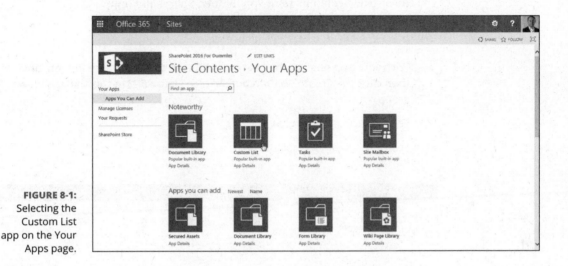

FIGURE 8-1:
Selecting the
Custom List
app on the Your
Apps page.

3. **Provide a name for the app in the Name text box.**

    To make things simple, you only need to give your new app a name. However, if you want to provide a description, you can click the Advanced Options link.

REMEMBER

The name you type here is used in the app's web address. Avoid using spaces in the name when you create the app. You can change the app's name to a friendlier name after you create it, as described in Chapter 7.

4. **Click the Create button.**

    SharePoint creates your new app and takes you automatically to the Site Contents page. Your new app has a green New! tag next to it to let you know it is a new app.

Adding Columns to Your App

A new custom app displays a single text Title column. The list also contains several behind-the-scenes columns that you can't see, such as ID and Version. To make the custom app your own, you have to add columns to the app.

Columns are like fields in a database table. When you add a column to your app, a data entry field appears in the app's New Form to give you a place to enter data into that column.

REMEMBER

A little planning goes a long way. You created a plan for your custom app, right? Because now is when you start adding the columns to your app that you listed in your plan.

You can also add columns to the predefined SharePoint apps.

Follow these steps to add columns to your custom app:

1. **With your app open in the browser, click the List tab on the Ribbon, and then click the Create Column button (see Figure 8-2) in the Manage Views group.**

   The Create Column window appears.

   You can also add new columns with the List Settings page.

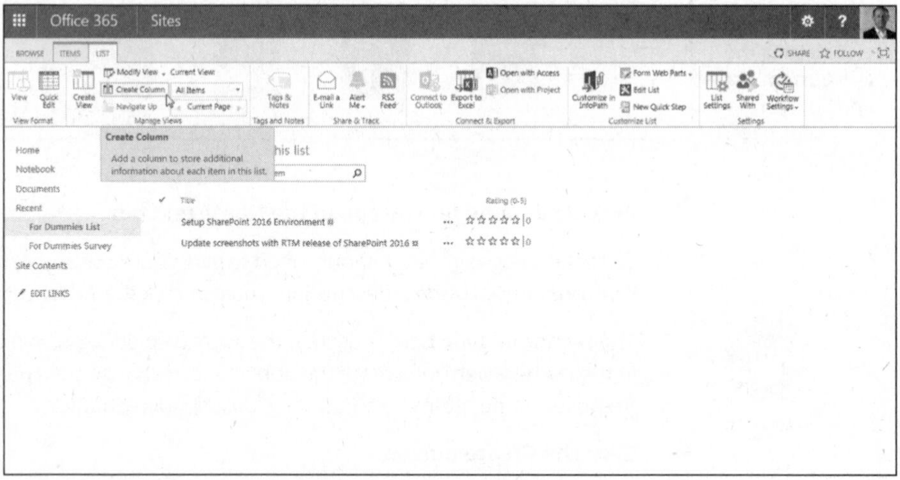

FIGURE 8-2:
Add a new column to your list.

2. **Type a name for your new column in the Column Name field.**

   The name you type is what users will see, so pick a name that's concise but meaningful. We don't recommend using spaces in your column names when you first create them. You can always add spaces later.

   Spaces entered in a column name become a permanent part of that column's *internal name* in SharePoint. Some of these internal names can get quite lengthy and downright nonsensical, which makes referencing them a real pain.

TECHNICAL STUFF

3. **Select the type of information you want to store in the column.**

The options given here are fairly intuitive — Single Line of Text, Number, Date and Time, and so on. See the later section, "Getting to know column types," for details on selecting the column type.

WARNING

Make sure you determine what kind of data you have when you first create the column. Changing the data type later may result in loss of data, or you may not have as many options when you change the type.

4. **In the Additional Column Settings section, select the options that further define your column's type.**

The column type you select in Step 3 determines what options you have available for configuring the column.

5. **(Optional) If you want SharePoint to test the values entered into your column, use the Column Validation section to enter your formula.**

6. **Click OK.**

SharePoint adds the column to your custom app.

You can change the column properties later and rearrange the order of the columns by using the List Settings page.

TIP

After you first create a custom app, use the List or Library Settings page to modify your app, where you have all the commands at your fingertips to power through the column creation — you can pick site columns, create your own columns, and rearrange them, as shown in Figure 8-3. After your app has been created and you need to add more columns, the Create Column button on the List tab of the Ribbon is a handy way to add one or two columns without leaving the main page.

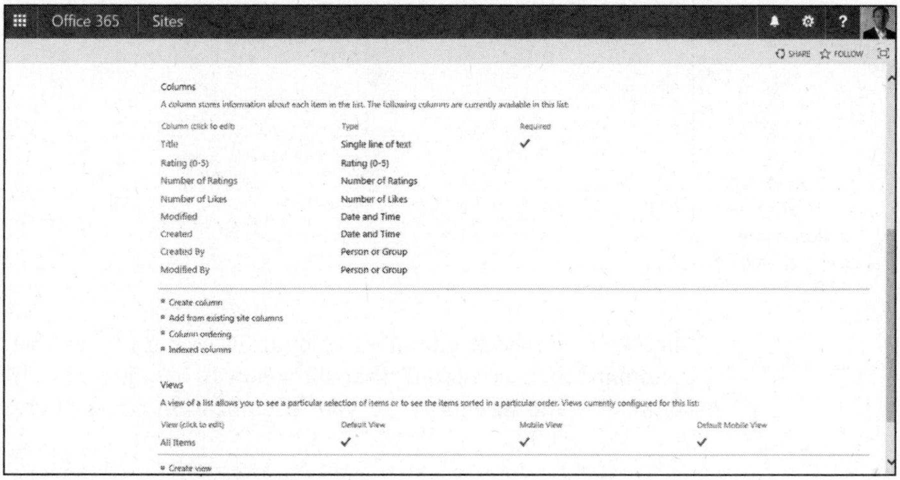

FIGURE 8-3:
Columns section of the List Settings page.

REUSING COLUMNS IN OTHER APPS

SharePoint actually has two kinds of columns — list columns and site columns. We show you how to create a *list column* (a column that's associated with one and only one app) in the "Adding Columns to Your App" section in this chapter. What if you like a column so much you want to reuse it on more than one app? That's when you create a *site column*. You define a site column once, and you can then associate it with as many apps as you want. SharePoint comes with a set of predefined site columns — those are the columns that are used in SharePoint's predefined apps. You can reuse any of those columns in your apps as well.

Getting to know column types

Columns are used to store data, and unlike a spreadsheet, you need to define the *type* of column as you create it, as shown in Figure 8-4. For those who work with databases, this is a familiar concept. By defining the type of column, you gain extra functionality based on that type, and you help to control the type of information that can be entered into the column and how that information is presented onscreen. For example, users can enter only a number in a Number column; they can't add miscellaneous text.

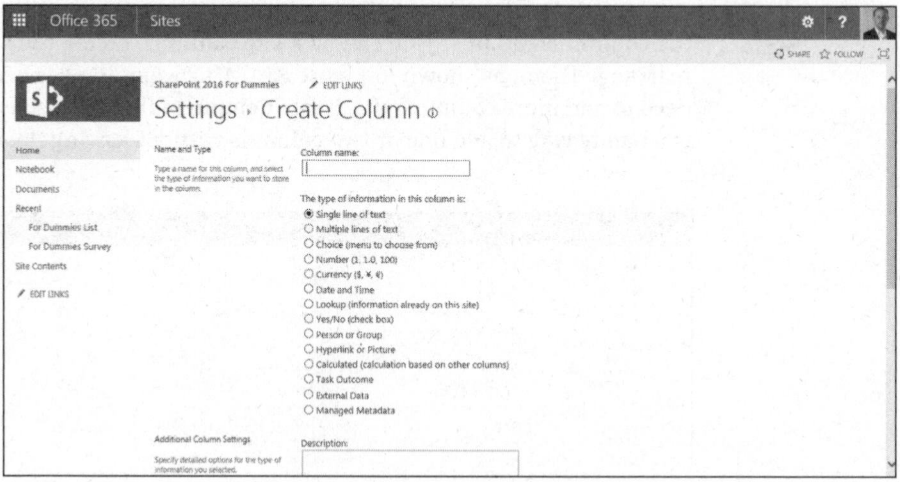

FIGURE 8-4: The Create Column page showing choices.

SharePoint provides a number of built-in column types that you can select for your apps, such as columns that know how to handle dates and URLs. Third-party companies and developers in your organization can also create custom column types that can be added to SharePoint. For example, if your company needs a column that handles a full zip code (the zip code plus four numbers), a developer could create it for you.

Table 8-1 lists common SharePoint column types and what they're used for.

TABLE 8-1   ## SharePoint Column Data Types

Column Data Type*	What It's Used For	Display on Form
Single Line of Text	Display text and numbers (such as phone or course numbers, or zip code) up to 255 characters.	Single-line text box (the text box may not show all 255 characters).
Multiple Lines of Text	Display multiple lines of text.	Select from Plain Text, Rich Text, or Enhanced Rich Text. Depending on the number of lines you select, this option shows as a text area of that size with additional toolbars to format text.**
Choice***	A defined list of choices; for example, categories or departments.	Drop-down list is the default and most common.
Number	Numerical values that can be used for calculations.	You can identify a min/max value number with a choice of decimal options.
Currency	Numerical values that represent money.	You can identify a min/max value currency. Includes options for decimal places and currency format.
Date and Time	Dates and times.	Date and/or Time-Calendar Picker.
Lookup	Values from another list — for example, categories could be stored in a lookup list for document metadata.	Drop-down list populated based on values from other list.
Yes/No	Boolean value of Yes or No.	Check box.
Person or Group	Directory listing information from SharePoint.	The person or group is shown as a hyperlink and can include presence information.
Hyperlink or Picture	Hyperlink (internal or external) or an image.	Hyperlink or picture.
Calculated	Data that can be calculated by formula.	Result of calculation; can be text or numerical.
Task Outcome	The outcome of a task such as Approved, Rejected, or Pending.	The Task Outcome presents a list of choices that you can define when creating the item.

(continued)

TABLE 8-1 *(continued)*

Column Data Type*	What It's Used For	Display on Form
External Data	Data stored in a data source; for example, a table or view in an enterprise database.	Usually filled in by the external source and not users.
Managed Metadata	Provides a common set of keywords and terms that can be used across the organization.	Users can simply start typing, and the options will fill in based on their input. The options are pulled from the metadata managed by SharePoint.

Most columns also include property options for Required, Allow Duplicates, Default Values, and Add to the Default View.

**Although you may set a number of lines for editing, this isn't a defined limit. Users can type or cut/paste a large amount of text into this control. You may want to use column validation to restrict the length.*

***Choice can also be shown on the form as radio buttons for a single choice or check boxes for multiple choices.*

In addition to the column data types in Table 8-1, other data types, such as Publishing HTML (an even richer form of text), can be selected when creating site columns in publishing sites. Publishing sites are beyond the scope of this book, but we would encourage you to dig further if you are in a large organization and need to have granular control on who can publish to which portions of a page.

REMEMBER

When you're creating columns for your custom app, you can change the order of the columns as they're shown in the Columns section of the List Settings page. Changing the column ordering in this section helps with organizing the app flow for owners and how they display on the app's form. However, changing the order on the List Settings page doesn't change the order of columns in the default view — you must modify the view separately.

TIP

Don't underestimate descriptions! Creators of lists often carry a lot of information in their heads about the content in the app. Users aren't mind readers. Make sure to type descriptions to help them understand the intent of the column and the data expected.

Validating data entry

Column validation options allow you to define additional limits and constraints for your data. For example, you may want to ensure that a value in one Date column occurs after another Date column. (So, for example, column validation can ensure that the date in the Date Finished column can't be earlier than the date in the Date Started column — you can't finish a project before it's begun!)

To use column validation on your app:

1. **In your app where you want to validate data entry, click the List Settings button on the List tab of the Ribbon.**
2. **Under General Settings, click the Validation Settings link.**
3. **Type a formula in the Formula text box, as shown in Figure 8-5.**

   The result of the formula must evaluate to `TRUE` to pass validation. The formula syntax is the same as calculated columns, which is similar to Excel syntax.

FIGURE 8-5: Entering a formula for list validation.

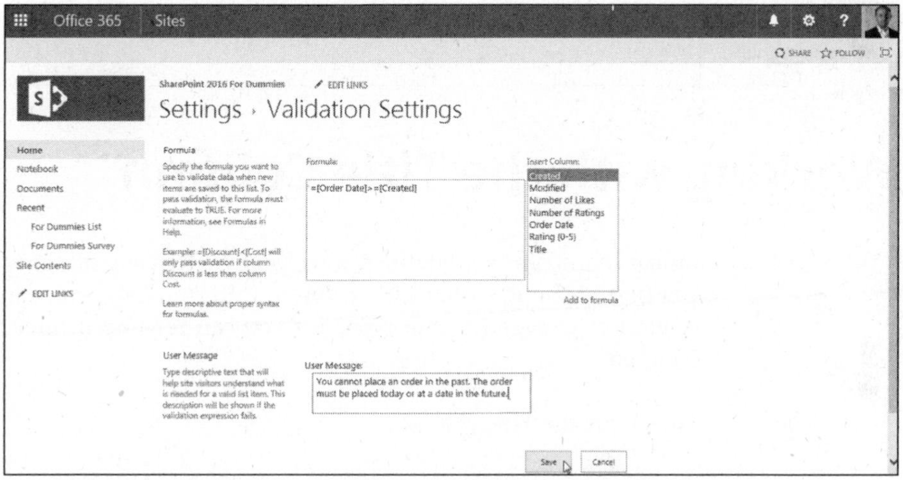

4. **Enter a user message that you want to appear if the validation formula fails.**

   The message should give the user an idea of how the formula works and how to fix the problem. (See the example message in Figure 8-5.)

5. **Click the Save button.**

When users enter data into your form, the validation formula is evaluated. If the formula evaluates to `FALSE`, your user message appears on the form, as shown in Figure 8-6.

You can add column validation to columns created at the app or site level. Validation created for site-level columns applies everywhere that column is used, although the formula can be overridden at the app where the site-level column is used.

Working with the Title Column

Unlike SharePoint's predefined apps, your custom app has only one column when you first create it — the Title column. Unfortunately, you can't delete the Title column or change its data type, but you can rename it, hide it, or make it not required.

To rename the Title column:

1. **Click the List Settings button on the List tab of the Ribbon.**

2. **Under the Columns heading, click the Title hyperlink.**

3. **Replace *Title* with your own title and make modifications to the other properties as desired.**

The Title column is used by the list as a means to access the data entry forms to view and edit the list item. You can opt to hide the Title column so that it doesn't appear on any of the app forms.

TIP

The hidden column will still appear in views unless you remove it from the view.

To hide the Title column:

1. **In your list, click the List Settings button on the List tab.**

2. **If the Content Types section isn't visible, enable management of content types by following these steps:**

a. *Click the Advanced Settings link on the List Settings page.*

b. *Select the Yes radio button under Allow Management of Content Types, and then click OK. The Content Types section becomes visible on the List Settings page.*

3. **In the Content Types section of the List Settings page, click the Item content type.**

   The List Content Type information appears.

   If you want to change the Title column in a document library, you click the Document content type. The Item content type applies to custom apps only. In a predefined app, such as a Tasks app, you click the Task content type.

4. **Click the Title column.**

   The Title column's properties appear.

5. **Under Column Settings, select the Hidden (Will Not Appear in Forms) radio button, as shown in Figure 8-7, and click OK.**

   The Title column doesn't appear on forms.

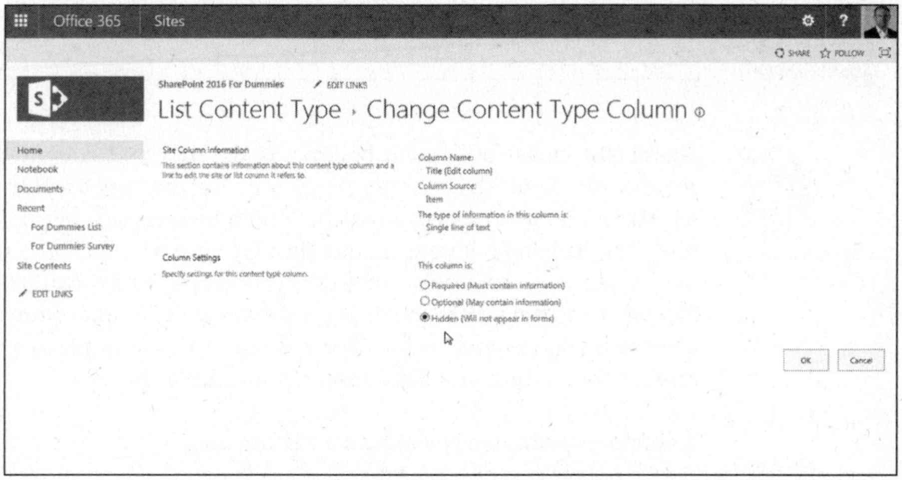

FIGURE 8-7:
Hide the
Title column.

Importing a Spreadsheet as an App

Already have data in a spreadsheet that you want to be a SharePoint app? You're halfway there! Before you start, make sure you do the following:

>> **Clean the spreadsheet.** Make sure your spreadsheet looks like a table, with no blank columns or rows.

>> **Make sure your spreadsheet has headers.** All columns in the SharePoint app need to have a column title.

>> **Make sure your data is consistent.** For example, if a cell has a comment in it, but it should contain a date, remove the comment text.

>> **Make sure your column heading in the first row is representative of the data.** SharePoint reads the headings in the first row and makes assumptions about the information in those columns.

Figure 8-8 shows an example of a clean spreadsheet ready for importing.

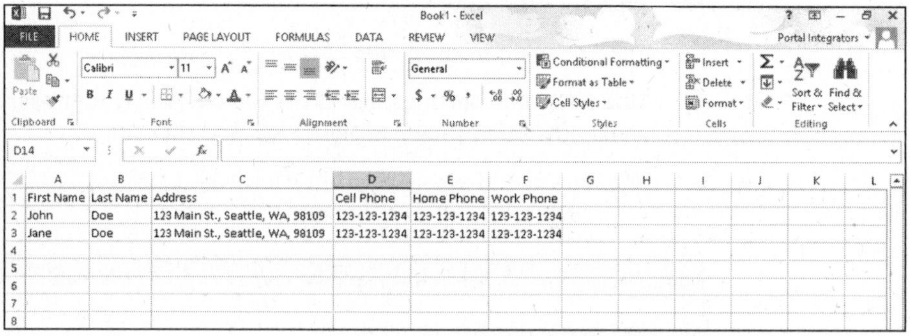

FIGURE 8-8: Cleaned spreadsheet ready for import into SharePoint.

WARNING

SharePoint looks for what it believes is the first text column and uses it as the pseudo-title field (the primary field in the list that has the Edit menu attached to it). Therefore, try to place a text field with unique data in the first column position. Unfortunately, if your unique field is a number, such as a serial number, this can cause issues. To work around the problem, create the app and copy and paste the data from the spreadsheet. (A good example of a first column is a unique name of a person or an item, such as Event Name. A bad example of a first column is the category of an item or a department of an employee.)

To import your spreadsheet into a custom app:

1. Click the Settings gear icon and choose Add an App.

You can also click the Site Contents link on the Quick Launch toolbar and then click the Add an App icon.

TIP

This feature requires the use of a browser that supports ActiveX. If you run into issues with this feature, such as seeing an unexpected error, then ActiveX Controls are not working properly with your browser.

2. Select the Import Spreadsheet App from the list of apps you can add.

3. **In the Name text box, enter a name for your app.**

   Follow the naming conventions outlined in this book for app names: Keep them short and eliminate spaces.

4. **(Optional) In the Description text box, enter a description of the app.**

5. **Click the Browse button, browse to your spreadsheet, select it, and click the Import button.**

   A dialog box appears that asks how your range is designated. The default is Table Range, but other options are Named Range or Range of Cells. If you haven't named the data as a range in Excel or set it as a table, select the Range of Cells option.

6. **If you chose the Range of Cells option, click the Select Range field in the dialog box, and then click your spreadsheet and highlight the desired cells.**

7. **Click the Import button in the dialog box.**

After you import your spreadsheet, verify the column types SharePoint chose for you. Generally, SharePoint assumes text, number, and dates. You may want to change some text fields to Choice, Yes/No, and so forth.

TIP

Don't have the patience to create all your custom columns one by one — but you don't have a current app in another format either? Create a spreadsheet with your column headers and at least one row of data, and then import this spreadsheet and modify the column properties as necessary.

Taking Your App to the Next Level: Calculated and Lookup Columns

Calculated columns are especially powerful for automatically generating data. Don't be intimidated — the web is full of great formula examples for SharePoint calculated columns. Some common uses include

» Adding days to a Date column to calculate an Expired or Due Date column

» Adding Number or Currency columns to get a total

» Using the Me function to automatically add the username to a field

Creating a calculated column

To create a calculated column, follow these steps:

1. **Select the Calculated column type in the Name and Type options in the Create Column dialog box.**

   The Additional Column Settings area changes to support entering a calculation (see Figure 8-9) and specifying column options.

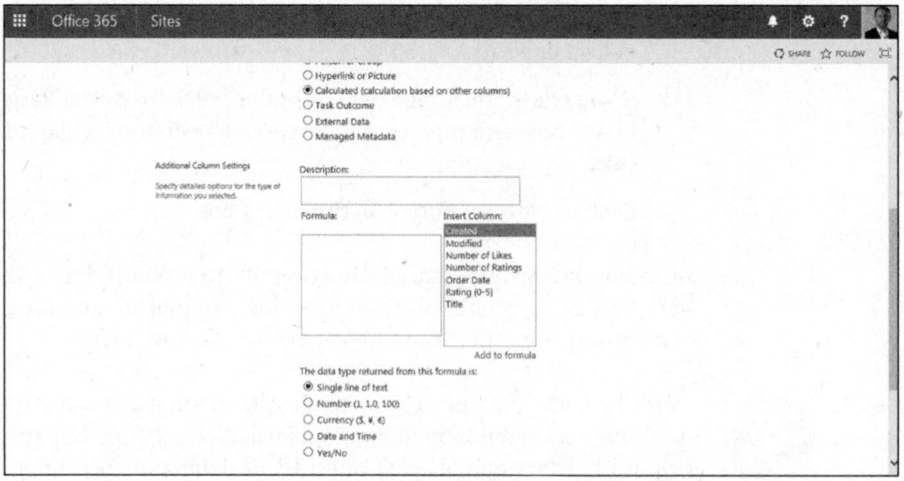

FIGURE 8-9:
Column settings
for a calculated
column.

2. **Type your formula using the proper syntax in the Formula text box.**

   If you're basing your calculation on another column in the app, you can reference that column using the square brackets reference syntax.

   For example, to calculate a Shipping Deadline value, add five days to the Order Date value in another column by entering **[Order Date]+5** in the Formula text box.

3. **Select the proper data type for the returned value and other data type property options, if available, from the Additional Column Settings section of the page.**

REMEMBER

   Not all return values are of the same data type as the input columns. For example, if you subtract one date from another, your returned value is a number (the number of days' difference between the two dates).

Other examples include

- Adding the current username to a field. Simply type the constant **[Me]** in the Formula text box.

- Using today as a date in a calculation to create a new date by entering **[Today]+7** in the Formula text box.

Using a lookup column

Maintaining all your options in a Choice field can be cumbersome and prone to error. SharePoint uses a similar model to relational databases by separating the *lookup* information from the *transaction* app. Think of all the lookup data that could be maintained in separate apps. For example, computer hardware inventory lookup apps could include hardware type, maintenance contract, and department location. These apps can be maintained independently of the transaction app — the inventory itself.

For example, you could create a Customer custom app with a single field — Title — and populate it with the names of customers. Then build an Order app (to track orders that customers place). Customer is a column in the Order app. Rather than build a Choice field, you could use the Lookup data type to connect to the Customer app and use the Title field as data for the Customer column in the Order app. The end result is that all your customers are separated from the orders. If a customer needs to change his or her name (maybe she got married, or his name was misspelled) you can just change the name in the Customer app instead of in every entry in the Order app.

You can also add other columns from the lookup app to the drop-down list to help users select the proper choice. When a user selects the value from the drop-down list, values for the additional columns also display. Figure 8-10 shows a scenario that uses a lookup column to display a customer's sales territory. The customer's name and sales territory are stored in one app and displayed in another app using a lookup column. Figure 8-10 also shows the use of inline editing in a Web Part.

For users familiar with databases and referential integrity, SharePoint 2016 includes additional options to support this implementation. Lookup columns can also be used to create a chain of joined apps that can be used to query and display values from additional columns.

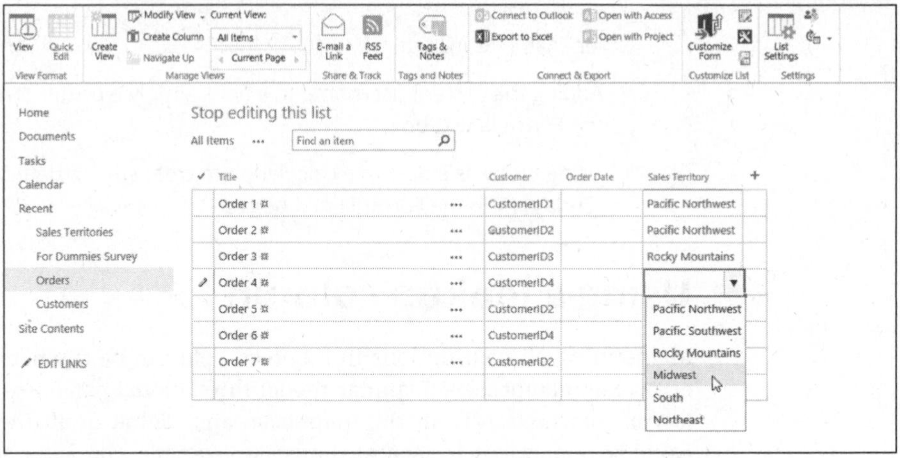

FIGURE 8-10:
Selecting a value
from a lookup
column.

Downloading Apps from
the SharePoint Store

In addition to the apps that come with SharePoint, you can also add apps from third parties. These third-party apps appear in the SharePoint Store. If you're using SharePoint Online, then you have access to the full store. If you're using SharePoint On-Premises, then your local IT administrators may have locked down the apps that you can add for security reasons.

The SharePoint Store can be found on the Your Apps page, as shown in Figure 8-11. You access the Your Apps page by clicking the Settings gear icon and then selecting Add an App. Take a look and see what SharePoint apps you have available in the store.

The SharePoint Store is shown in Figure 8-12.

You can choose to view all apps or only those that are free by selecting the Price refiner on the left side of the page. You can also sort apps by clicking a category link. If you want to purchase an app, click it and then click the Buy It button. After you click the Buy It button, you have to log in with your Microsoft account. If you already have a credit card on file with your Office 365 subscription, then you can purchase and download the app. Otherwise, you are prompted to enter your credit card information.

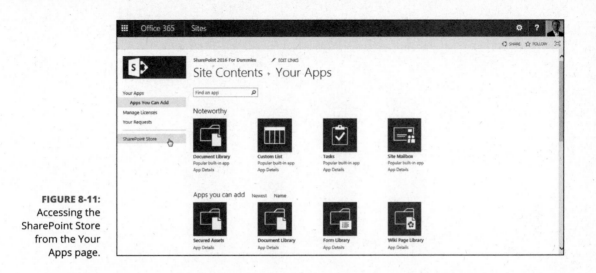

FIGURE 8-11:
Accessing the
SharePoint Store
from the Your
Apps page.

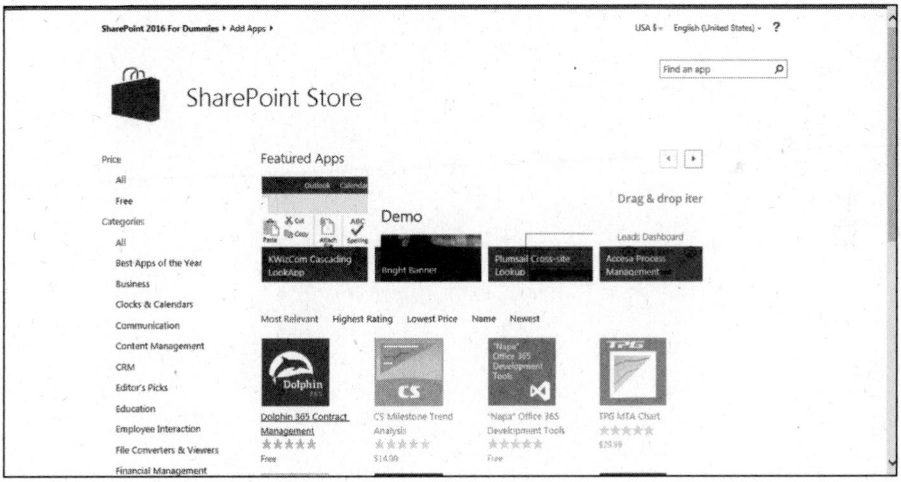

FIGURE 8-12:
The SharePoint
Store.

IN THIS CHAPTER

Knowing when to create a view

Understanding view formats

Working with various views

Managing views that already exist

Displaying views by using Web Parts

Chapter 9

Viewing Data in Your Apps

A number of apps ship with SharePoint, and you can also create custom apps (as discussed in Chapter 8). SharePoint also lets you create additional pages, or *views*, that you can use to customize the display of the information in apps. In Excel, you might hide rows and/or columns to create a new view of the data. In a database, you may query only certain fields and use criteria to create a specific snapshot of data. The concept is similar with views.

Common reasons for creating new views include showing only active items, only tasks associated with a certain person, only documents in a certain category, and so on. These views help users find or focus on certain data in the app without having to see everything, all the time.

In this chapter, you discover how to manually create new views and how to modify existing views.

Viewing the View

Each SharePoint app comes with at least one view, the All Items view, which is a public view available to app users. Document Library apps start with the All

Documents view. Certain apps come with several more predefined views, such as the Discussion Board app, which has special views for showing threaded discussions.

You use the SharePoint Ribbon to access the options for changing an app's views. Figure 9-1 shows the List tab under List tools (use the Library tab under Library tools in Library apps), where you can see the commands available for changing the current views or creating new views.

You can easily switch among views in an app. The current view is displayed at the top of the page, and additional views are displayed next to it with links to those views, as shown in Figure 9-2. Just to the right is an ellipsis for modifying or managing the views.

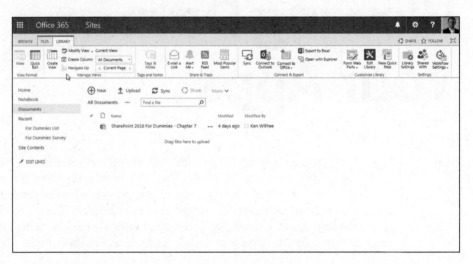

FIGURE 9-1:
Use the Ribbon to manage views.

Anyone with Design and Full Control permissions (Designers and Owners) can make Public and Personal views for the app. However, Site Members (Contributors) can create only Personal views for their own use.

TIP

Use a view instead of folders. When you organize files on your network, folders are the predominant method of subdividing your content. In SharePoint, you gain great power in using columns in combination with views to hide or show what users need to see. Folders take extra effort for the user to drill down and then navigate back up to look for other content. Views coupled with built-in sorting and filtering header options enable the user to easily and quickly find different content by toggling back and forth between views.

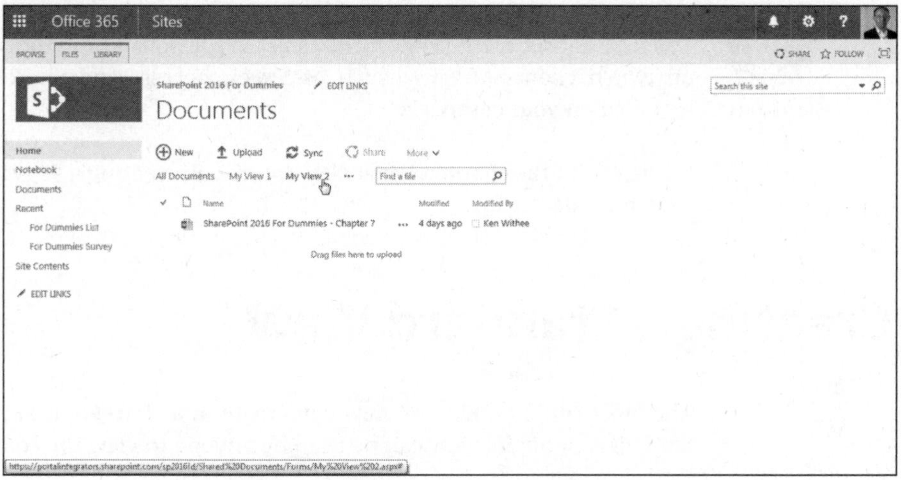

FIGURE 9-2:
Switching among
views in an app.

Getting to Know Your View Formats

SharePoint provides six predefined formats for creating new views. These formats jump–start your view creation experience by determining how information appears on the web page:

- ≫ **Standard:** This is the default view when you first access an app. The document or title item is in hyperlink format with an Edit menu for accessing properties and other options, and the rest of the list resembles a table without borders.

- ≫ **Datasheet:** An editable spreadsheet format. Although any app has the option to edit information in a datasheet format using the Quick Edit button on the List or Library tab, certain views may make sense to be created in this format if users will edit multiple items at a time.

- ≫ **Calendar:** As you would expect, this view displays as a calendar. You need at least one date field in your app to create a Calendar view.

- ≫ **Gantt:** If you are familiar with project management charts, you recognize the Gantt view as showing tasks along a timeline. This view makes it possible to do simple project-management tracking using a SharePoint app.

- ≫ **Access view:** This view creates an Access database with a linked table to your SharePoint app so that you can create a form or report in Access based on your SharePoint app. Lookup tables and a user app are also linked as tables with this option.

- ≫ **Custom View in SharePoint Designer:** If you have SharePoint Designer installed on your computer, you have the option to use it to create custom views.

REMEMBER

You may not see all the view formats listed previously. Your options are dependent on which client software, such as Excel, Access, and SharePoint Designer, is installed on your computer.

In the rest of the chapter, we walk you through creating a view using each of these view formats.

Creating a Standard View

The most common kind of view you create in a SharePoint app is a public, Standard view. A public view can be used by anyone to view the contents of an app.

Standard views have the following traits:

>> They're accessible by all browsers, including Firefox, Chrome, and Safari.

>> They have the most configuration options, such as filtering, grouping, and editing options.

>> They're available for all apps.

>> They don't require any special columns for configuring the view. Other view formats, such as a Calendar view, require date columns.

To create a new Standard view:

1. **Browse to the app where you want to create the new view.**

2. **Click the List or Library tab of the Ribbon to access options for managing views.**

    In a Calendar app, click the Calendar tab to manage the app's views.

3. **Click the Create View button.**

    A list of view format options appears.

4. **Click the Standard View link to create a view that looks like a web page.**

    After selecting your view format, the Create View page displays your options for creating the new view.

5. **In the View Name field, type the name you want to call this view.**

    The View Name field has two purposes:

    • It provides the friendly name that can be selected to display the view.

    • It provides the filename for the web page, which is part of the web address.

We suggest giving the page a name that's easy to remember. For example, if your view will group products by department, entering the name **GroupByDepartment** creates a web page named GroupByDepartment.aspx. You can change the friendly name after the filename has been created.

6. **To set this view as the default view for the app, select the Make This the Default View check box.**

   If this isn't the default view, users can select the view from a drop-down list on the Ribbon.

7. **In the View Audience field, select the Create a Public View radio button.**

   Optionally, you can create a private view that only you can see. You must have at least Designer or Owner permissions to create a public view.

8. **In the Columns section of the page, select the Display check box next to any columns you want to display, as shown in Figure 9-3.**

   You can also indicate the relative order that columns appear on the screen by selecting the appropriate number in the Position from Left drop-down lists. See more on choosing columns in the "Choosing columns for your view" section, later in this chapter.

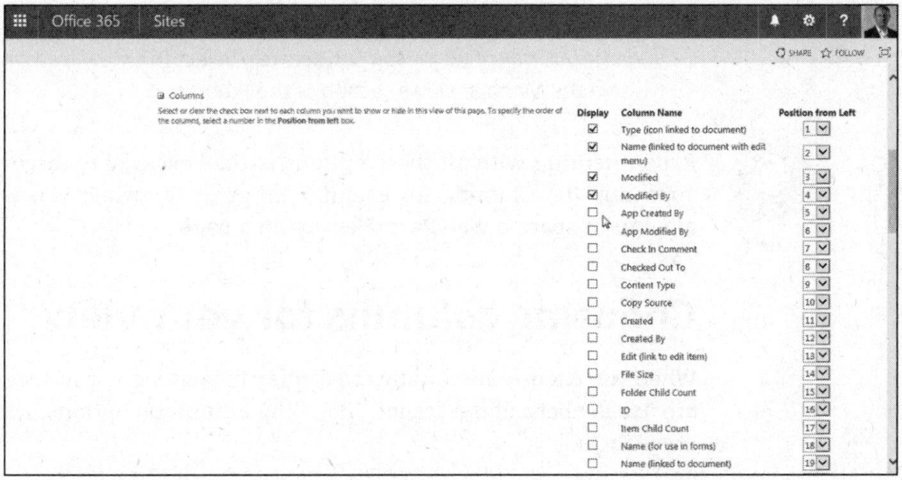

FIGURE 9-3: Create a new view and select the columns you want to show.

9. **(Optional) In the Sort section, use the drop-down lists to select the first column you want to sort by and then select the second column to sort by.**

   The default sort option is ID, which means that items will be sorted by the order they were entered in the list.

10. **Select the remaining options to configure your view, such as the columns you want to filter or group on.**

Some of the options you can choose from are

- Select Tabular View to include check boxes next to items for bulk operations.

- Select the style that the view will take. For example, Boxed, Shaded, Newsletter, Preview Pane, or Basic style.

- In the Totals section, select which columns to aggregate using Count, Average, Minimum and Maximum functions.

- In the Folders section, specify whether items should appear inside folders or flat as if the folders don't exist.

- Item Limit allows you to limit the items displayed on a single page. This can improve the performance of the view.

We discuss additional options in more detail in the "Filtering apps with views" and "Grouping results" sections, later in this chapter.

11. **Click OK to create the view.**

The new view appears in the browser.

If you created a public view, SharePoint creates a new web page using the name you specified in Step 5. Users can select this view from the drop-down list in the Manage Views section of the Ribbon.

TIP

Experimenting with all these options is the best way to discover what works for your site. Item Limits, for example, is great for when you want to control the amount of space a Web Part takes up on a page.

Choosing columns for your view

When you choose the columns to display in your view, you see many columns that are usually behind the scenes, including Edit menu options. For a List-based app, these include

>> **Edit (Linked to Edit Item):** Displays an icon that a user can click to edit the item. This column is useful when you don't want to display the Title column.

>> **Title (Linked to Item):** Displays the Title column with a hyperlink to the list item or document. When a user clicks the hyperlinked title, a web page opens and displays the app item or opens the document.

>> **Title (Linked to Edit with Edit Menu):** When a user hovers his mouse over this column, the Edit menu appears.

We may want Edit menu columns on our app page for a member to modify items, but we generally don't want them in our app Web Parts on home pages and publishing pages (in that case, we just want users to click a link to open a document or only view the app data as a table).

Other columns you may have available to add to your view include

>> **ID** displays the identity number of the item. The ID number is used to display the item's values in a form.

>> **Version** displays the version number of the item or document. This allows you to easily see what the latest version of a document is.

>> **Checked Out** shows who has the document checked out. Document Library based apps will have this column by default.

>> **Folder Child Count** displays the number of folders contained within a folder.

>> **Item Child Count** displays the number of items contained within a folder.

>> **Content Type** displays the content type associated with the item or document.

When you create a view, you often realize that you want to display a column that's based on a value calculated from another column. For example, if your app displays an anniversary date, you may want to calculate years of service. You can do that by creating a new column and then displaying it in your view. (See Chapter 8 for details on working with calculated columns.)

In the past, you could use SharePoint Designer to work with views. SharePoint Designer might still work with SharePoint Server 2016, but Microsoft is moving away from it. They didn't ship it with Office 2016, so if you want to try to use it with your site, you need to use SharePoint Designer 2013. In 2013, SharePoint Designer was mostly used for building workflows, so it is best to stick with the web browser experience we just described to develop your List and Library app views.

Filtering apps with views

You can use the filtering options of views to limit the items displayed. You can choose which columns to filter on and how to apply the filter. You can use filters to display app data where a certain column is equal to some value or not equal to some value, or where an item was created between certain date ranges.

You can create filters using columns that are based on String, Number, Currency, or Choice data types. However, you can't filter on lookup columns or multiline text fields.

Building a filter is like writing an equation; for example, $x > y$. In this case, x is the column you want to filter on, and y is the value you want to test the column contents against. The operator in between determines what the test evaluates. This test gives the system a TRUE or FALSE response to your equation.

Available operators are

>> **Equality:** Is Equal To or Is Not Equal To

>> **Comparison:** Is Greater Than or Is Less Than

>> **Substring:** Contains or Begins With

The filtering equation is evaluated for each item in your app. If the equation is TRUE, the item is included in the view; if the equation is FALSE, the item is excluded.

TIP

If you don't see the results you expect to see in your view, your filter is probably evaluating to FALSE.

For numerical values, you usually use the Equality or Comparison operators. When you create filtered views based on string (text) values, you want to be familiar with your data before trying to create the filter. For example, if you want to filter a Contacts app to display only those contacts in the U.K., you have to ask how the value for the U.K. has been entered in the app. Is it U.K., United Kingdom, or both? You can use a Datasheet view to quickly scan the data to determine the range of possible values.

TIP

One way to get around this problem is by validating your data when it's being entered. You can use Choice columns to do that or use SharePoint 2016's validation features. (See Chapter 8 for details.)

Say you discover that your data include both values — U.K. and United Kingdom. You could go through and make all the data consistent. Or you could filter for both values using the Or option, as shown in Figure 9-4.

You can also use the constants Today and Me to filter your columns. (See Chapter 8 for details on using these constants.)

Grouping results

You can configure your view to group together items based on a common value in a column. For example, you can group a listing of contacts that all share the same department or company.

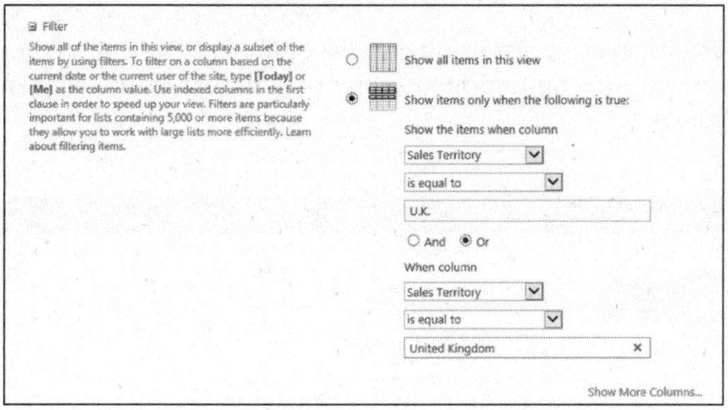

FIGURE 9-4:
Select the column
to filter the view.

Figure 9-5 shows the grouping options. You can indicate whether to automatically collapse or expand grouped items and how many items to display per page. Figure 9-6 shows a listing of contacts grouped by department. Use the toggle arrows to the left of each group header to expand or contract the grouped items.

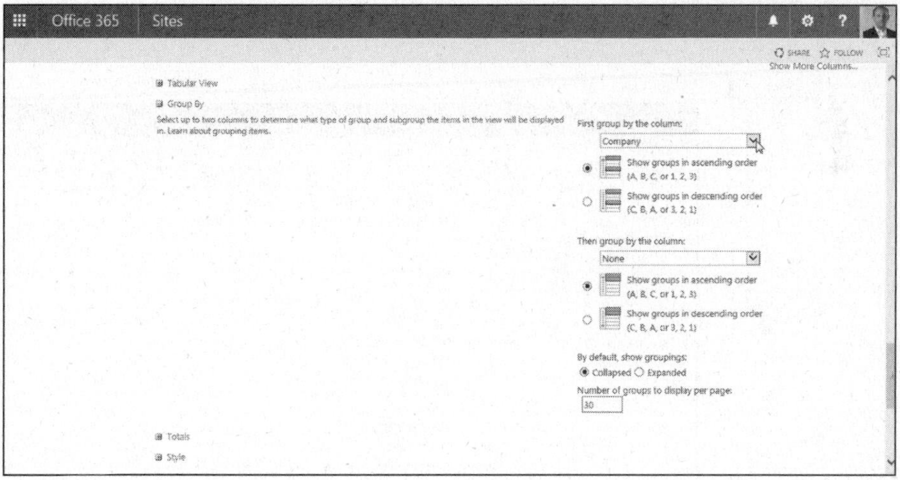

FIGURE 9-5:
You can group
items based on a
shared value.

Don't forget the Totals option! Often when grouping data, you want to create totals. For example, grouping on Inventory by Category and totaling the Quantity creates subtotals for the Category grouping as well as an overall total for the app.

Quickly edit app data with Quick Edit

In past versions of SharePoint, you had to create special views if you wanted to do things like inline editing and multiple item selection. In SharePoint 2016, this functionality is baked right into every app in the form of Quick Edit. Quick Edit is available on every app based on a list or library. The Quick Edit functionality takes the form of a button on the List or Library tab of the Ribbon, as shown in Figure 9-7.

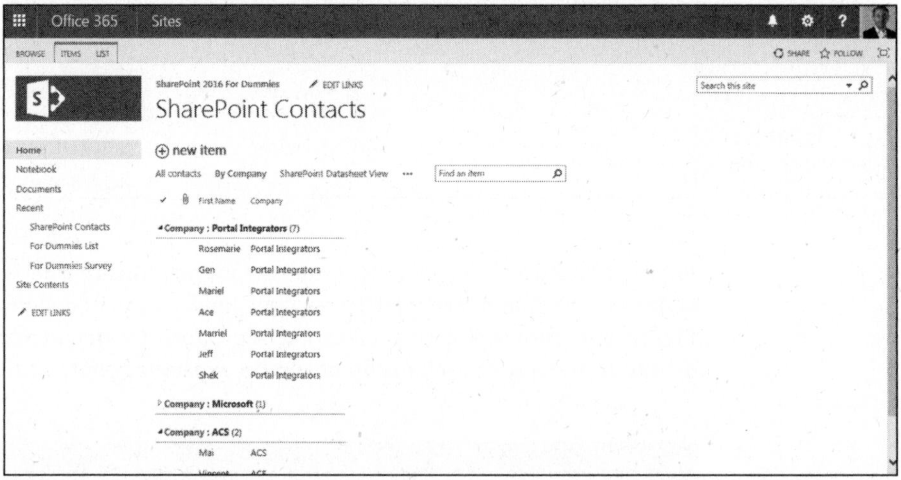

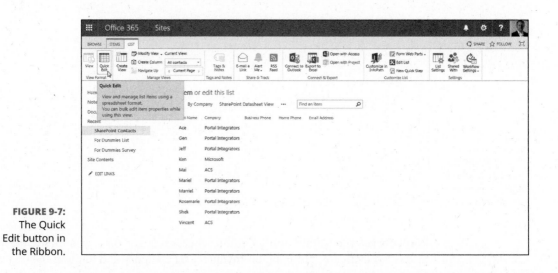

FIGURE 9-6:
Expand or contract grouped items.

FIGURE 9-7:
The Quick Edit button in the Ribbon.

When you click the Quick Edit button, you're presented with the data in the app in an easily editable form. You can make changes right on the pages and with multiple items. An app displaying data in Quick Edit is shown in Figure 9-8.

FIGURE 9-8:
Using Quick Edit
in an app.

Choosing a display style

SharePoint 2016 provides several preformatted view styles that you can use to control the display of your view. The default view style displays your app data in rows. You can use several additional styles. Many of these are especially helpful in configuring app Web Parts:

» **Basic Table** displays app data in a simple table.

» **Boxed** and **Boxed, No Labels** display items as a series of cards, with or without column labels. This display is similar to the Address Card view in Outlook.

» **Newsletter** and **Newsletter, No Lines** display a table with a streamlined format.

» **Shaded** displays items in rows, with each alternate row shaded.

» **Preview Pane** displays items on the left and previews the details on the right. This is a great way to display a lot of information in a compact display.

TIP

Many users overlook these effective display styles. Again, experimenting is the best way to find out how a display style can improve a user's experience with the data.

Figure 9-9 shows the style options you can choose from when configuring your view.

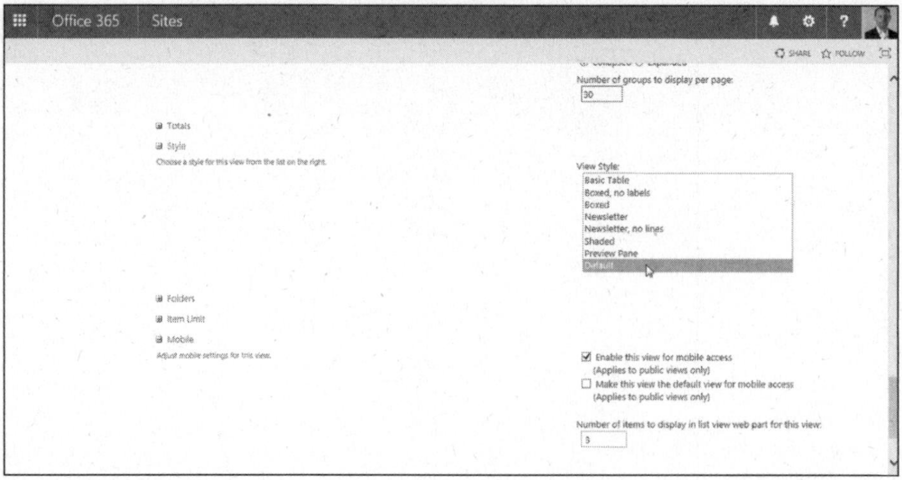

FIGURE 9-9:
You can
change the
format of
the view.

Managing App Data in a Datasheet View

Datasheet views are great for performing bulk updates on items and document properties. A Datasheet view displays app data in a web-based spreadsheet.

With Datasheet views, you can

>> Support most column types including Text, Choice, Date, Number, and Lookup columns. Not all column features work as expected in a Datasheet view. In short, when Datasheet views work, they work great. You just have to test your column types before getting overly ambitious.

>> Use the arrow keys to move around in the view like a spreadsheet.

>> Copy and paste values, which is another great way to make bulk updates to an app. We often use this approach instead of importing a spreadsheet as a custom app.

>> Choose View App Data in a Datasheet view on the fly from any Standard view by clicking the Quick Edit button on the List tab of the Ribbon.

You create a Datasheet view just like you create a Standard view, although you have fewer configuration options. You can sort, filter, display totals, and set the item limit on Datasheet views.

Figure 9-10 shows a Contacts app in a Datasheet view. If a column can't be edited because of the column's data type, the contents of the cell turn gray when you click in the cell to edit the data.

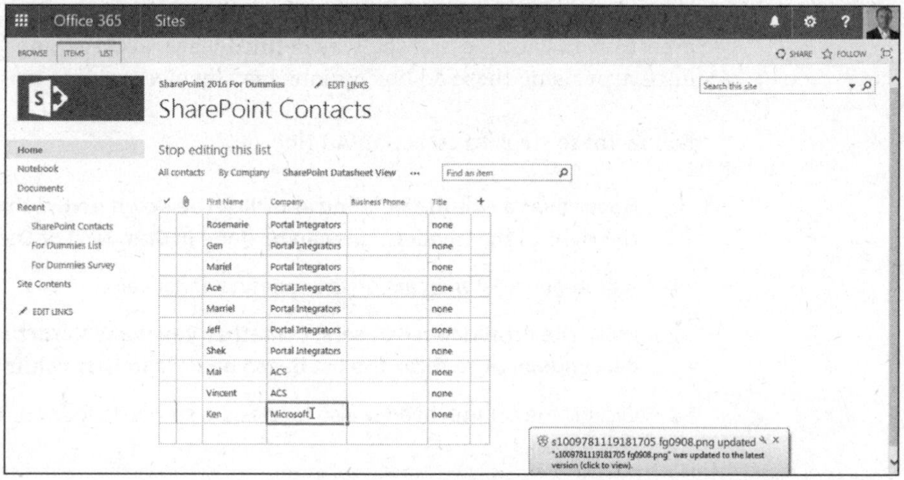

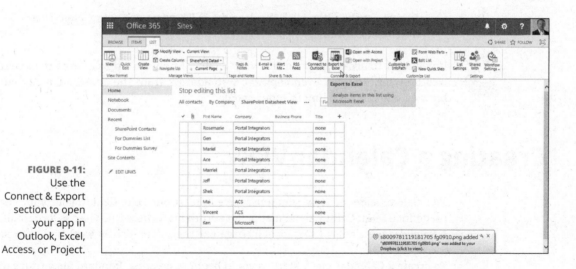

FIGURE 9-10:
Use a Datasheet view to update data.

Depending on which Office applications you have installed, you may be able to access additional options for managing app data in Datasheet view. You can access these options in the Connect & Export section of the Ribbon, as shown in Figure 9-11. Notice you can connect the app to Outlook, export the data to Excel, and open the app with Access or Project.

FIGURE 9-11:
Use the Connect & Export section to open your app in Outlook, Excel, Access, or Project.

Using Ad Hoc Views

Users can make Ad Hoc views in any Standard or Datasheet views by using the headers of the columns to sort and filter the data on the fly. These ad hoc changes aren't saved with the app the way defined views are. Helping your users be productive by using these ad hoc options may involve training tips or help support.

Follow these steps to create an Ad Hoc view:

1. **Hover over a column heading and click the down-arrow that appears on the right of the header. This can be done in Standard or Datasheet view.**

   A drop-down list appears on the column header cell.

2. **From the drop-down list, select whether you want to sort ascending or descending, or to filter the list based on data in that column.**

   Clicking the column header also toggles the sort order between ascending and descending.

   Filtering options appear as distinct data from the values in the column (for example, if Marketing appears ten times in the column, it appears only once as a filter choice).

3. **Select a value from the Filter list.**

   Filtering hides rows that don't contain that value.

   A Filter icon appears in the column header to indicate a filter is applied.

4. **To remove the filter, click the drop-down list again and select Clear Filter from *[Column Name]*.**

TIP

If you want to access your Ad Hoc view again, simply save it as a favorite in your web browser. You can even copy the web address from the address bar in your browser and send the link to other people.

Creating a Calendar View

To create a Calendar view, you must have at least one Date field in your app. The predefined SharePoint Calendar app, not surprisingly, uses this view as its default. A Calendar view helps users visually organize their date-driven work and events.

To create a Calendar view, start as you'd begin to create a Standard view (refer to the earlier section, "Creating a Standard View"), but in Step 4, click the Calendar View link. Like the Gantt view (which we describe in the following section), you see new options on the Create View page. You have a section for Time Interval, where you select the date column to use as the Begin and End fields for the view.

You also have selections to make for Calendar columns, including Month/Week/Day Titles and Week/Day Sub Heading Titles (optional). Choose the column of data you want visible on those days in the different calendar layouts.

There is also a scope option for the default display — Month, Day, or Week. As expected, several options aren't available for Calendar views including sorting, totals, item limits, and styles; however, filtering choices are important and are often used with Calendar views.

TIP

Calendar views can also be used with Calendar overlays, which allow you to display more than one calendar view in a calendar.

Displaying Tasks in a Gantt View

To create a Gantt view, your app needs to contain task/project management information relative to that view format. The predefined SharePoint Tasks app contains these default types of columns, including Task Name, Due Date, and Assigned To.

The Create View page includes Gantt view options not seen in other views based on the five columns mentioned previously.

The Gantt view is a *split view* (see Figure 9-12), where you see a spreadsheet of data on the left and the Gantt chart on the right. A split bar between the two views can be moved by users to see more or less of one side. You can create a custom list or modify the Tasks list to add more columns for this spreadsheet side if you want.

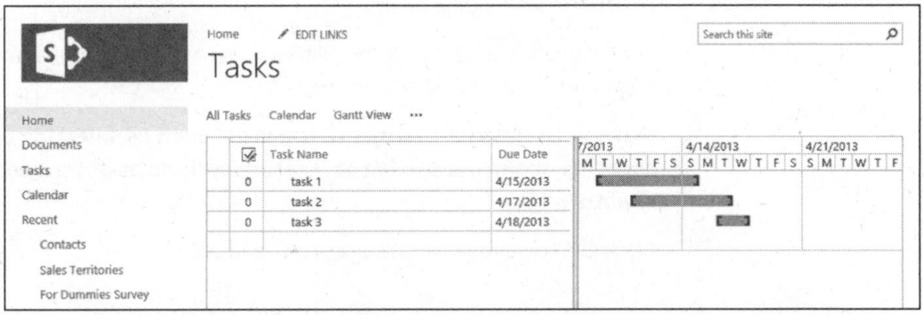

FIGURE 9-12:
The Gantt chart
columns available
in Gantt view.

TIP

You can synchronize tasks with project plans in Microsoft Project 2016. In Project, choose Save & Send ⇨ Sync with Tasks List and enter the URL for your tasks list.

Managing Existing Views

Chances are that you'll want to modify your views over time. In the following sections, we explain how to modify your views and set one as the default view that users see when they browse to an app. SharePoint also provides a couple of built-in views that you may want to customize.

Modifying your views

After creating your fabulous new view, you may find that you need to change it. Maybe you forgot a column, it doesn't sort the way you want it to, or the grouping is just all wrong.

To modify a view, follow these steps:

1. **Browse to the app where you want to modify the view.**

2. **Display the view you want to modify.**

   To change the view that is currently displayed:

   a. Click the Library or List tab on the Ribbon.

   b. In the Manage Views section, click the Change View drop-down list and select the view you want to modify.

   Alternatively, you can click the view name at the top of the page.

3. **Click the Modify This View button in the Manage Views section of the Ribbon.**

   A View Properties page similar to the Create View page appears, enabling you to edit the view's properties.

   Alternatively, you can click the ellipsis next to the view name at the top of the page and choose Modify This View.

4. **Make your desired changes to the view, such as selecting or removing columns or setting sorting or filtering options as described earlier in this chapter.**

5. **Click OK to save your changes to the view.**

REMEMBER

Public views are visible to everyone, but private views can only be used by the person who creates them.

Setting the default view

To change the default view, select the Make This the Default View check box when you create or modify a view. If you are modifying the current default view, you don't see the Make This the Default View check box.

Most apps have only one default view; the exception is the Discussion Board list, which has both subjects and replies as default views. Keep in mind that if you make a view a default view, it must be a Public view.

Other SharePoint built-in views

In addition to the other view formats we discuss earlier in this chapter, two other options fall under the view discussion:

>> **Mobile:** Simplified, text-only views of your apps for use on a mobile device. Mobile is actually a section on the Create View page. You can enable a view to be a Mobile view or set it as the default Mobile view. (Mobile views must be public.)

   You can also set the number of items to display for Mobile views. If you don't see the Mobile section in your Create View page, this type of view can't be displayed in Mobile format.

>> **RSS:** SharePoint generates RSS feeds for apps. (See Chapter 16 for more on how users subscribe to and view SharePoint RSS feeds.)

Displaying Views via Web Parts

Throughout this chapter, we make references to app Web Parts to point out what view properties are helpful and applicable to a view displayed in a Web Part. You want to display your app data with other text and Web Parts in multiple locations, such as team site home pages, Web Part pages, or publishing pages. In these situations, you don't want your users to interact with the app itself with all the editing options. You just want them to see several columns to access a document or view an item.

Chapter 6 goes into detail about using Web Parts, including linked Web Parts, connections, and master/detail settings. However, you need to know that each app generates a Web Part that can be used on SharePoint pages. Each of these Web

Parts has a Properties panel that allows you to change the view in that instance of the Web Part.

Predefined SharePoint apps may have specific views that are defaults for Web Parts (for example, the Announcements app has a special default view that can't be re-created in the browser for other apps). Custom apps generally show all columns when first generated.

After selecting the Edit Web Part command on the Web Part, you can use the Selected View drop-down list in the Web Part Properties panel to apply another view (Current View is selected by default), or you can also click the Edit the Current View hyperlink to modify the view on the fly. Depending on the complexity of your choices, creating a view first to apply to the Web Part(s) may be a better long-term maintenance strategy.

Figure 9-13 shows the Selected View options in a Web Part for a Tasks app.

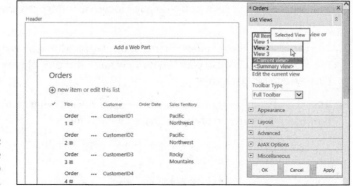

FIGURE 9-13:
Change the view in an app Web Part.

3
Becoming a SharePoint Administrator

Chapter 10

Getting Familiar with Site Settings

I t used to be that website administration was done by the same web developer geeks that created the site. This made life simple for the information worker. If something was wrong with the site, call IT! If something needed to be changed, call IT! If a new site needed to be created and developed, call IT!

SharePoint has shifted the paradigm of website administration. No longer do you need to involve IT in your website administration. This relieves the pressure on IT and also empowers you to take control of your own site. Wasn't it a line in *Spider-Man*, that with great power comes great responsibility? Well, the same is true with SharePoint. If you are a site administrator, you have great power at your fingertips. Just be prepared; the website users will now come to you instead of IT. No need to fear, though; SharePoint makes website administration straightforward. Everything is done using your web browser from a centralized settings page called Site Settings. Yes, you use SharePoint to administer SharePoint. How convenient!

In this chapter, you go through the settings available for a SharePoint site. You find out how to find the Site Settings page and gain familiarity with the many different settings categories.

Finding Site Settings

Thankfully, finding the Site Settings page is as easy as two clicks of the mouse. Click the Settings gear icon and choose Site Settings, as shown in Figure 10-1.

When the Site Settings page loads, you see a number of links all grouped into various categories, as shown in Figure 10-2. The Site Settings page can be daunting and overwhelming. Don't worry, though. As you administer a SharePoint site, you will become familiar with all the various settings pages and become an expert before you know it.

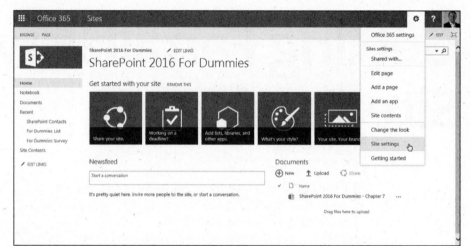

FIGURE 10-1:
Opening the Site Settings page.

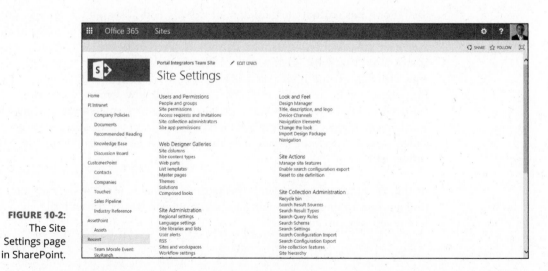

FIGURE 10-2:
The Site Settings page in SharePoint.

Different settings links appear and disappear, depending on your particular permissions and the type of site you are administering. For example, if you're a site collection administrator, then you see the Site Collection Administrators link under the Users and Permissions section. If you're not, then you won't see this link or even the entire Site Collection Administration section.

TIP

If you read about a settings page but can't find it, then chances are you don't have permissions or you are working with a site that does not have that particular setting. This can occur, for example, if the publishing feature is activated or not. In general, SharePoint shifts around links and names depending on how the site is set up.

Digging into Site Settings

The Site Settings page for a site based on the Team Site template contains seven settings categories: Users and Permissions, Web Designer Galleries, Site Administration, Search, Look and Feel, Site Actions, and Site Collection Administration.

Users and Permissions

SharePoint security is a broad topic. In SharePoint, you can create groups, add roles, and set permissions. You can add users to those groups and set permissions for sites and apps. The Users and Permissions section of the Site Settings page is where you administer SharePoint security. (Refer to Figure 10-2 to see the Users and Permissions category.)

The Users and Permissions section contains links to the following settings pages:

>> **People and Groups:** Click to view settings for all the users in your site. Using the People and Groups settings page, you can create new groups, add and remove users from groups, and set permissions for groups.

>> **Site Permissions:** Click to see a page where you can create groups, add roles, change access request settings, and view current roles. In addition, you can add, edit, view, and remove permissions from users.

>> **Site Collection Administrators:** Click this link to set which users have site collection administrator permissions. Site collection administrators have permissions to all the sites contained in the Site Collection. This could be many sites, depending on how your SharePoint farm is set up. If you're a site collection administrator, be very careful who you give this permission to. (This link does not appear if you're not already a site collection administrator on the site.)

>> **Site App Permissions:** Click to provide permissions to the site for SharePoint apps. This is important for third-party apps that you install on the site that need to access your data.

TIP

SharePoint security can take some time to comprehend. Sometimes things just don't seem to work the way they should. Hang in there, though. We talk more about SharePoint security in Chapter 14.

UNDERSTANDING ADMINISTRATION

SharePoint is a very complex product. This book covers only a small sliver of SharePoint that is the user perspective. In addition to the users of SharePoint, a complete infrastructure also makes up a SharePoint environment. If you use SharePoint Online, then Microsoft handles most of the infrastructure (your organization is still responsible for its own Internet access). If you use SharePoint on your own premise, then there is a small army of administrator roles that need to be considered.

In this part of the book, you find out how to administer a SharePoint site. In addition to site (and site collection) administration, there are also SharePoint farm administrators. A *farm administrator* takes care of all the settings for the entire SharePoint farm. A *farm* is made up of multiple web applications that can each contain multiple site collections. Depending on the size of your organization, you may have multiple farm administrators.

SharePoint runs on Windows and uses the Microsoft database product SQL Server. These are complicated products in their own right and often have their own administrators. In particular, a database administrator is a very specialized role, and many companies have more than one of them.

SharePoint environments are often made up of multiple servers. And then you have all the users that each have a device that needs to connect to these servers. To make all the communication happen, you need network administrators. Network administrators live in a completely separate world from the rest of the administrators and focus on the wires (and wireless), switches, hubs, and routers that connect all the devices together.

A lot of administrators make up a SharePoint environment. Organizing them all and making everything work properly is one of the reasons SharePoint is considered enterprise-class software. And trust us, mobilizing this army isn't cheap. Using SharePoint on your premise gives you more control over the environment, but using SharePoint Online offers a cost-effective alternative, and SharePoint Online is often the only real choice for small- to medium-sized organizations.

Web Designer Galleries

A common theme throughout SharePoint is reusability. When you spend the time to develop something, you want to be able to use it over and over again. In SharePoint, reusability takes the form of things like data containers, templates, layouts, and solutions. The Web Designer Galleries is where you manage all these reusable components. The components are stored in galleries and are designed to hold the pieces you use when designing your websites. With that in mind, Web Designer Galleries is such a perfect name. (What a nice break from other horribly named technology and acronyms like XSLT, HTML, and CSS.)

The Web Designer Galleries section of the Site Settings page includes the following links:

- » **Site Columns:** A gallery that contains columns you can use throughout the site. For example, you might create a column called Product Name that you could add to any app in the site. SharePoint ships with a number of existing site columns.

- » **Site Content Types:** This gallery stores site content types (which are a collection of columns) so that you can use them throughout the site. For example, say you want to store all the information about a product. A product might contain many different data fields (called site columns) such as Product Name, Product Description, Product Bar Code, Product ID, and probably a lot more. You could create the site column for each data field and then group all of the data fields together into a content type. Now, rather than adding each data field to every app throughout the site, you can simply add the content type when you want to work with a product, and all the columns come along with it. SharePoint ships with a number of content types out of the box. The content types are grouped into categories for easy reference.

- » **Web Parts:** The gallery where all Web Parts (both out of the box and third-party) are stored. *Web Parts* are functional components that can be added to pages. (Web Parts are covered in Chapter 6.)

- » **List Templates:** The gallery where an app saved as a template is stored. (List Templates is a bit of a naming snafu. In SharePoint 2016, all lists and libraries are called apps, so this gallery would more aptly be named App Templates.) Each app based on a list has a link on the List Settings page. Under the Permissions and Management section is the Save List as Template link. When you save a list app as a template, it is then stored in the List Templates gallery. You can then take the template and upload it to this gallery on a different SharePoint site. After it's uploaded, you see a new app type on the Your Apps page, and you can then create apps based on the uploaded template. This is handy when you spend a lot of time building a list app just the way you want it and need to transfer it to another location.

» **Master Pages:** This gallery contains all the master pages and page layouts. A *master page* is a template type page that provides a consistent look and feel throughout every page in the site. For example, notice how in every out-of-the-box SharePoint site, the navigation is on the left, there is a header at the top, and the pages are in the middle? That is all due to the master page that ships with SharePoint. (Creating custom master pages for your organization is best left to developers — master pages are a lot of work and can quickly turn into a nightmare project. SharePoint also requires the master page to contain certain things and behave in a certain way.) A page layout is a similar concept to a master page but is designed to be a template for a single page. (Page layouts are a feature of the publishing components of SharePoint and are covered further in Chapter 18.)

» **Themes:** A gallery that holds SharePoint themes. A *theme* is a collection of colors and fonts. When you apply a theme, your SharePoint site magically changes. A number of themes ship with SharePoint, and you can also have a web developer build your own custom themes. (Changing the look and feel of your site is covered further in Chapter 13.)

» **Solutions:** A gallery that stores custom SharePoint solutions. A *SharePoint solution* is a bunch of custom-developed functionality all packaged together. The entire package is called a Web Solution Package (WSP). A SharePoint solution might be developed by your in-house developers or purchased from a third party. For example, the company Portal Integrators has deveoped a number of SharePoint solutions for clients all over the world. When they send the final product to a client, they send them the WSP. One of these solutions is geared towards Human Resources. If you purchase it, you get a WSP with all sorts of SharePoint functionality designed for Human Resources. Upload the WSP to this gallery, and your Human Resources department now loves SharePoint.

» **Composed Looks:** A gallery that has to do with the look and feel of your site. A *composed look* is relatively new in SharePoint; it expands on the idea of themes and adds a background image and a master page. A number of composed looks ship with SharePoint (and are explored in Chapter 13). To give you a sneak peek, SharePoint ships with composed looks called Sea Monster, Breeze, and Immerse. You can look forward to spicing up your SharePoint site, if you so desire.

Refer to Figure 10-2 to see the Web Designer Galleries category.

Site Administration

The Site Administration section is where you manage options that are specific to this individual site. The changes you make in this section won't affect other sites in the same site collection container. This is different than the Web Designer Galleries section of the Site Settings page. The Web Designer Galleries section includes components that are used throughout the site collection. So if you upload a solution, it will be available to other sites in the site collection.

REMEMBER

It's easy to get confused about which site the Site Administration page affects. This is especially true if you manage multiple sites or are a site collection administrator. When working with the Site Administration settings, make sure you are on the correct site.

The Site Administration section contains a large number of settings, so many that we can't cover them all in this book. We encourage you to explore these settings. Among the settings in the Site Administration section are Regional Settings, User Alerts, Workflow Settings, Term Store Management, Popularity Trends, and even Translation Status (which is only available when SharePoint Server Publishing Feature is active).

(Refer to Figure 10-2 to see the Site Administration category.)

Search

The Search section is where you manage all the search functionality for your site. Search can be an incredibly powerful productivity tool. It's worth spending the time to discover the capabilities of SharePoint search.

The Search section contains the following links:

» **Result Sources** is a settings page where you define where SharePoint search should look for content. You can set sources to local SharePoint content, remote SharePoint content, Exchange, or any other external system that supports the OpenSearch protocol.

» **Result Types** is where you define how a result will look based on the type of content displayed. For example, you might want the results of a person to look different from the results of an Excel or Word file. A number of prepackaged types ship with SharePoint, and you can also define your own. For example, you might want all your products to display in a search result in a particular way. You might want the picture on the left and a description and price on the bottom. You might then want a link to the product page and also a link to the product documentation. You define this with a custom search result that uses a custom template. Building these isn't simple, but it is possible with the right technical resources.

- ❯❯ **Query Rules** is a place where you can promote important content into search results. This is valuable because most people are looking for common content. The search engine doesn't know the difference between an actual marketing template and a hundred other documents that might include the words *marketing template*. Using the query rules, you can let SharePoint know that the actual marketing template is what people are looking for when they search the term and that it should be displayed at the top. You can also show additional blocks of search results based on a search that you might think someone is trying to find. For example, if someone searches for *sales decks,* they might really mean *sales PowerPoint documents*. Query rules are very powerful, and it's worth taking the time to figure out the capabilities to provide the best search experience.

- ❯❯ **Schema** is where you can manage properties and map the properties that the search engine uses when searching. A *property* is a piece of data about the thing that you search for. For example, if you search for a person, you might create a property to hold the person's department. The search engine can then reference that property when you look for a person in a particular department. Managing properties is only available to site collection administrators.

- ❯❯ **Search Settings** is where you define the general search settings for the site. You can point the search results to a special site called a Search Center or a specific custom page you have developed to show search results. In addition, you can configure navigation for moving between search and the rest of the site.

- ❯❯ **Searchable Columns** is a where you define which columns you want the search engine to reference when you search. (Creating a new column is covered in Chapter 8.) You can use this settings page to let SharePoint know it should use a particular column of metadata when searching for content. The Searchable Columns link is available only when the SharePoint Server Publishing Feature is active.

- ❯❯ **Search and Offline Availability** allows you to ban the site content from appearing in search results, set fine-grained search permissions, and even allow items from the site to be downloaded to offline clients.

- ❯❯ **Configuration Import** lets you import a search configuration file. A search configuration file can contain all the settings and details that you have already spent the time to set up. You definitely wouldn't want to go through the entire exercise on every site, so you can use configuration files to move settings between sites.

- ❯❯ **Configuration Export** is used to export a search configuration file after you have everything set up just how you want it. You can then use the Configuration Import setting to import on the new site.

SharePoint search is a very broad topic and it takes some time to get familiar with its capabilities. It is well worth the effort, however, because search can greatly improve your organization's productivity. (We discuss SharePoint search in more detail in Chapter 19.)

(Refer to Figure 10-2 to see the Search category.)

Look and Feel

The Look and Feel section of the Site Settings page includes links for managing things like the color, title, and landing page. You can easily change a number of things to customize your site and make it your own.

WARNING

The Look and Feel section of the Site Settings page is a perfect lesson in Share-Point frustration. The links that appear in this section depend on whether you have the SharePoint Server Publishing feature activated. Not knowing this could cause you frustration because you may read about a settings link, but when you look at your own SharePoint 2016 site, that link is nowhere to be found. To make matters worse, the links are different depending on whether SharePoint Server Publishing is activated at the site collection level or the site level. For example, you could have SharePoint Server Publishing activated at the site collection level but not activated at the site level. You will still see the Navigation link in the Look and Feel section, as opposed to the Top Link bar and Quick Launch navigation links that appear if the publishing feature was deactivated at the site collection level. (Activating and deactivating SharePoint features is covered in Chapter 12.)

The Look and Feel section contains the following setting links (when the Share-Point Server Publishing feature is not active at the site collection or site level):

>> **Title, Description, and Logo** is where you can change the title of your site, add or edit the description, and insert a logo. Just changing the title and logo is often enough to make a business site your own. With this simple change, your site looks professional and unique to your team or organization. You can then get on with the productivity benefits that SharePoint has to offer.

>> **Quick Launch** enables you to configure the navigation on the left side of the page. You can add headings, links, and change the order.

>> **Top Link bar** enables you to configure navigation at the top of the page.

>> **Tree View** is where you enable or disable the Quick Launch (left navigation) or turn on a special type of navigation on the left side that shows a tree of the site's content.

>> **Change the Look** is where you choose the colors and design of the site. There are some exciting and outrageous looks such as Sea Monster and Immerse. The looks available to choose from are in the Composed Looks gallery (see the earlier section, "Web Designer Galleries").

When you activate the SharePoint Server Publishing Infrastructure feature at the site collection and site level, the Tree View and Top Link bar setting links disappear and are replaced with a single Navigation link. In addition, the following settings links appear in the Look and Feel section.

>> **Design Manager** is a web-based tool that you can use to create your own SharePoint site designs. The tool is wizard based and walks you through uploading design files, editing your master page, changing page layouts, and publishing and packaging your design.

>> **Device Channels** enables you to specify certain characteristics of your site based on the device used to view the site. A channel can be optimized for the device to display the site in a specific way. For example, you can set up a channel for smartphones (such as an iPhone or Windows Phone). You could set up a different channel for the iPad or Surface tablets. And finally, you can set up a channel for laptops and desktop browsers.

>> **Import Design Package** enables you to import a design package developed by a third party or in-house designer.

>> **Navigation** enables you to manage navigation links and also change how the navigation behaves. You can configure global navigation (top of page) and also current navigation (left side of page). The Navigation settings page also enables you to change the sorting order of the navigational links and show and hide the Ribbon.

>> **Master Page** is where you choose which master page the site uses and which master page the system uses. The system master page is for pages used by the system, such as when you view an app.

>> **Page Layouts and Site Templates** enables you to control which page layouts and site templates are available for users of the site. All the page layouts are contained in a gallery (see the earlier section, "Web Designer Galleries"). This settings page enables you to limit the page layouts and site templates that users of the site can use.

>> **Welcome Page** is the landing page for a publishing site. You can use this settings page to determine which page should be used for the landing page.

>> **Image Renditions** is where you determine how images and video should render. You can choose a particular width and height for each type of image or video.

We cover changing the look and feel of your site in Chapter 13 and cover Share-Point navigation in Chapter 11.

The Look and Feel category, with the SharePoint Server Publishing feature activated, is shown in Figure 10-2.

Site Actions

The Site Actions section is where you manage the SharePoint features for the site. You can activate or deactivate particular features using the Manage Site Features link. This is important because some features show up only when certain features are active. For example, the Save Site as Template link and the Enable Search Configuration Export option show up when the SharePoint Server Publishing Feature is not active but disappear when it is active. In addition, you can reset the site to its original template definition or delete the site completely.

We cover activating and deactivating SharePoint features in detail in Chapter 12.

(Refer to Figure 10-2 to see the Site Actions category.)

Site Collection Administration

A *site collection* is a container for multiple sites. SharePoint allows organizations to delegate different levels of administration. For example, you might be a site collection administrator, and there might be an administrator for each site. This delegation of duty is important for offloading the work required to keep a large number of websites running smoothly.

The Site Collection Administration section of the Site Settings page is used to administer the overall site collection. The result is that any changes made to these settings pages affect all sites in the site collection. In addition, you can activate or deactivate a feature here to make it available or remove it from all the sites in the collection. The next step up in administration from site collection administrator is SharePoint farm administrator. A SharePoint farm administrator uses a tool called Central Administration, and the changes they make at the farm level affect all site collections in the SharePoint farm.

TIP

In order to see this section, you must be a site collection administrator.

There are over 30 links to settings pages in the Site Collection Administration section. Most of the links are similar in nature to the Site Administration section but affect all sites in the collection and not just the current site. Keep in mind that having a feature active or not causes links to appear or disappear. For example, activating the SharePoint Server Publishing Feature alters this settings page.

The Site Collection Administration category is shown in Figure 10-3.

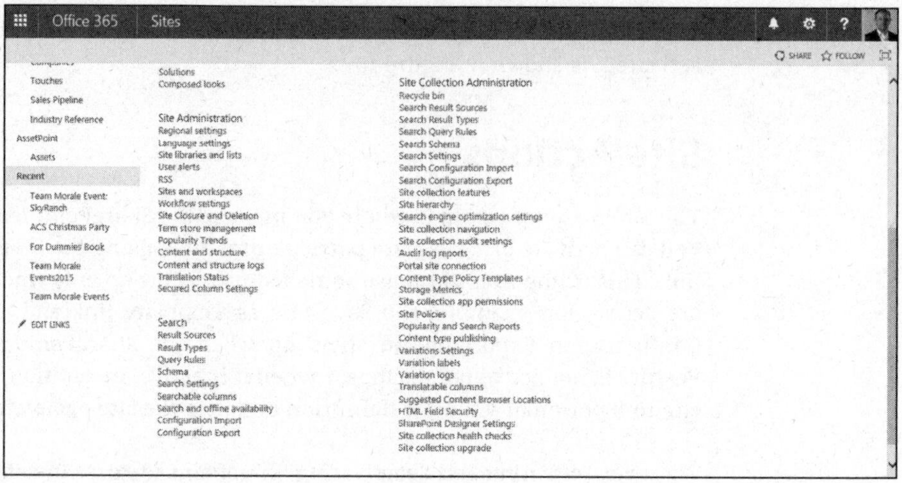

FIGURE 10-3:
The Site
Collection
Administration
category of
the Site
Settings page.

Chapter 11

Configuring Site Navigation

SharePoint handles navigation by default. When you create a site based on a template, you already have navigational links to pages such as your Documents app, the home page, and the contents of the site. As you get more advanced with SharePoint, you may want to start modifying the default navigation and customizing it to fit your needs.

In this chapter, you see how to configure SharePoint navigation. You add your own links not only to SharePoint pages, but also to anywhere on the World Wide Web. You discover the differences between dynamic and static navigation. Finally, you delve into some of the options available when configuring navigation in your SharePoint site.

Understanding How to Configure SharePoint Navigation

SharePoint navigation is fairly straightforward until you turn on the SharePoint Server Publishing Infrastructure feature. This feature is activated and deactivated at the site collection level. When the feature is not active for the site collection, you manage SharePoint navigation in a straightforward manner. When it is activated, you manage SharePoint navigation in a more advanced manner. In addition, the name of the navigation settings links on the Site Settings page change when the feature is activated. To see exactly how the SharePoint Server Publishing Infrastructure changes the names of the links, check out the section about Look and Feel settings in Chapter 10.

In this chapter, we focus on navigation when the SharePoint Server Publishing Infrastructure feature is activated for the site collection. Without this feature, you can simply add, remove, and order links. With this feature activated, a whole world of SharePoint navigation is flung open. (To find out more about navigation when the SharePoint Server Publishing Infrastructure feature is not turned on, check out Chapter 13.)

Configuring SharePoint Navigation

The navigation options in a publishing site allow you to manage both the top navigation and the site's Quick Launch navigation on one page. SharePoint enables you to manage the two major kinds of navigation found on most websites:

>> **Primary navigation** is what your site visitors use to reach the main areas in your site, no matter where they are in your site. Primary navigation is usually positioned somewhere in the top of the page and is consistent across every page in your site. SharePoint calls this *global navigation*.

>> **Contextual navigation** is usually found in the body of the page, usually on the left, and provides access to pages within each major area of your site. This navigation is considered contextual because the navigation items may change, depending on where the visitor is in the site. SharePoint calls this *current navigation*.

SharePoint provides two navigation menus that correspond with global and current navigation. The Top Link bar is the global navigation menu that's usually present at the top of publishing pages. The Quick Launch menu provides the current navigation that appears along the left side of most pages.

SharePoint's publishing site assumes that you want global and current navigation menus created dynamically based on site hierarchy. To that end, configuring navigation in a publishing site requires two things:

>> **A site hierarchy that matches your navigation requirements.** In other words, you have subsites for the major items in your global navigation and pages for the items below. Any time you want to create a new grouping of pages in the navigation menu, you have to create a new subsite.

This often leads to extensive nesting of sites, which we recommend you avoid. This is one reason that people start looking for alternative approaches to navigation.

>> **The ability to think in terms of the current site you're setting navigation options for, its parent site, its sibling sites, and any children sites that may exist.** This can be extremely confusing to people, which is one reason why we see many people abandon dynamic navigation. It's too hard to keep track of what's happening where.

Configuring global navigation

In most publishing sites, you want all pages and sites to display the same navigation settings. SharePoint can dynamically display all subsites and pages within a subsite in your global navigation. Pages display in a drop-down list.

Each site in your publishing site can have its own global configuration settings. So you need to perform the following steps for each site. The settings you make in a subsite, such as whether to display pages, impacts navigation for the entire site, not just what the visitor sees when they're on that site. Follow these steps:

1. **Browse to the publishing site or subsite you want to configure global navigation for.**

2. **Click the Settings gear icon and choose Site Settings, and then click the Navigation link in the Look and Feel section.**

   The Site Navigation Settings page appears.

3. **In a parent site, such as the top-level site, use the Global Navigation section to indicate whether you want to display navigation items that are below the parent site.**

   Select the Show Subsites options to display each subsite in the global navigation. To show the pages that have been created in the parent site, select Show Pages.

   Scroll down to the Structural Navigation: Editing and Sorting section of the page to get a sneak peek at your global navigation hierarchy.

4. **In a child site, use the Global Settings section to determine whether the subsite will display the same global navigation items as its parent site.**

Select the Show Subsites and Show Pages options to display subsites and pages on the current site and any other site (parent or child) that opts to display navigation for the site you are configuring. Figure 11-1 shows the global navigation options for a child site.

A child site can be a parent site to another site.

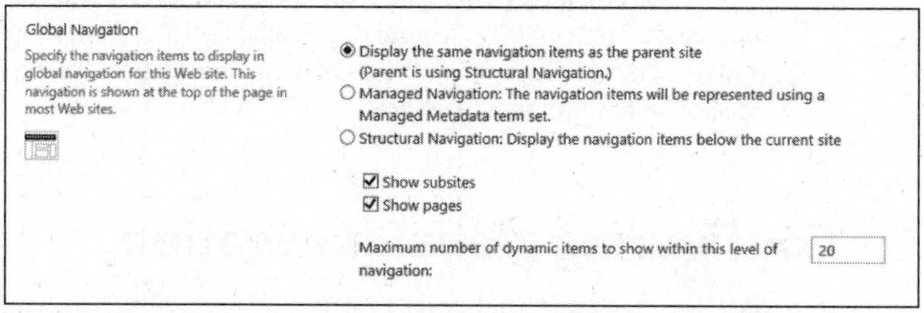

REMEMBER

Global Navigation

Specify the navigation items to display in global navigation for this Web site. This navigation is shown at the top of the page in most Web sites.

○ Display the same navigation items as the parent site
(Parent is using Structural Navigation.)
○ Managed Navigation: The navigation items will be represented using a Managed Metadata term set.
○ Structural Navigation: Display the navigation items below the current site

☑ Show subsites
☑ Show pages

Maximum number of dynamic items to show within this level of navigation: [20]

FIGURE 11-1:
Global Navigation
settings.

For example, you might create a subsite in your publishing site called MyPubSubSite. If you enable Show Subsites and Show Pages, the top-level home site will also display any pages and subsites of the MyPubSubSite navigation option. Figure 11-2 shows the MyPubSubSite navigation menu from the parent site when the Show Pages option is selected.

FIGURE 11-2:
The MyPubSub-
Site navigation
menu and global
navigation
settings for a
parent site.

← → http://intranet.portalintegrators.com/parent/Pages/default.aspx   🔍 ▾ C   SharePoint   Home

SharePoint

Parent Site   MyPubSubSite   ▾

Home   Subsite Page

5. **Click OK to save your global navigation settings.**

We usually have two browser windows open when we configure navigation. We use one browser window to configure the navigation and another to view the changes we made.

TIP

Figure 11-2 shows the global navigation menu for a typical publishing site. This site's parent site is configured to show subsites and pages. The subsite, MyPub-SubSite, is configured to show pages. Table 11-1 summarizes typical global navigation settings.

TABLE 11-1 **Typical Global Navigation Settings**

When You Select This Option	This Appears in Global Navigation
Select the Show Subsites check box in each site in your hierarchy.	Subsites automatically appear in the global navigation as soon as they're created. If this option isn't selected in the parent site, no subsites appear in your global navigation.
Select the Show Pages check box in each site in the hierarchy.	Pages automatically appear in the global navigation as soon as they're approved. If this option is selected in the parent site, the parent's sites pages appear as siblings to any subsites in the global navigation.
Select the Display the Same Navigation Items as the Parent option.	All sites have the same global navigation. Make sure that you select this option in each site's global navigation settings.

Configuring current navigation

Configuring current navigation settings for each site is similar to global navigation. You have the same options to automatically show pages and subsites. As shown in Figure 11-3, you have these options to determine what items appear in the site's current navigation:

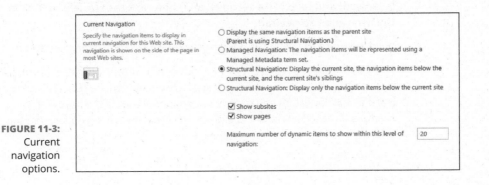

FIGURE 11-3:
Current
navigation
options.

>> **Display the Same Navigation Items as the Parent Site:** This option displays the current navigation items using the settings of the parent site.

>> **Managed Navigation:** This option enables you to manage navigation using a set of terms you define called Managed Metadata. When you select this option, your site will show sites and subsites based on the terms you have defined and not the subsites and pages in the site. When you select the Managed Navigation option, the option to show subsites and pages disappears.

>> **Structural Navigation:** This option gives you the choice to display subsites and pages below the current site.

REMEMBER

Choosing the Show Pages and Show Subsites options in the Global Navigation section makes navigation items show for pages and subsites in the top navigation. Choosing the Show Pages and Show Subsites option in the Current Navigation section shows the navigational links in the left navigation.

Configuring Static Navigation

Most clients we work with don't want pages and subsites showing automatically in their navigation. They usually want a static menu that doesn't change when someone publishes an article page.

You can opt to use a static navigation menu by deselecting the Show Pages and Show Subsites options in the navigation settings for each site. You can then manually enter whatever navigation you want to appear in the global and current navigation for each site.

To manually configure your navigation items:

1. **Browse to the site you want to configure, choose the Settings drop-down (gear icon) and select Site Settings, and then click the Navigation link in the Look and Feel section.**

2. **Scroll down to the Structural Navigation: Editing and Sorting section.**

   This section shows a hierarchy of your global and current navigation items, as shown in Figure 11-4. The items you see here depend on the settings you make in the global navigation and current navigation settings of the page. For example, if you select the Show Subsites in Global Navigation option, you see subsites listed in this section of the page.

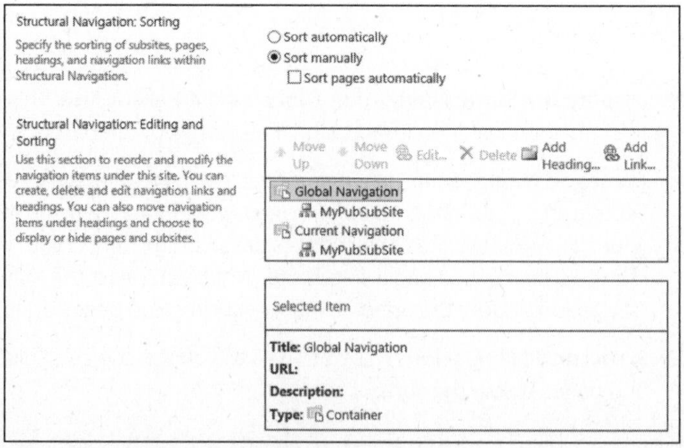

FIGURE 11-4:
View the navigation hierarchy.

Structural Navigation: Sorting

Specify the sorting of subsites, pages, headings, and navigation links within Structural Navigation.

○ Sort automatically
◉ Sort manually
   ☐ Sort pages automatically

Structural Navigation: Editing and Sorting

Use this section to reorder and modify the navigation items under this site. You can create, delete and edit navigation links and headings. You can also move navigation items under headings and choose to display or hide pages and subsites.

↑ Move Up   ↓ Move Down   ✎ Edit...   ✕ Delete   Add Heading...   Add Link...

Global Navigation
   MyPubSubSite
Current Navigation
   MyPubSubSite

Selected Item

Title: Global Navigation
URL:
Description:
Type: Container

3. **To add a new navigation to your global or current navigation, click the place in the hierarchy where you want to add the item.**

4. **Click the Add Heading button to add a new heading, or click the Add Link button to add a new link.**

   Figure 11-5 shows the Navigation Heading dialog box. The Add Link dialog box looks exactly the same. A heading doesn't require a web address or URL. That is, you can use a heading to contain links without requiring that the heading point to anything in the browser.

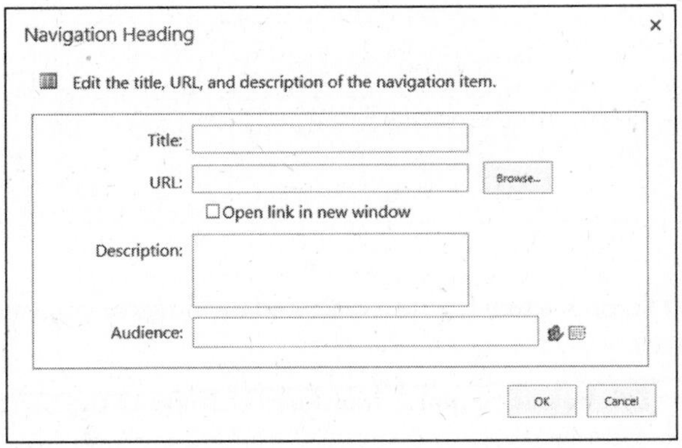

FIGURE 11-5:
Adding a
new heading to
your current
navigation.

Navigation Heading ✕

▦ Edit the title, URL, and description of the navigation item.

Title:
URL: Browse...
☐ Open link in new window
Description:
Audience: ✿ ▦

OK   Cancel

5. **Enter the details for the navigation item.**

   You have these options:

   - *Title:* The text you enter in this field appears in the navigation menu.

   - *URL:* Enter the page where the item links to. This is an optional field for headings.

   - *Open Link in New Window:* Select this check box to open the link in a new window.

   - *Description:* The text you enter in this field displays as a tooltip when someone hovers the cursor over the navigation item.

   - *Audience:* Use this text box to filter the navigation item so that only members of the selected audience can see the navigation item.

   Get creative about adding navigation items. We often add static links to the current navigation for common tasks that people need to perform, such as managing a group's membership.

TIP

6. **Click OK to save your heading or link.**

The heading appears in the site's navigation hierarchy, as shown in Figure 11-6. Use the Move Up or Move Down buttons to reposition the item in the hierarchy.

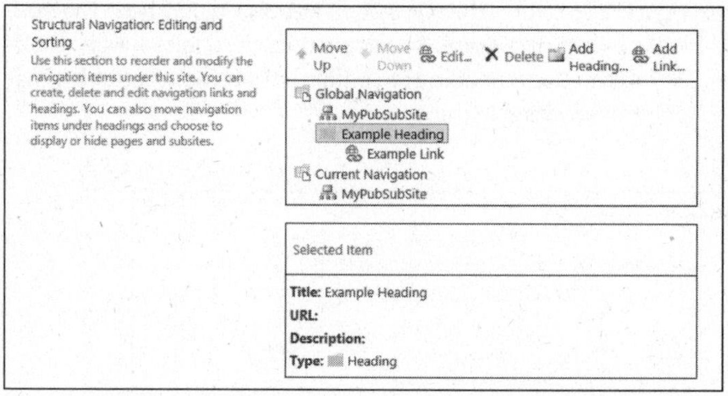

FIGURE 11-6: Your item appears in the navigation hierarchy.

7. **Repeat Steps 3–6 to add more links and headings to your navigation hierarchy.**

8. **Use the Edit button to make additional changes to the hierarchy.**

Click the Edit button to modify the Title, Description, URL, or Audience for a navigation item.

9. **Click OK to save your navigation settings.**

Navigation Using Web Parts

It'd be naïve to expect that you only need to use two kinds of site navigation. In reality, webmasters and site visitors expect lots of ways to get to content. In Chapter 6, we discuss the Content Rollup Web Parts. These Web Parts are often used to provide the additional navigation options that you want to see inside your web pages, not just in the header and along the side.

One such Web Part, the Table of Contents Web Part, can be used to create a sitemap. A considered best practice is to provide a sitemap, and the Table of Contents Web Part dynamically generates it for you.

**TECHNICAL
STUFF**

Advanced web developers can use a custom master page to control where the site's navigation menu appears on the page. For example, if you want the current navigation on the right instead of the left, you can have it moved there in the master page. Customizing master pages is not an easy task and should be left to SharePoint master page experts. SharePoint expects certain controls and behaviors from a master page, and if it is customized in the wrong way, SharePoint will throw errors.

Understanding Managed Navigation

In many cases, people want more control over the site navigation than SharePoint provides out of the box. Publishing sites provide great options for dynamically displaying the navigation based on the site's hierarchy, but what if you want to display navigation based on metadata?

SharePoint 2016 includes Managed Navigation. Managed Navigation allows you to drive SharePoint navigation based on managed metadata. Managed metadata is hierarchal in nature and is managed at the site collection level. When you tie navigation to this hierarchy, you can be sure that every site in the site collection will subscribe to the same structure. When you need to update the hierarchy, you update it for the entire site collection, and every site automatically updates navigation as well. The Managed Navigation option on the navigation settings page is shown in Figure 11-7. You access the Navigation settings page from the Look and Feel section of Site Settings.

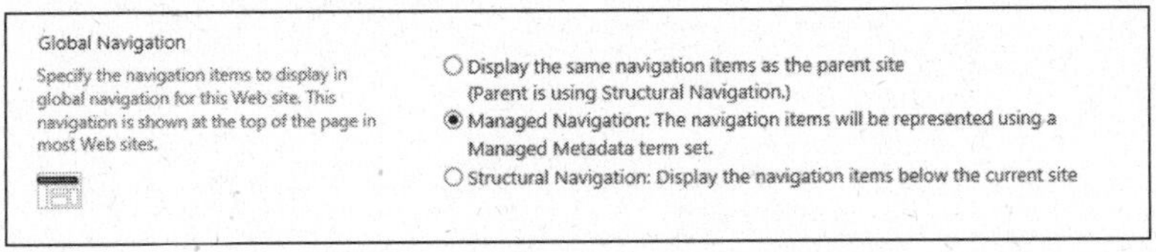

FIGURE 11-7:
The Managed
Navigation
option.

Global Navigation

Specify the navigation items to display in global navigation for this Web site. This navigation is shown at the top of the page in most Web sites.

○ Display the same navigation items as the parent site
(Parent is using Structural Navigation.)
◉ Managed Navigation: The navigation items will be represented using a Managed Metadata term set.
○ Structural Navigation: Display the navigation items below the current site

**TECHNICAL
STUFF**

If you still need more navigation control, you can always bring in developers. SharePoint is built on ASP.NET and allows developers to use special controls for modifying navigation. Because this involves writing code, it's best left to professional developers — but you should at least know it's possible.

IN THIS CHAPTER

Figuring out how a SharePoint feature works

Discovering some of the features that ship with SharePoint 2016

Using features to extend SharePoint

Chapter 12

Understanding SharePoint Features

As you can read in Chapter 3, the term *feature* can be a bit confusing in SharePoint. You often hear people talk about functionality in terms of features. The term feature has a double meaning in SharePoint. The first meaning is in the traditional sense, so you could say web-based administration is a feature of SharePoint. The second meaning of feature is technical and specifically means a package of code that can be activated and deactivated (turned on and off).

In this chapter, you discover SharePoint features. You see how a feature works and which features are active by default. You also find out how to activate and deactivate features and explore some of the most common and helpful ones. Finally, you see how SharePoint can be extended with custom features.

Getting a High-Level View of SharePoint Features

We have to admit that SharePoint features took us a long time to really understand. The reason is that a feature can do anything in SharePoint. A feature is just a collection of code that alters SharePoint in some manner. For example, say you want to write some code that adds a new item to the drop-down list that appears when you click the Settings gear icon. SharePoint lets you do this in code. Now, how do you deploy it to SharePoint? How do you let site administrators turn it on and off? The answer is that you package that code up in a SharePoint feature. When the feature is installed, an administrator can activate (turn on) or deactivate (turn off) the feature. The result is that your custom item appears in the Settings drop-down list when the feature is activated and disappears from the drop-down list when the feature is deactivated.

SharePoint ships with a number of features out of the box. In fact, features can be a major source of frustration. Take the earlier example of a feature that makes an item appear on a menu when the feature is activated. The way you reach navigation in SharePoint (covered in Chapter 11) depends on whether a particular SharePoint feature is activated. That feature is the SharePoint Server Publishing Infrastructure feature. This feature does a lot of things when you activate it, including altering the settings links for navigation. Before you activate the feature, the navigation links on the Site Settings page in the Look and Feel section are displayed as Quick Launch and Top Link bar. When you activate the SharePoint Server Publishing Infrastructure feature, it removes those two links and adds one called Navigation.

You will find that the answer to a SharePoint question is often that it depends on which features are activated!

Turning On and Off Features

You turn on and off features by activating and deactivating them. Features are activated at two different levels. The first is a site collection; the second is a site. Features activated at the site collection level affect all sites contained within the site collection. Features activated at the site level only affect that particular site.

When a feature is active (turned on), a blue Active status indicator appears next to the feature on the right side of the page. See the Access App row in Figure 12-1 and note the Active button in the status column. When a feature is inactive (turned off) the status column is empty, as shown in the second row (Announcement Tiles Feature) in Figure 12-1.

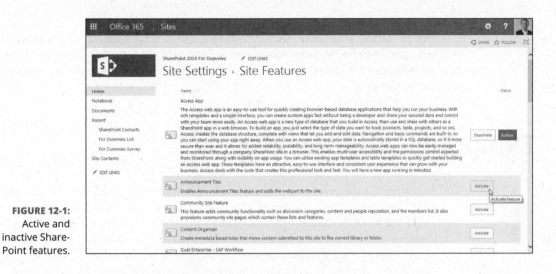

FIGURE 12-1:
Active and
inactive Share-
Point features.

To view a listing of all features for a particular site:

1. **Click the Settings gear icon and choose Site Settings.**

The Site Settings page appears.

2. **In the Site Actions section, click the Manage Site Features link.**

A listing of all the features for this particular site is displayed. Each feature includes an icon, name, description, Activate/Deactivate button, and status column.

To view a listing of all features for a particular site collection:

1. **Click the Settings gear icon and choose Site Settings.**

The Site Settings page appears.

2. **In the Site Collection Administration section, click the Site Collection Features link.**

A listing of all the features for this particular site collection is displayed. Each feature includes an icon, name, description, Activate/Deactivate button, and status column.

If you don't see the Site Collection Administration section on the Site Settings page, then you do not have Site Collection Administrator permissions.

WARNING

It's easy to get turned around when working with SharePoint features. For example, if you are in a subsite and go to the Site Settings page for that subsite, you don't see all the settings links in the Site Collection Administration section. You instead see a link that takes you to the settings page for the site collection. When you click that link, the Site Settings page reloads for the site collection, and you see all the Site Collection Settings links. (A site collection is also a site.) So if you then click the Manage Site Features link, you are actually managing the features scoped for only the site collection site and not the subsite where you originally started.

Exploring Common Features

Exploring all the features that ship with SharePoint could fill a book unto itself. Each feature on the settings page includes a name and description. We wish we could tell you that they are all straightforward, but they are not. Some features are massive and complicated and others are simple. For example, the SharePoint Server Publishing Infrastructure feature can do a mind-boggling number of things. Conversely, the Site Feed feature simply enables the use of site feeds on a site.

A couple of the most common features are the SharePoint Server Standard Site features and the SharePoint Server Enterprise Site features. These features include functionality for the different editions of SharePoint Server (Standard and Enterprise). The Standard Edition features include functionality such as user profiles and search, and the Enterprise Edition features include functionality such as Visio Services, Access Services, and Excel Services.

TIP

If you're looking for functionality such as Excel Services, and you can't find it, then check to make sure the SharePoint Server Enterprise Site feature is activated for your site.

Extending SharePoint with Features

Microsoft ships a ton of features with SharePoint 2016, but the product can always be extended further. If your organization has a dedicated development team, they can build features specific for your organization. For example, a company might use in-house developers to create custom SharePoint features for different groups within the company. For example, some features could provide functionality for the sales department, others for human resources, and still others for engineers. Each team in the company can then choose whether to activate or deactivate the features based on whether they need the specific features for their relevant workload on the SharePoint site.

Alternatively, third-party companies also develop features to extend SharePoint for a particular audience. For example, Portal Integrators has a Human Resources

Solution, shown in Figure 12-2, that can be activated to extend SharePoint with human resources functionality. After installing a third-party feature, it shows up right alongside the features that Microsoft ships with SharePoint.

FIGURE 12-2: A third-party feature that extends SharePoint with human resources functionality.

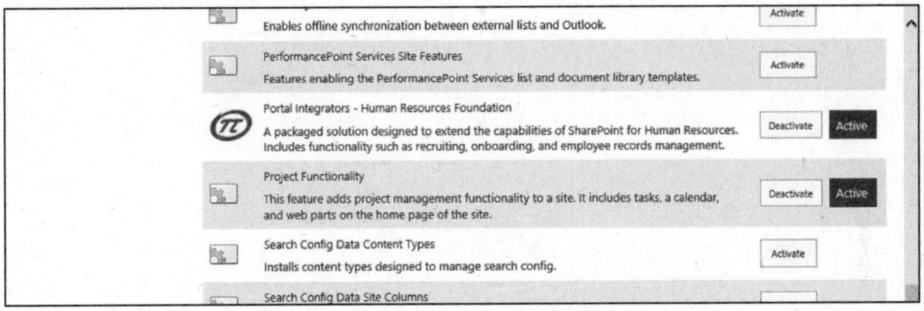

Chapter 13

Changing the Look and Feel of Your Site

Changing the look and feel of a site can be very powerful. The standard SharePoint colors work just fine, but perhaps you want to change the color palette for a holiday or to match your team's color scheme. SharePoint provides some very powerful features for changing the look and feel of your site. You don't need web designers or any specialized technical skills.

Usability experts have a lot to say about the look and feel of a site. After users are familiar with the look and feel of a site, it's best not to change it. Creating change when it isn't required causes a productivity loss. However, it can be a good idea to spice things up a bit by changing some of the colors for a holiday or special day. You just shouldn't go too crazy (unless you want your users to do the same).

In this chapter, you find out how to change the look and feel of a SharePoint site. You see how themes are used for colors and fonts and how composed looks are used. Finally, this chapter delves into editing the Top Link bar and Quick Launch navigation on a team site.

The Look and Feel Section of Site Settings

You change the look and feel of your site using settings in the Look and Feel section of the Site Settings page, shown in Figure 13-1. You can access the Site Settings page by clicking the Settings gear icon and choosing Site Settings.

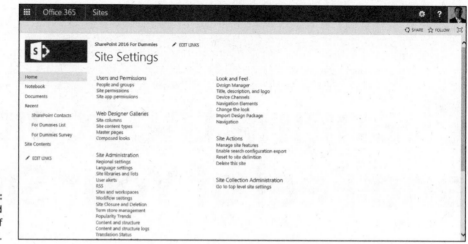

FIGURE 13-1:
The Look and Feel section of Site Settings.

The Look and Feel section contains a number of links for changing things on your site such as navigation, title, description, logo, and most importantly, the look of your site. The links in the Look and Feel section of Site Settings differ depending on which SharePoint feature is active. For example, activating or deactivating the Publishing Infrastructure Feature changes the links in the Look and Feel section. (To find out about the available links in the Look and Feel section and how features affect these links, see Chapter 10.)

Changing Your Site Icon

SharePoint team sites contain a site icon in the upper-left corner. The default image in a team site is a blue rectangle with the SharePoint 2016 logo. SharePoint has a setting that allows you to change this image.

TIP

In the past, you had to worry about the exact size of your logo. SharePoint 2016 dramatically simplifies the process by letting you choose a logo image from your computer or from a Library app somewhere on your SharePoint site. SharePoint then automatically resizes the image to the optimal size for the logo.

To change the site icon:

1. **Navigate to the Site Settings page by clicking the Settings gear icon and choosing Site Settings.**

The Site Settings page appears. You see all the options available in the Look and Feel section.

2. **Click the Title, Description, and Logo link in the Look and Feel section.**

The Title, Description, and Logo page appears, as shown in Figure 13-2.

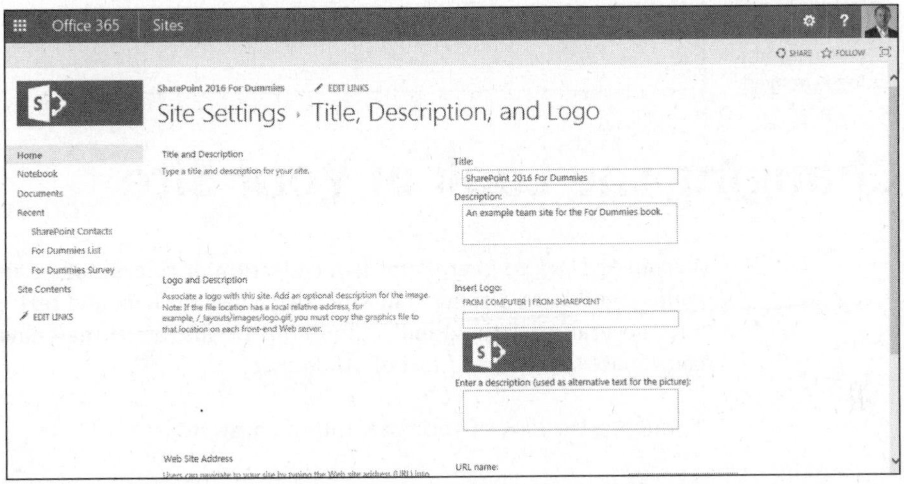

FIGURE 13-2:
The Title, Description, and Logo page. Note the Web Site Address field is only available in SharePoint Online.

3. **Click the From Computer link and browse your computer for the image you want to use as a logo.**

When you browse and select an image, SharePoint automatically uploads it to your SharePoint site for you. After the image is uploaded, you see the URL for the image and also a preview of the image.

4. **Type a short description of the image in the Enter a Description (Used as Alternative Text for the Picture) text box.**

Alternative text is important for accessibility software such as screen readers.

5. **Click OK to commit your changes.**

You see your new logo in the header area, as shown in Figure 13-3.

TIP If you want to return to the default SharePoint logo, you can simply clear the logo URL and click OK. SharePoint automatically updates the site with the default SharePoint logo.

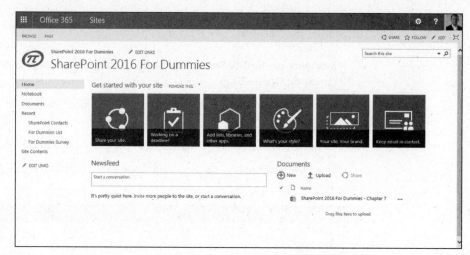

FIGURE 13-3:
A team site
with the site
logo changed.

Changing the Look of Your Site

A *composed look* in SharePoint is a collection of colors, fonts, and layouts that all come together to display your site with a certain look and feel. SharePoint comes with several predefined looks, and your organization may have added others to coordinate the look and feel of other sites.

To change the look of your site, follow these steps:

1. **Click the Settings gear icon and choose Site Settings; in the Look and Feel section of the Site Settings page, click the Change the Look link.**

   The Change the Look page appears, as shown in Figure 13-4, with a preview of many different site looks. Some examples include Sea Monster, Lime, Nature, City, Orbit, Immerse, and Wood. Each preview pane shows you a sample of the site look.

2. **To try out a look, simply click the preview image.**

   The preview image is enlarged and settings are displayed so you can change the background image, the color palette, the site layout, and the font combinations used in the site, as shown in Figure 13-5.

3. **Click the Try It Out link in the top-right corner of the page to see what your actual site will look like.**

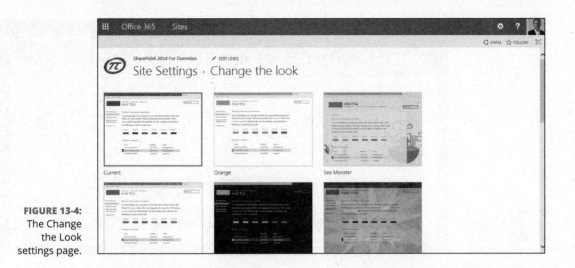

FIGURE 13-4:
The Change
the Look
settings page.

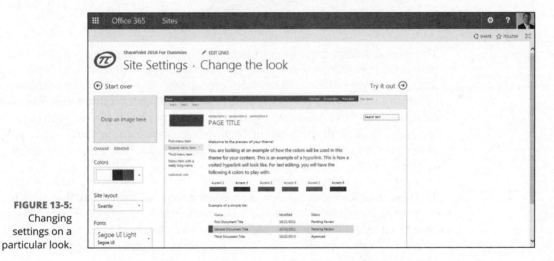

FIGURE 13-5:
Changing
settings on a
particular look.

SharePoint does some work and shows your site with the new look in place. The top of the page lets you decide whether to keep the site (by clicking Yes, Keep It) or to revert to the original settings and make more changes (by clicking No, Not Quite There), as shown in Figure 13-6.

4. **When you're satisfied with the new look of your site, click Yes, Keep It.**

Your site loads with the new look and feel.

TIP

If you want to go back to the original look of a SharePoint 2016 site, you can always change back to the Office look.

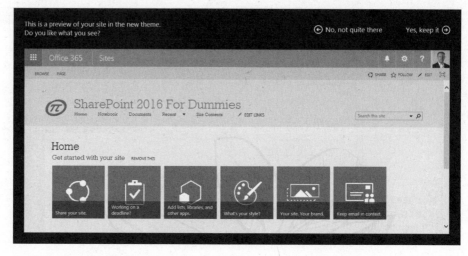

This is a preview of your site in the new theme. Do you like what you see?

⊖ No, not quite there   Yes, keep it ⊕

FIGURE 13-6:
Previewing a particular look for your site.

A note on fonts

The most common fonts used in web design used to be of two families — ones with *serifs* (the strokes that extend from letters), such as Times New Roman, and *sans-serif* (those without strokes from the letters), such as Arial and Verdana. You couldn't guarantee what fonts users had on their computers, so those fonts were a safe default. They're also recognized as fonts with good readability. (For those reading this book that can't wait to pick Gigi, Jokerman, or Curlz MT, and you know who you are, you may want to hold up and read the "A word on usability" section, later in this chapter.)

The best practice when we first learned to design web sites was that serif fonts were good for paragraph text and sans-serif fonts were good for very large and very small text (like headings and footer notes). The trend today for many sites is to use only sans-serif fonts, or in the case of SharePoint, the Segoe UI Light and Segoe UI fonts.

Many companies have a large amount of font styles available on employee computers, especially as the options in Microsoft Office have grown. However, if your users don't have the font you selected, the browser will convert to a default font.

When you're customizing a look (as we describe earlier in this chapter in the "Changing the Look of Your Site" section), you can choose different font combinations. The font combinations have been matched for each packaged site look.

A new trend in Microsoft technology is the use of Segoe UI fonts. The Segoe font family is used across all Microsoft products such as Windows Phone, Windows 10, the new Surface tablet and Surface book, and of course Office.

The default look of a SharePoint site uses the Segoe font family.

A word on usability

We suppose the reason you have a SharePoint site is that you and your team are *using* it, and a big part of using a site is being able to read it. The following common checkpoints for websites might apply to your site look choices or perhaps your content on the team site pages as well:

>> **Make sure there is a strong contrast between the background colors and the text.** Dark text on a white background is generally considered the easiest to read. The second best is very light text on a very dark background.

One area of SharePoint that this has been a problem with in the past is the Quick Launch menu or left navigation area, where the contrast between the background and links isn't distinct enough. Be careful with your selections. Even if red and green are holiday colors, red text on a green background isn't very readable.

>> **Choose a font that's simple and easy to read.** No matter that the Chiller font looks cool at Halloween, a whole page of Chiller will have your users running for the door, or at the very least not reading your site.

>> **Use only a few colors.** Even though it seems like the theme palette has a lot of color options, many of them are similar in hue. Using the entire rainbow makes it hard for your users to focus on what's important.

>> **Make link colors obvious.** If the text is black and links are navy blue or brown, it becomes difficult to identify them.

>> **Make the *followed* (or visited) link color different enough from the unvisited link color.** A red hyperlink that changes to maroon when visited may not be enough of a visual cue to users that they've followed that link.

Microsoft took the liberty of helping you choose decent combinations when it created the out-of-the-box looks. Some of the looks are downright scary, though. Don't believe me? Try changing your site to the Sea Monster look and see how your users run away, or maybe run to you, screaming.

The benefits of composed looks

Composed looks are a big step up from previous versions of SharePoint. Composed looks allow you to change the background image, colors, site layout, and fonts. Best of all, composed looks can dramatically change the look and feel of your site with just a few clicks of the mouse. You don't need to worry about breaking SharePoint by fiddling with a master page.

Whenever a discussion of branding occurs, you should take note to pose a major question. Can you achieve what you need with an out-of-the-box composed look, or do you need to create a completely custom look? If you need a completely custom composed look, then be prepared to bring in web designers and developers. Depending on your needs, a custom look can be a considerable investment and involves creating custom master pages, CSS files, and themes.

The Composed Looks link is found on the Site Settings page in the Web Designer Galleries section.

Changing Team Site Navigation

Chapter 11 covers navigation when using a site with the SharePoint Server Publishing Infrastructure feature enabled. If you don't have this feature enabled, then navigation is much more straightforward. You can add links to the top of the page (called the Top Link bar) or to the left side of the page (called the Quick Launch).

The Top Link bar can be used to link all your subsites together. So in other words, every subsite would have the same top link navigation. A common scenario is to put links to each site across the Top Link bar. This allows users to navigate among subsites with minimal frustration. The Quick Launch is unique to each site. The Quick Launch contains links for apps and pages that live in the current site.

Figure 13-7 shows these navigational elements for a SharePoint team site.

A polished team site may look good, but if people can't find anything, then it isn't very helpful. Lucky for you, most of these navigation settings are easy to change in a team site.

The SharePoint Server Publishing Infrastructure feature is activated for a site collection. If you're a site administrator, then it may be out of your hands whether this feature is activated or not. You will know right away if the feature is activated by looking at the links in the Look and Feel section on the Site Settings page. If you see the Navigation link, then the Feature is activated. If instead you see the Quick Launch and Top Link bar links, then the feature is not active.

All SharePoint Online sites have a common set of navigational elements that appear at the top of the site's page. This includes the 'waffle'-like Start button on the left, an Office 365 link, and a Sites link. The Start button is called a waffle button because it looks like a grilled waffle. When you click it, you see all of the Office 365 apps you can use, such as Mail, Calendar, and OneDrive, to name a few. (If you are using SharePoint On-Premises, then you won't see the waffle button.)

The Office 365 apps in the waffle menu deserve a book all to themselves — in fact, Rosemarie is writing one called *Office 365 Apps For Dummies* at the same time we are writing this SharePoint book!

Top Link bar

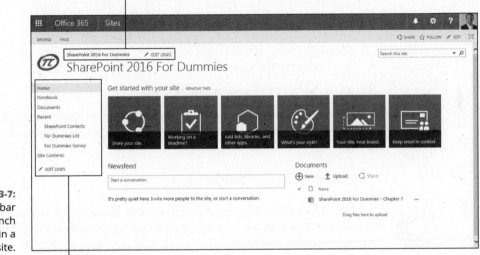

FIGURE 13-7:
The Top Link bar
and Quick Launch
navigation in a
team site.

Quick Launch menu

Going global with the Top Link bar

Each team site has its own *Top Link bar* — a common navigational element used to provide access to resources across all subsites. The Top Link bar is a series of tab links that run across the top of the page. The links that appear in the Top Link bar often display the titles of all the subsites. A common source of confusion though is that you can edit these links to point to anything you want. For example, you might include two links to the two subsites, a link to BBC News, and a link to the Documents app in the main site. This might seem like it makes sense, but it will really confuse users. We know it really confused us when we first started with SharePoint!

REMEMBER

Rather than randomly adding links across the Top Link bar, maintain usability by only linking to subsites. If you need external links, add them to a Web Part and put them in the middle of the page with a clear heading. That way, users know they are going to an external location if they click the link.

The following steps apply only to team sites. (See Chapter 12 for details on configuring navigation for publishing sites.)

You manage the Top Link bar with the Top Link bar settings page. To access the page, follow these steps:

1. **Browse to the site where you want to modify navigation, and then click the Settings gear icon and choose Site Settings.**

The Site Settings page appears.

2. **In the Look and Feel section, click the Top Link bar link.**

The Top Link bar settings page appears. You must be an administrator of the site to edit the Top Link bar.

3. **Click the New Navigation Link button.**

4. **Enter the web address and name for the link you want to appear on the Top Link bar in the Web Address and Description text boxes, respectively.**

5. **Click OK.**

The link appears on the Top Link bar.

TIP

The Top Link bar is also often referred to as the global navigation bar. This is because the Top Link bar is often used to navigate between different sites and is therefore globally available across all sites in the site collection. Keep in mind that you can modify the Top Link bar to include any links you want.

To remove or modify an existing tab in the Top Link bar:

1. **Browse to the site where you want to modify navigation, and then click the Settings gear icon and choose Site Settings.**

The Site Settings page appears.

2. **In the Look and Feel section, click the Top Link bar link.**

The Top Link bar settings page appears.

3. **Click the Edit button next to the item you want to modify.**

The Edit button looks like a piece of paper with a pencil across the bottom-right corner.

4. **Edit the entry or click the Delete button to remove the tab altogether.**

TIP

As a shortcut to managing the Top Link bar, you can click the Edit Links button next to the Top Link bar, as shown in Figure 13-8. You must be on the top-level site collection in order to see the Edit Links button. If you're on the top level site collection and you still don't see the Edit Links button next to the Top Link bar links, then you're not an administrator of the site.

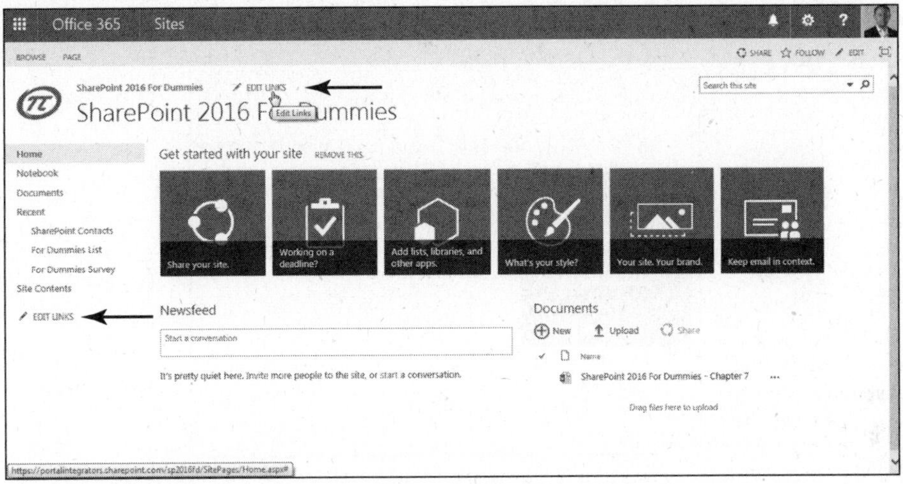

FIGURE 13-8:
Edit the Top Link
bar with the Edit
Links button.

Staying local with Quick Launch

SharePoint team sites display a list of navigation links on the Quick Launch navigation along the left side of the page. The Quick Launch, also known as the Current Navigation, displays links to featured site content such as apps and pages. By default, the team site Quick Launch includes three very important links:

>> **Home:** A link back to the main start page for the team site.

>> **Documents:** A direct link to the Documents app.

>> **Site Contents:** A link to the Site Contents page. The Site Contents page shows all the apps in the site.

TIP

The Quick Launch navigation takes up valuable space. Depending on the device you're using, you might want to hide the Quick Launch while working with an app. You can hide the Quick Launch and take over the entire screen by clicking the Full Page Expansion button in the upper-right corner of the screen, as shown in Figure 13-9.

You can manage Quick Launch in the same way you manage the Top Link bar; however, the Quick Launch doesn't have the capability to inherit from the parent site. Instead, the items that appear in the Quick Launch are determined by the apps you add to the site and the links you manually add to the Quick Launch. Each app contained in a site can display a link to itself on the Quick Launch.

Full Page Expansion button

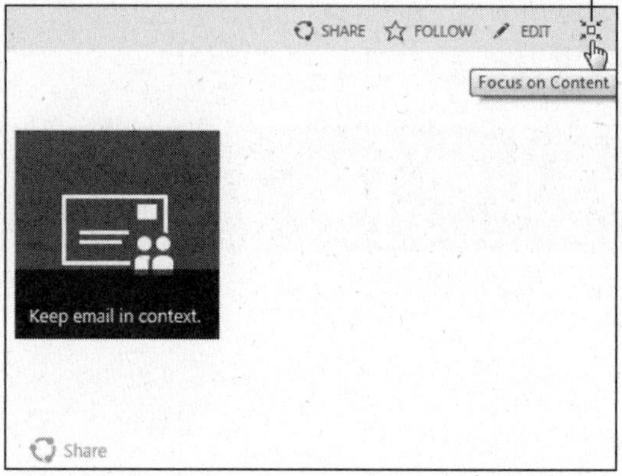

FIGURE 13-9:
Expand an App to
take over the
entire page.

You can easily add or remove an app from the Quick Launch using the app's settings:

1. **Browse to the app you want to add or remove from the Quick Launch.**

   For example, click the Documents app on the Site Contents page.

2. **Click the Library tab in the Ribbon and then click Library Settings.**

   The Library Settings page appears.

3. **In the General Settings section, click the List Name, Description, and Navigation link.**

   The General Settings page appears.

4. **In the Navigation section, indicate whether to include the list or library on the Quick Launch by selecting Yes or No.**

5. **Click the Save button.**

   The links in the Quick Launch update to reflect your changes.

You also can disable the Quick Launch entirely for a site. You can add a site hier-archy called a *Tree View* to the left navigation panel instead of the Quick Launch. If you leave the Quick Launch enabled, the Tree View appears below the Quick Launch. To perform either of these tasks, follow these steps:

1. **Click the Settings gear icon and choose Site Settings for the site you want to manage.**

2. **In the Look and Feel section, click the Tree View link. (If you are using SharePoint Online, then the link is called Navigation Elements instead of Tree View.)**

The Tree View / Navigation Elements page appears. Figure 13-10 shows the Tree View / Navigation Elements page.

3. **Choose whether to enable the Quick Launch or the Tree View or both by selecting the Enable Quick Launch and/or Enable Tree View check boxes.**

4. **Click OK.**

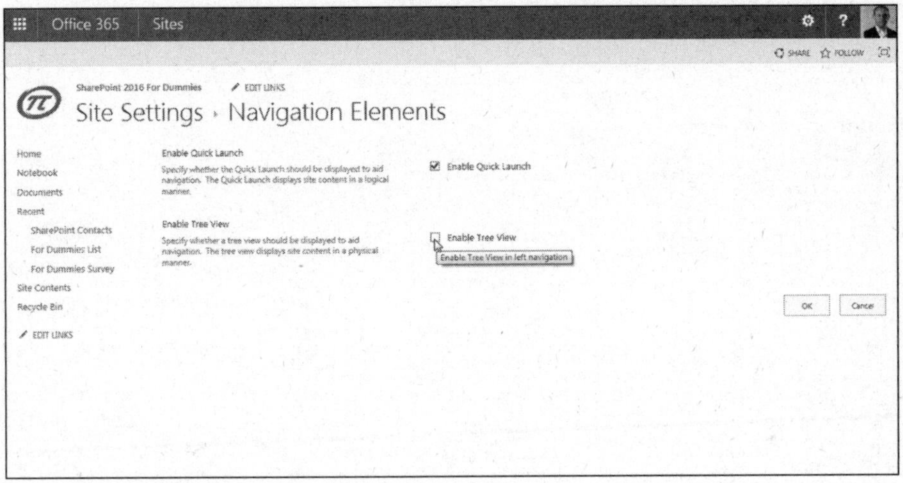

FIGURE 13-10:
The Tree View/
Navigation
Elements page is
used to enable or
disable the Quick
Launch and the
Tree View.

Chapter 14

Securing Your SharePoint Site

SharePoint is a great tool for storing documents and managing calendars and contacts. But how do you know that your information is secure? Although your IT department makes sure that your network and servers are secure, managing the security for your SharePoint content falls on you as the site administrator.

When securing your site, you need to perform three basic tasks. We list them here in the order of the frequency you perform these tasks, from most often to seldom:

>> **Managing SharePoint group membership:** When it comes to that dreaded time to manage SharePoint security, what you really need to be thinking is, "To which SharePoint group do I need to add this person?" If you don't have an existing group and you find yourself descending into a morass of permission levels, inheritance, and other such incomprehensible stuff, back away from your browser. The reality is that assigning permissions — breaking inheritance and assigning groups — should be a rare event, if done right.

>> **Assigning permissions to sites, apps, or folders:** Deciding which groups get access to what is an important task, and one you only want to think about infrequently — most usually at the time (or ideally before) you create your site. In other words, granting Read Only, Edit, and Delete permissions to the content in your site should be a set-it-and-forget-it task if you make those assignments

to SharePoint groups. When these permission assignments are granted to your SharePoint groups, you only have to manage who is in each group.

>> **Managing administrative access:** Even less frequently do you need to grant or revoke administrative access to your site.

In this chapter, we explain these three tasks.

Using SharePoint Groups

SharePoint uses groups to manage the process of granting someone access to the content in a site. Each *SharePoint group* maps to a set of permissions that define the tasks that a user can perform. Most users fall into one of SharePoint's three default groups:

>> **Site Visitors:** Grants read-only access to the site and allows users to create alerts. Users who need read access to a site but don't need to contribute content are visitors.

>> **Site Members:** Confers the Contribute permission level for users, which allows them to add, edit, and modify items and browse sites. Most end users fall into this category for a site.

>> **Site Owners:** Grants full control. A site owner may or may not use the site on a regular basis, but the site owner can delegate administrative and design tasks to others. Also, a site owner may or may not be a technical person.

REMEMBER

Access to your site and its content is managed through *group membership*. Adding and removing users from SharePoint groups is the most efficient way of granting and revoking permissions.

A top-level site has a single set of Site Visitors, Site Members, and Site Owners. The actual names of the groups are determined by the name of the site. For example, if your site is named *Sales*, SharePoint calls your groups Sales Visitors, Sales Members, and Sales Owners.

These three groups are created and named when the top-level site is created. All the apps and subsites that are created below the top-level site use these groups and have the same set of people inside the groups. By default, all the content and subsites in your top-level site have the same permissions, dubbed *permissions inheritance*.

Adding users to a group

For people to access your site, you must share it with them by adding them to one of these default groups. For example, to add users to the *Site* Members group, follow these steps:

1. **Log in to the site as a Site Owner, and then click the Share button in the upper-right corner of the page.**

   The Share dialog box appears, as shown in Figure 14-1.

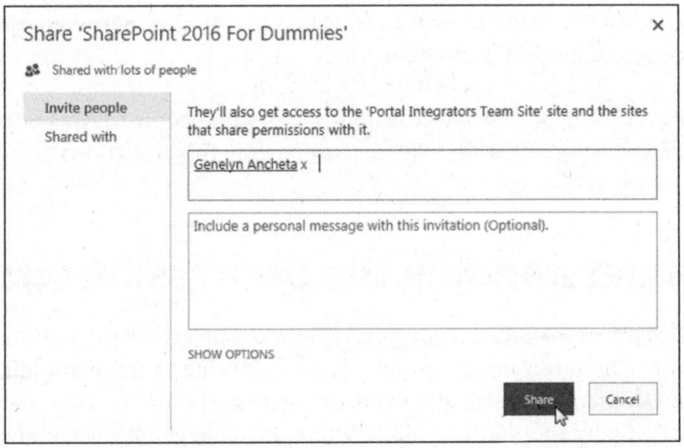

FIGURE 14-1: The Share dialog box is used to add users to the site.

TIP

Alternatively, you can add users to groups on the Site Settings page by clicking the People and Groups link in the Users and Permissions section.

2. **Enter the names of the users you wish to add to the site.**

   You can enter names or email addresses of users that SharePoint can add to the site.

   Type the names in the form of domain\account. For example, if your domain name is PORTALINTEGRATORS and the name is Rosemarie Withee, type **PORTALINTEGRATORS\rosemariewithee**. You can also just type **Rosemarie Withee**, and SharePoint will try to resolve the name to the account.

   If you don't know the names of user accounts, you can type the email addresses. SharePoint tries to map the email address for the account. For example, the email address rosemarie.withee@portalintegrators.com resolves to PORTALINTEGRATORS\rosemariewithee in our domain. Chances are that you can use the email addresses from your address book in Outlook.

3. **Include a personal message that will be included with the invitation.**

   This step is optional. If left blank, users will be emailed a generic welcome message.

   If you don't see a dialog to enter a personal message, then email has not been configured for the SharePoint environment.

4. **Decide if you want to send the users a welcome email message by selecting or deselecting the Send an E-mail Invitation check box.**

5. **Click Show Options to select the group where you want to add the users.**

   By default, the dialog box adds users to the *Site* Members group.

6. **Click the Share button to add the users to the SharePoint group and thus share the site with them.**

With Office 365, you have the ability to invite people to use your site who are outside your organization. We discuss using this functionality to create a client extranet in Chapter 23.

Understanding the permission structure

Members in the Site Owners SharePoint Group create the permission structure for a site. The Site Owner should have a pretty good understanding of which users need to access the site and what that access should be. This means that members of IT usually shouldn't be Site Owners. Instead, you want members of the business departments to take responsibility for site ownership.

Permissions are contained within a site collection. Therefore, all the people, groups, and permission levels defined for a site collection are available to every site and app within the collection. Permissions inheritance is in place by default, so all the content and subsites in SharePoint inherit permissions from their parents.

Web sites, apps, folders, and list items are all securable with permissions in SharePoint.

When a subsite is created, all the content structures within the site inherit permissions from the site collection. For example, when you create a new site using the Team Site template (see Chapter 4), all the apps in the site inherit permissions from the site collection. The default permissions configuration for a site collection is as follows:

» The Site Owners, Site Visitors, and Site Members groups are created.

» The primary and secondary site collection administrators are added to the Site Owners group. These administrators are specified when the site collection is created.

The site collection administrator takes responsibility for planning the permissions. If desired, the site collection administrator can delegate the responsibility of implementing the permissions to the Hierarchy Managers group in publishing sites. In team sites, the owner has to create a new permission level that confers the Manage Permissions permission to those individuals and groups assigned to it.

SharePoint also provides the following set of specialized administrative groups for sites based on publishing templates that enable the site's owner to delegate responsibility:

>> **Approvers:** Enables Approve permissions, which allow users to approve items and override document check-outs.

>> **Designers:** Grants permission to change the look and feel of sites with style sheets and themes.

>> **Translation Managers:** Grants permission to change the translated text of a page. This role works in conjunction with the translation features, which are part of the Publishing Infrastructure Feature.

>> **Hierarchy Managers:** Enables Manage Hierarchy permissions, which makes it possible to manipulate the site's hierarchy and customize lists and libraries.

In addition to providing several kinds of administrative roles, SharePoint 2016 provides the following groups for restricting access:

>> **Everyone:** Enables access for every SharePoint user.

>> **Excel Services Viewers:** Enables users to view Excel documents in a page. This is required so that the page they are viewing can read the Library app where the Excel document is located.

>> **Quick Deploy Users:** Moves content from one server to another, such as from a staging server to a production server. Available only when Publishing Infrastructure Feature is active.

>> **Restricted Readers:** Enables users to view only items and pages but doesn't show any item history.

>> **Style Resource Readers:** Enables users to read from the master page gallery and style library. Available only when Publishing Infrastructure Feature is active.

There are a number of other specialized groups to choose from in addition to the primary groups mentioned here. You can view all of the groups in your site by clicking on the People and Groups link in Site Settings. You will see a list of groups in the left hand navigation. Clicking the More link at the bottom loads all of the groups into the main page so you can read about the group. Figure 14-2 shows common SharePoint groups, their permission levels, and their permissions.

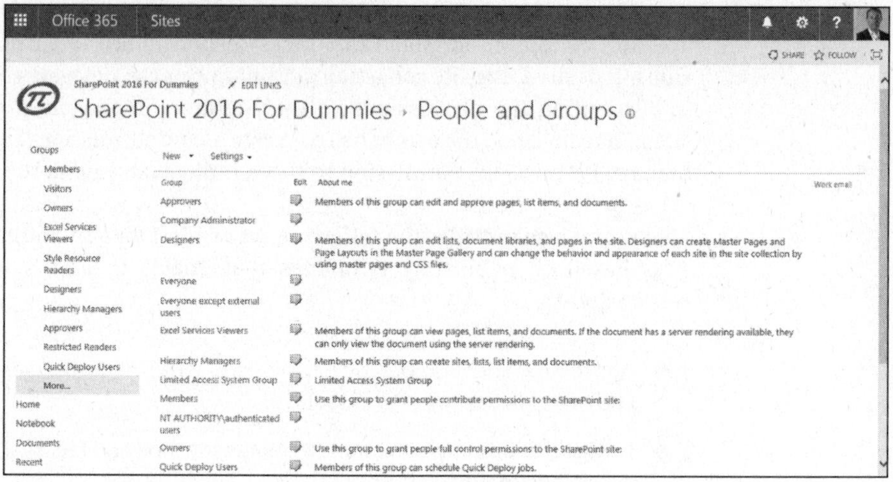

FIGURE 14-2:
The People and
Groups page for
a site based on
the Team Site
template.

Securing a site collection

After you know how to add new users and domain groups to a SharePoint group, finish setting up security for a site collection by doing the following:

1. Add user accounts or domain groups to the *Site* Visitors group.

The *Site* Visitors group has Read permissions, which enables this group to view the site collection's content.

We suggest you add the Authenticated Users domain group to the *Site* Visitors group. This enables all your network users to access your site collection (assuming you want to allow them, of course).

2. Add user accounts or domain groups to the *Site* Members group.

Members of the *Site* Members group have Contribute permissions, which allow them to add content to the site collection.

3. Add users to the Hierarchy Manager and Designers groups in publishing sites.

You may want to create a separate permission level for consultants. SharePoint team sites don't have these groups by default, but you can create similar groups if you need that kind of role.

4. Configure unique permissions for content structures in and below the top-level site.

You have to stop inheriting permissions from the top-level site before you can create unique permissions for subsites and apps. See the section, "Creating unique permissions for a subsite," later in this chapter, for details.

5. Add subsites to the main site collection site.

You can inherit permissions or use unique permissions when you create the site.

REMEMBER

Remember that everything *in* the site collection inherits *from* the site collection by default. Make sure your site collection permissions don't grant too many people access.

Securing Apps, Folders, Documents, and Items

In theory, you could set up security once for a site collection and allow everything to inherit. In reality, you may not want everyone to have the same access. In order to create unique permissions for a site, app, folder, or item, you have to stop inheriting permissions from the parent.

Creating unique permissions for a subsite

TIP

You must be in a subsite to create unique permissions; the following steps don't make sense otherwise.

To stop inheriting permissions in a subsite from a parent site, follow these steps:

1. **Browse to the Site Permissions page for a site by clicking the Settings gear icon and choosing Site Settings and then clicking the Site Permissions link in the Users and Permissions section.**

    The Site Permissions page is displayed with a message reading This website inherits permissions from its parent (<parent site name>). If you wish to change permissions for the entire site collection, click the <parent site name> link.

2. **Click the Stop Inheriting Permissions button in the Permissions tab on the Ribbon.**

    A message window appears reading, in part, You are about to create unique permissions for this website.

3. **Click OK.**

    The Set Up Groups for this page is displayed. Choose the groups you want to use in the site. By default, the page uses the groups from the site collection.

4. **If you need your own groups for this site, then you should select the Create New Group radio button.**

5. **Set groups for Site Visitors, Site Members, and Site Owners by selecting an existing group from the drop-down list.**

6. **Click OK to create the new unique groups for the site.**

   The main home page for the site reloads, and your site now has unique permissions. Repeat Step 1 to return to the Site Permissions page. You see that there is now a `This website has unique permissions` message. Any permissions changes you make on this site are now unique to this site. No other sites in the site collection will be affected.

WARNING Be careful about adding users to SharePoint groups at the site or app level. You're actually adding users to the entire site collection group. Individual subsites and apps don't have their own SharePoint groups. This behavior causes a great deal of confusion. To drive the point home, do the following. When you stop inheriting site permissions and are on the page, to set up groups (Step 4 in the preceding list) choose to create new groups for the site. After you have finished, go to the Site Permissions page for the site collection. You see the groups you created in the site are in the site collection. This is because all groups in SharePoint are located at the site collection level, even if they are only used by a subsite that is set to use unique permissions.

To reinherit permissions from the parent site, choose Inherit Permissions in Step 2. Any changes you've made are discarded, and the site inherits the parent's permissions.

TIP After you stop inheriting permissions, the parent's permissions are copied to the site.

WARNING Be extremely careful when deleting groups and permissions! If you are in a site that is inheriting permissions and you delete a group, you are actually taken to the site collection to delete the group. We have seen highly trained IT administrators make this mistake and wipe out the entire permission structure for the entire site collection. Before you delete a group, make certain that your site isn't inheriting permissions and you're not deleting all the permissions at the site collection level by deleting the group at the site level.

Removing existing permissions

Follow these steps to remove existing permission assignments:

1. **Browse to the Site Permissions page for a site by clicking the Settings gear icon and choosing Site Settings and then clicking the Site Permissions link in the Users and Permissions section.**

2. **Place check marks next to the permission assignments you want to remove.**

   Remember to leave yourself with permissions; otherwise, you won't be able to access the site.

3. **Click the Remove User Permissions button, and then click OK to confirm the deletions.**

   All the permissions are deleted for the selected permissions assignments.

Creating unique permissions for an app or document

Allowing a site's content structures to inherit permissions from the site is usually sufficient. Don't try to secure everything individually. But at times, you need to secure a folder in an app or limit access to an app. You may want to delegate ownership of an app, thus pushing administrative responsibilities for the app to an app administrator.

TIP

To manage permissions, the user must have the Manage Permissions permission. You must be a member of the Hierarchy Managers group to edit permissions.

To create unique permissions for an app, follow these steps:

1. **Browse to the app, click the Library or List tab of the Ribbon, and click the Library or List Settings button in the Settings group.**

2. **Click the Permissions for This Document Library link in the Permissions and Management section.**

   The Permissions page appears.

3. **Manage the permissions as you would for a subsite by breaking inheritance and managing the permissions uniquely for the list.**

   Managing permissions on apps is the same as managing permissions for subsites — see the earlier section, "Creating unique permissions for a subsite."

You can also give unique permissions for an individual document, folder, or list item. You do this by sharing the particular item with a person and selecting their level of permissions in the Share dialog box. Accessing the Share dialog box depends on the item you are sharing. For example, you can share a site by clicking the Share button in the upper right corner of the screen. Alternatively, you can share a document by using the Share button located in the ellipsis next to that document as outlined in the next procedure.

TIP

With SharePoint Online, you can even share a document without requiring the other person to log into your SharePoint site.

Follow these steps to give permissions for a document, item, or folder in an app library:

1. **Browse to the app where the item, document, or folder is located.**

2. **Click the ellipsis next to the item and click Share, as shown in Figure 14-3.**

   The Share dialog box appears.

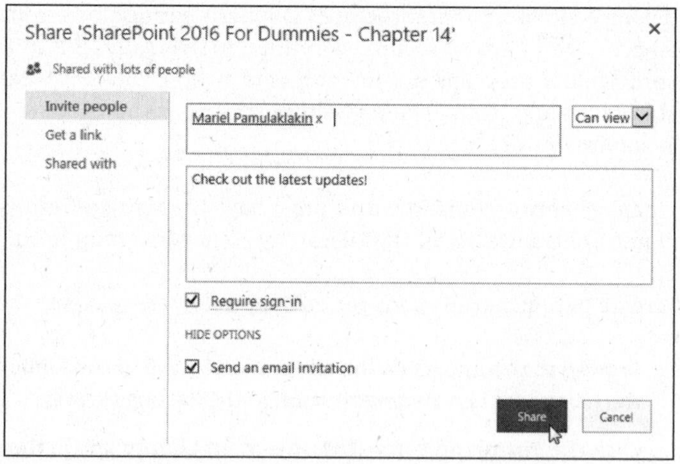

Share 'SharePoint 2016 For Dummies - Chapter 14'   ×

Shared with lots of people

Invite people	Mariel Pamulaklakin x	Can view ▾
Get a link		
Shared with	Check out the latest updates!	

☑ Require sign-in

HIDE OPTIONS

☑ Send an email invitation

Share   Cancel

FIGURE 14-3:
Click Share for a document in a Library app.

3. **Enter the name, email address, or group, and then select the permission you wish to give — Can Edit or Can View.**

4. **Click the Share button to give permissions.**

TIP

For an item in a list app, the process is a bit different. For individual list items, you manage permissions separately in much the same way you would for a subsite. To access the permissions for the individual list item you want to manage, click the ellipsis next to the item and choose Manage Permissions from the Advanced drop-down. However, you cannot share out list items individually like you can actual documents because the list item is part of SharePoint, whereas the document is a file unto itself.

Managing permissions scenarios

Managing permissions is tricky, and the steps we outline in this section are our recommendations. These aren't the only ways to manage permissions. Try a scenario to help you better understand permissions. Assume you have a site with the SharePoint groups we outline here.

SharePoint groups	Members
Site Members	John, Bill, and Steve
Site Visitors	Mary, Sue, and Sally

Everything in the site inherits from the top-level site. In this scenario, those in the Site Members group have Contribute permissions, whereas those in the Site Visitors group have Read permissions.

Assume you create a new subsite, and you only want your Site Members to access it. You don't want Site Visitors to even know the subsite exists. In this case, you create unique permissions on the subsite and remove the Site Visitors group.

Assume you have an app for policy documents, and you want John and Sally to have Contribute permissions. We recommend creating a new Policy Reviewers SharePoint group at your top-level site and then adding John and Sally as members to the group. You aren't done here, however. You haven't actually granted the group permission to anything yet. You have to browse to the app, break inheritance from its parent, and then grant the Policy Reviewers SharePoint group the Contribute permission level.

Why not just add John and Sally to the app and grant them the Contribute permission level? That approach will certainly work, but it's hard to manage. That approach obscures that John and Sally have some permissions granted outside the context of a SharePoint group. We like to be able to look at our SharePoint groups and have a good idea of what the role of that group is, based on their names on the site. If you start adding users individually to subsites, apps, documents, folders, and items, it becomes difficult to get a big-picture view of how your permissions for the site are configured.

Viewing a group's permissions

You can easily check the permissions for a given group to see everything that group has been granted access to in your site. You must repeat these steps at each site in your site collection. To do so:

1. **Browse to the top-level site in your site collection.**

2. **Open the People and Groups page for the top-level site by clicking the Settings gear icon and choosing Site Settings, and then clicking the People and Groups link in the Users and Permissions section.**

   The list of SharePoint groups appears on the Quick Launch.

3. **The list of groups is truncated. Click the More button at the bottom of the listing of groups in the Quick Launch.**

The list of all SharePoint groups in the site collection appears in the main part of the page.

4. **Click the name of the group for which you want to view permissions.**

5. **Choose Settings ➪ View Group Permissions.**

The View Site Collection Permissions window appears, as shown in Figure 14-4. All the sites, lists, and libraries that the group has permission to access appear in the list.

REMEMBER

Everyone who is a member of the group has the permissions shown on the View Site Collection Permissions window.

View Site Collection Permissions -- Webpage Dialog

SharePoint For Dummies
View Site Collection Permissions: Designers

Use this page to view the permission assignments that this SharePoint group has in this site collection. In addition to the listed URLs, this group has access to any sites, lists, or items that inherit permissions from these URLs.

URL	Permission Level
http://intranet.portalintegrators.com	Design, Limited Access
http://intranet.portalintegrators.com/_catalogs/masterpage	Design, Limited Access
http://intranet.portalintegrators.com/Cache Profiles	Read
http://intranet.portalintegrators.com/DeviceChannels	Design
http://intranet.portalintegrators.com/PublishedLinks	Design, Limited Access
http://intranet.portalintegrators.com/Relationships List	Limited Access
http://intranet.portalintegrators.com/Style Library	Design
http://intranet.portalintegrators.com/teamsite	Design, Limited Access
http://intranet.portalintegrators.com/Translation Status	Read

OK

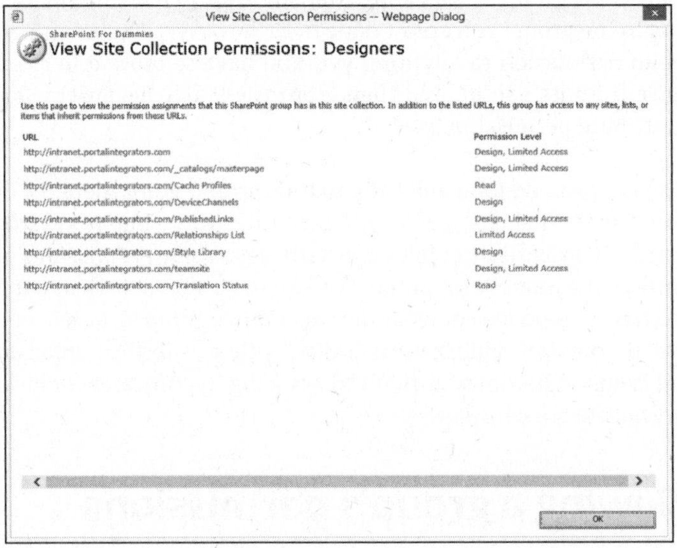

FIGURE 14-4:
The View Site Collection Permissions window.

Checking a user's permissions

Sometimes, you just want to know who has permission to do what in a given site. SharePoint 2016 provides just such a method:

1. **Browse to the site where you want to check a user's permissions.**

This command only checks permissions within a single site. You have to check each site manually.

2. **Browse to the Site Permissions page for a site by clicking the Settings gear icon and choosing Site Settings, and then clicking the Site Permissions link in the Users and Permissions section.**

3. **Click the Check Permissions button on the Ribbon.**

4. **Enter the name of the user or group whose permissions you want to check for the current site in the User/Group field, and then click the Check Now button.**

   The permissions appear in the bottom of the window, as shown in Figure 14-5.

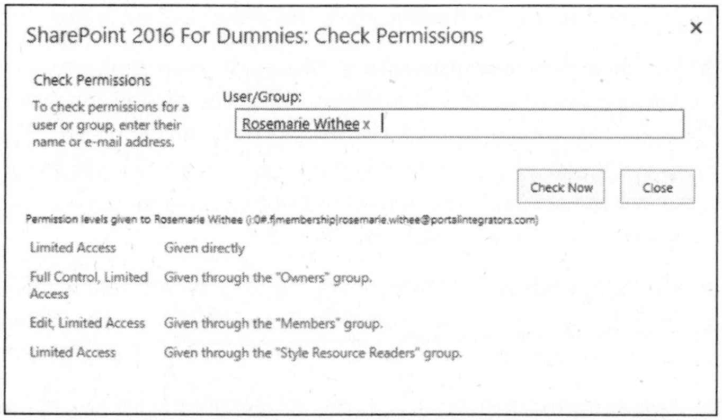

SharePoint 2016 For Dummies: Check Permissions

Check Permissions

To check permissions for a user or group, enter their name or e-mail address.

User/Group:

Rosemarie Withee x |

Check Now   Close

Permission levels given to Rosemarie Withee (i:0#.f|membership|rosemarie.withee@portalintegrators.com)

Limited Access	Given directly
Full Control, Limited Access	Given through the "Owners" group.
Edit, Limited Access	Given through the "Members" group.
Limited Access	Given through the "Style Resource Readers" group.

FIGURE 14-5:
View a user's permissions to the current site.

PUTTING IT ALL TOGETHER

We often encourage site owners to create their own SharePoint groups instead of using the built-in Visitors and Members. There's something about naming your own groups that makes managing them more intuitive (maybe because you don't refer to your coworkers as *members*).

By creating your own groups, you can very easily add a new employee to a particular group when someone asks, "Hey, can you add the new guy to the Accounting Clerks group in the team site?" Because you've already assigned proper permissions to the Accounting Clerks group throughout your site, the new guy is guaranteed to have all the access he needs. When the not-so-new guy gets promoted a year later, you can change his membership to the Accounting Supervisors group and get back to important stuff.

Granting Administrative Access

You'll find a number of different administrator levels in a SharePoint deployment. Administrators usually have full access over the area they've been charged with administering. The levels of administrators in SharePoint are

>> **Server administrators:** By virtue of having local administrator access to the physical server, a server administrator can do anything from the server console. Server administrators are usually members of the technical staff.

>> **Service administrators:** Administration of SharePoint's services, such as Search or User Profiles, can be delegated. This allows administrators to specialize.

>> **Site collection administrators:** These administrators can access everything within a site collection. SharePoint allows you to appoint a primary and secondary administrator for each site collection, who both receive email notifications when the site hits its storage quota or is slated for deletion due to lack of use. Site collection administrators also manage all the features that affect the entire site collection.

>> **Site administrators:** Members of the *Site* Owners SharePoint group are the site administrators. If subsites inherit permissions, a site administrator has full access to each site.

>> **App administrators:** Permissions can be unique for an app, which allows for the delegation administration. Depending on the size of your department or team, you might have different people administer different apps.

>> **Document/item administrators:** For extremely sensitive documents and items, you can use unique permissions that in effect enable someone to administer just that document or item.

In Office 365, the server administrator role is replaced by the SharePoint Online administrator. Microsoft Online manages the entire infrastructure for you, so you just have to manage SharePoint Online.

The primary and secondary site collection administrators are determined at the time the site collection is created. Additional site collection administrators can be added to the site collection itself.

To set the site collection administrators for a site:

1. **Browse to the top-level site in your site collection.**

2. **Open the Site Collection Administrators page by clicking the Settings gear icon and choosing Site Settings, and then clicking the Site Collection Administrators link in the Users and Permissions section.**

The Site Collection Administrators page appears.

3. **Add or remove users from the Site Collection Administrators box by typing in their names or deleting their names using the backspace key, and then click OK.**

    Users are separated by semicolons.

REMEMBER

Assigning users to be site collection administrators is one time when it's acceptable to use individual user accounts instead of domain groups.

Viewing Site Permissions

A site can have all the elements of an *authorization model* — people, groups, and permissions, in other words — but still not be secure. The deciding factor in securing SharePoint's content lies with the permission assignments made on securable objects such as sites, apps, folders, documents, and items. A permission assignment consists of permissions, *principals* (users and groups), and securable objects.

Permissions are the smallest unit for managing security in SharePoint. Permissions confer rights a user may have, such as View Pages rights or Add Items rights. In SharePoint, you deal with following three permission types:

>> **App (List or Library):** Permissions related to accessing apps, folders, documents, and items.

>> **Site:** Permissions related to accessing sites, pages, and permissions.

>> **Personal:** Permissions related to creating personal views of web pages.

When managed properly, you never have to work with permissions on a case-by-case basis because permissions are never assigned directly to principals. Rather, they're assigned to *permission levels*, which are assigned to default SharePoint groups. You can also assign permission levels directly to user accounts or custom SharePoint groups you create.

Follow these steps to view a list of permission levels for a site:

1. **Browse to the Site Permissions page for a site by clicking the Settings gear icon and choosing Site Settings, and then clicking the Site Permissions link in the Users and Permissions section.**

    A list of groups and their corresponding permission levels appears, as shown in Figure 14-6. Note that this shows up only when the Permission Levels button on the Ribbon is clicked (step 2 below).

REMEMBER

If you've assigned permission levels to user accounts or domain group accounts outside SharePoint groups, you see them listed here.

Each site inherits its site permission assignments from its parent site or has its own unique permission assignments.

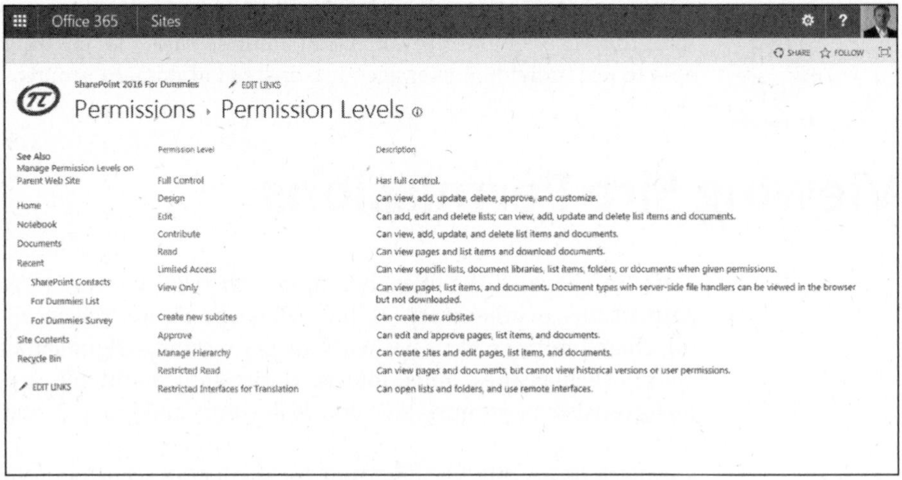

FIGURE 14-6:
View the site's permission assignments.

2. **Click the Permission Levels button on the Ribbon.**

   The Permission Levels page appears. You can use this page to create new permission levels or modify existing ones. You will only see the Permission Levels button in the Ribbon if you have broken inheritance. Otherwise, the site inherits permissions from the parent, and to see the Permission Levels button you need to go to the parent where those permissions originate.

3. **Click a permission level, such as Contribute, to view or modify the permissions in the permission level, as shown in Figure 14-7.**

   Note: The permissions you see might not be the entire set of permissions available in SharePoint. The server administrator can limit the list of permissions available to a web application using Web Policies.

TIP

Keep in mind that the Permissions Levels page doesn't really show individual permissions. Instead, the page shows permission levels.

Table 14-1 lists the permission levels, the rights they grant, and the SharePoint group they're assigned to by default. Note that the last four permission levels are specific to sites with the Publishing Infrastructure Feature active.

TABLE 14-1   **Permission Levels**

Permission Level	Rights Granted	SharePoint Group Assigned to by Default
Full Control	Wield administrative access	Site Owners
Design	Change the site's look and feel	Designers
Edit	Add, edit, and delete apps as well as the items and documents contained within the apps	Site Members
Contribute	Add and modify content	Site Members
Read	View all content, including history	Site Visitors
Limited Access	Open (same as guest access)	Quick Deploy Users
View Only	View items and pages	Viewers
Approve	Approve content	Approvers
Manage Hierarchy	Manage the site's structure and permissions (this is only available in the site collection when the SharePoint Server Publishing Infrastructure feature is active)	Hierarchy Managers
Restricted Read	View and open	Restricted Readers
Restricted Interfaces for Translation	Open apps and use remote interfaces	Restricted Interfaces for Translation

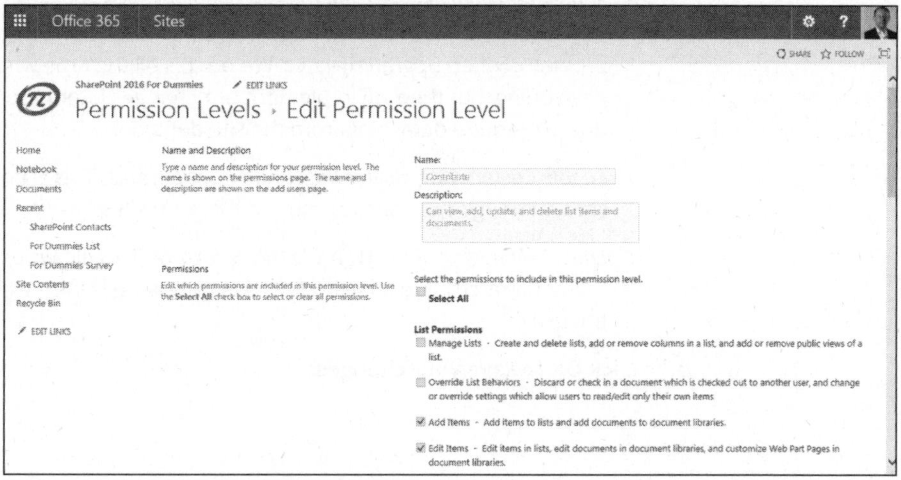

FIGURE 14-7:
View permission levels.

Managing SharePoint Designer Access

SharePoint 2016 allows you to configure which users can use SharePoint Designer to access your site. Before you jump to the conclusion that you don't want anyone doing that, bear in mind that the role of SharePoint Designer has changed. SharePoint Designer is the primary tool used for developing workflow. Workflow has a number of powerful abilities that maximize processes.

TIP

SharePoint Designer 2013 is used to develop workflows for SharePoint 2016. Microsoft decided not to rebrand the SharePoint Designer tool. Speculation is that at some point they will move away from a separate tool, like SharePoint Designer, to a web-based app contained within SharePoint that workflow developers can use. There are also a number of really amazing workflow creation tools on the market such as those made by Nintex (www.nintex.com) and K2 (www.k2.com).

To grant a user the right to use SharePoint Designer with your site:

1. Browse to the top-level site of your team site, click the Settings gear icon, and choose Site Settings, and then click the SharePoint Designer Settings link in the Site Collection Administration section.

2. Select the options that you want to enable:

   - *Enable SharePoint Designer:* Users who are *Site* Owners or who have Design permissions can use SharePoint Designer to access your site.

   - *Enable Detaching Pages from the Site Definition:* We advise against allowing this unless you have a good reason to do so. Detaching pages can cause problems when upgrading later. We do this all the time when we're developing, but then we implement our changes later in such a way that doesn't require detaching from the site definition.

   - *Enable Customizing Master Pages and Page Layouts:* This is fine for publishing sites, although not usually required for team sites.

   - *Enable Managing of the Web Site URL Structure:* This allows users to see the folder hierarchy. We usually allow this unless we think it will overwhelm the user.

3. Click OK to save your changes.

4

Getting Social and Going Mobile

Chapter 15

Taking Control of Your Personal Profile and Content

Throughout this book, you can read about SharePoint sites and how they can be used with teams and organizations. SharePoint also provides individualized benefits designed specifically for you. In particular, you can customize your own individual space and take control of your SharePoint experience.

In this chapter, you explore how your personal SharePoint space works. You find out about some pretty cool apps and explore how to work with these apps using only your web browser. You discover how to aggregate news and create a blog with Newsfeed, sync and organize documents with OneDrive for Business, and add and follow specific sites. Finally, you explore and set up your personal profile.

Organizing Your Personal Content with OneDrive

Your personal cloud storage location, also known as OneDrive, is where you store and organize your documents. You access OneDrive by clicking on the waffle menu (officially called the app launcher) in the upper-left corner of your screen and then choosing OneDrive, as shown in Figure 15-1.

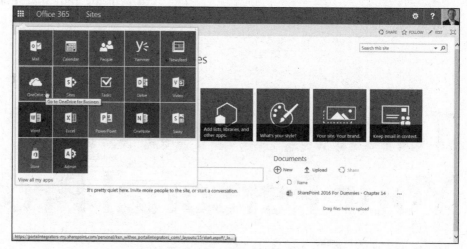

FIGURE 15-1:
Accessing your
OneDrive site.

When you land on your OneDrive site, the heading OneDrive appears at the top of your browser, and your personal site loads, as shown in Figure 15-2. Congratulations, you are now working in your own personal SharePoint storage location! This is your own personal domain, and everything here is private unless you choose to share it with others.

TIP

There are some slight differences between OneDrive in SharePoint Online and OneDrive in SharePoint On-Premises. One example is the action link (New, Upload, Sync, Share, More) which can be found below the status bar at the top in the Online version but below the Documents heading in the On-Premises version.

OneDrive includes a number of features right out of the gate that you access in the left-hand navigation tools. You have a Library app in which you can store documents, a view of any recent documents you have worked on, including in other SharePoint sites, a view of documents that are shared with you, and any documents or sites you are following. You also have a recycle bin for anything you deleted that you want to resurrect.

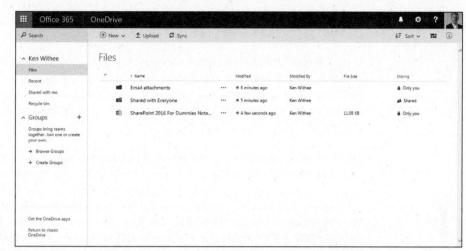

FIGURE 15-2:
The personal
SharePoint
storage location
called OneDrive.

MY SITE, ONEDRIVE, AND ONEDRIVE FOR BUSINESS

If you have heard of My Site, then you are already familiar with what we refer to as OneDrive, Newsfeed, and Sites. In past versions of SharePoint the personal site feature was called My Site, but recently Microsoft changed the name and divided the functionality into three different apps (OneDrive, Newsfeed, and Sites).

This can be a bit confusing because there are actually two different things known as OneDrive now. One is a consumer version for personal file storage called OneDrive and the other is a business version called OneDrive for Business.

OneDrive for Business, Newsfeed, and Sites are really just components of a personal SharePoint site in which you can, among other things, store digital content. On the waffle menu (also known as the app launcher) the app just says OneDrive even though it is actually OneDrive for Business (part of SharePoint). The Newsfeed and Sites apps are more straightforward since there isn't a consumer version of these with the same name.

Throughout this chapter we use the term *OneDrive* to refer to the OneDrive that is part of SharePoint, called OneDrive for Business. So if you are already familiar with SharePoint, think of the combined OneDrive, Newsfeed, and Sites apps as the old My Site. If you are not familiar with SharePoint, then just think of these apps as your personal SharePoint space. And if you are familiar with the consumer-based OneDrive, then distinguish it by thinking of it as an online storage location for your family pictures and other personal files. As for OneDrive for Business, remember it is part of SharePoint, and it is where you put your work stuff.

Saving stuff with OneDrive

Your personal storage location, known as OneDrive, is designed as a place to store, organize, and share your documents, such as, for example, a carpool list you're working on or a potluck spreadsheet. You might also be working on business documents that don't really fit into any specific app in SharePoint. Your OneDrive is the catch-all place you can store it.

Think of your OneDrive as your personal Documents folder on your computer. The difference is that the personal Documents folder on your computer is only on that single computer. If you're using a different computer, you can't access those documents. In addition, if your computer crashes and you have not backed up your Documents folder, then those files are lost. OneDrive is designed to be a secure and safe place to store all your documents. What if your device crashes or is stolen? With your documents stored in OneDrive, you just log in again from a different device and continue working on your documents.

WARNING

Your OneDrive files are only secure and backed up if your IT team sets up the infrastructure that way. If you're using SharePoint Online, then you can be assured that Microsoft is doing this for you. If your local IT team is running SharePoint for you, then check with them to make sure they back up and secure your OneDrive documents.

Your OneDrive is designed to live in the cloud and to be accessible by any device you happen to be working on. For example, if you start a document at work and then have to stop working on it when you leave to pick up your kids, you can log in and continue working on the document when you get home. And if you later have to take your mother-in-law to the doctor, and you take your tablet with you, you can log in from your tablet while you're waiting in the doctor's office. Finally, if, you drop off your mother-in-law and make a quick stop at the grocery store, and you get an email on your smartphone asking about a detail in the document you have been working on, you can connect to your OneDrive on your smartphone and view the document so you can respond to the inquiry. Being this connected isn't always the best way to spend your off-time, but OneDrive enables you to decide when and where you want to work. The idea behind OneDrive is that when you need your documents, you can access them as long as you can connect to the Internet.

TIP

The OneDrive discussed in this chapter is called OneDrive for Business, and it is designed for organizations and is part of SharePoint. A consumer version of One-Drive is also available at `https://onedrive.live.com`, but it is not part of Share-Point. It is a completely separate offering designed for general consumers, not organizations and business. When using the consumer version, your files are stored in the cloud on Microsoft servers. The consumer version of OneDrive is similar to other cloud storage services such as Dropbox and Google Drive.

Creating or uploading documents in your OneDrive

When you first land on your OneDrive page, you are presented with a notice letting you know that OneDrive for Business is a place to store, sync, and share your documents. You can add documents to OneDrive by following these steps:

1. **Navigate to your OneDrive page by clicking the OneDrive app in the waffle at the top of the SharePoint window (refer to Figure 15-1).**

TIP

   If you are using SharePoint Online, then you won't have any trouble finding OneDrive because Microsoft has already set it up for you. If you are using SharePoint On-Premises, then you will only find the waffle menu and the OneDrive app in the waffle menu if your administrator has set it up for you. If you don't see the waffle menu, or if you don't see the OneDrive app in the waffle menu, then contact your administrator to get things set up.

2. **Click the New link at the top of the page and select the type of document you want to create, as shown in Figure 15-3.**

   If you are using SharePoint Online, then you already have the Office document types (Word, Excel, PowerPoint, and OneNote) integrated with your OneDrive site because Microsoft has already set it up for you. If you are using SharePoint On-Premises, then you will only see these document types if they have been set up. If the integration has not been set up, then you will see a dialog box that lets you choose to upload an existing file already.

3. **The document you created opens and you can add content.**

4. **On the other hand, if you want to upload an existing document, you can click the Upload button instead of the New button (Step 2) and then browse to the document you want to add to OneDrive and click OK to add the file.**

You can choose to overwrite the document if a document with the same name already exists. If versioning is turned on, a new version of the document will be created and the existing document will be the previous version. If versioning is turned off, then overwriting will result in the loss of the existing document with the same name.

TIP

The OneDrive site contains a number of views. You can see all of the documents you have recently worked on and all of the documents that are shared with you. You access these views by clicking on the links in the left hand navigation (refer to Figure 15-2).

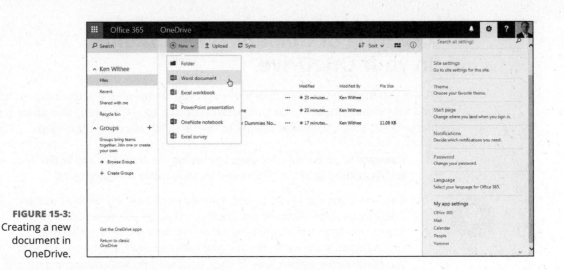

FIGURE 15-3:
Creating a new
document in
OneDrive.

Aggregating SharePoint Activity with Your Newsfeed

Your Newsfeed is an aggregation of SharePoint activity such as news, mentions, and likes. When you enter the Newsfeed app, you're presented with a dashboard of your relationships and connections throughout the organization. In addition, you can see which hashtags are trending and how many people, documents, sites, and tags you are following.

TIP

A *hashtag* is a way to track a theme throughout multiple conversations. A hashtag is the hash symbol (#) followed by a word or phrase without spaces. For example, you might use the hashtag #companypicnic2017. All postings that use this hashtag will be grouped together. You can see the most popular, or trending, hashtags on the Newsfeed landing page in the Trending #tags section.

To access your Newsfeed, click the waffle icon and choose the Newsfeed app, as shown in Figure 15-4.

After the Newsfeed app loads, a dashboard of your SharePoint life appears. Here you find people, documents, sites, and tags you are following as well as places where people have mentioned you in other parts of SharePoint (think of the @ name in Twitter or Facebook), and in conversations you are having with people. The Newsfeed landing page is shown in Figure 15-5.

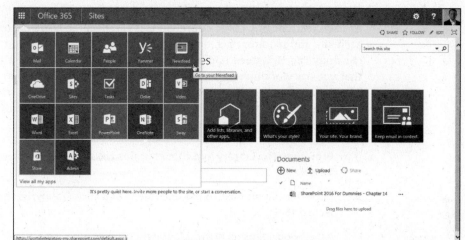

FIGURE 15-4:
Opening the
Newsfeed app.

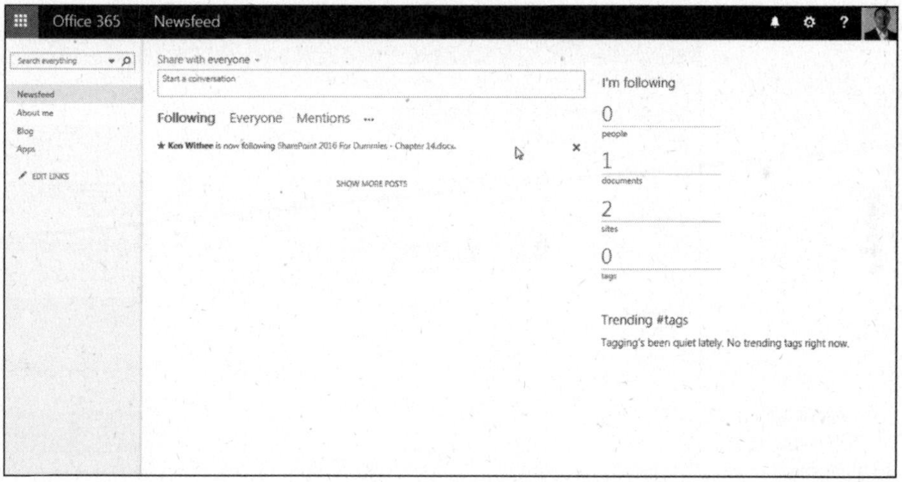

FIGURE 15-5:
The Newsfeed
landing page.

From the Newsfeed landing page, you can post a status update with everyone or with specific sites for which you have permissions. As people see your post, they can like it or reply to continue the conversation. You see these replies on your Newsfeed page and can thus stay interconnected with your organization in one place without clicking around through each site of every team.

Following a document from another site

A modern organization generates an unbelievable amount of digital content. The sheer number of digital documents can be beyond comprehension. SharePoint is a product that was developed from the beginning to help manage digital content.

As each team begins using SharePoint, it can become burdensome to navigate to each site and monitor each document. You might get carpal tunnel from so much clicking! The Newsfeed app pulls together into one nice view all the documents that you are working on, that have been shared with you, or that you are following. Accessing these views can be achieved by clicking the waffle button and choosing the Newsfeed app. To follow a document and add it to the Followed view on your Newsfeed, follow these steps:

1. **Browse to the Library app that contains the document you want to follow.**

2. **Click the ellipsis next to the document and click Follow, as shown in Figure 15-6.**

   A dialog box pops up in the upper-right corner of the screen, letting you know you are now following the document.

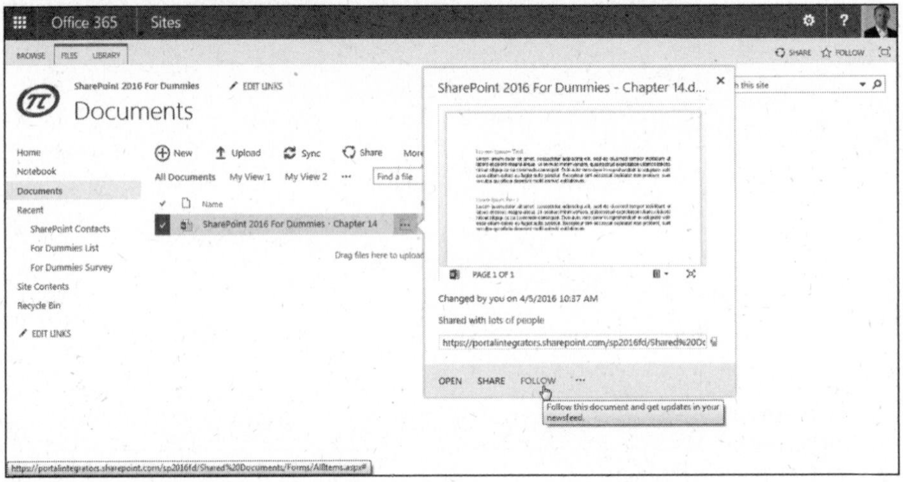

FIGURE 15-6:
Following a document in a SharePoint site.

3. **Navigate to your Newsfeed by clicking the waffle and choosing the Newsfeed app.**

4. **The document you just followed appears front and center under the Following view, as shown in Figure 15-5.**

   The documents you follow are displayed along with the web address of the document. To the right of the link you can click an X to stop following the document.

Reaching out with a blog

You can share information within your company in many ways. You can send an email, publish a document to your portal, or maybe go old-school and leave a hard copy on everyone's desk.

But nothing really compares to a good blog. It's a bit like reading a book with really short chapters. As shown in Figure 15-5, your Newsfeed has a link to your own personal blog. Clicking that link actually does just that — it creates your very own blog site with an entry that lets everyone know to stay tuned to hear from you.

TIP

Your blog is provisioned when you first click the Blog link on your Newsfeed page. The direct URL to your blog is configured based on how SharePoint was set up. An example is

```
http://portalintegrators.com/my/personal/rosemarie/Blog/
```

Your blog posts show up on your Newsfeed and the Newsfeed of anyone following you.

As shown in Figure 15-7, your blog site contains some useful links. Notice that you see Categories on the left side and a link to add a new category. You also see an Archives section that shows you past months. This makes is easy for readers of your blog to navigate through and find topics of interest.

On the right side, you have links to the blog tools. Here you can create, edit, and delete posts and manage comments that people make on your blog.

FIGURE 15-7:
A SharePoint blog site.

So what is so special about a blog? Nothing, really, except for the content you create in it. Blogging is not for everyone, but if you feel like sharing your thoughts with your colleagues, and you know that you can post at least a few times a month, your blog might be compelling to your coworkers.

Writing in your blog is a great way to communicate what you're working on, your ideas about the latest company initiative, or what's going on in your life that you think others may find interesting. The topic of your blog can be about a single thing or can range from the Amazon to Zambia. It doesn't really matter (unless you start violating some company blogging policies), but what matters to your readers is that you create posts that are interesting to read and you're updating your blog on a somewhat regular basis.

Tracking Your Favorite Sites

The number of sites being used throughout your organization can be overwhelming. You might be a user on sites for sales, human resources, various departments, carpools, child care, product development, and so on. As SharePoint gains momentum in your organization, the number of sites you might participate in will grow quickly. The Sites app is designed to help you solve this site overload issue. You access the Sites app by clicking the Sites app in the waffle menu. The Sites app loads and a navigation reminder appears at the top of the page that says Sites. This lets you know you are looking at SharePoint sites (as opposed to another app such as OneDrive or Newsfeed which were discussed previously). The Sites app landing page is shown in Figure 15-8.

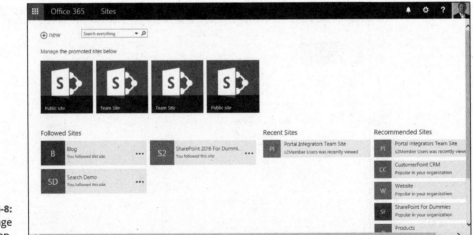

FIGURE 15-8:
The landing page
for the Sites app.

To help you keep track of your sites, the Sites app aggregates all the sites you follow. In addition to keeping track of your sites, the Sites app allows you to create new sites and even suggests sites that you might be interested in following based on the sites you currently follow. In other words, the Sites app is a one-stop sites shop and a sites dashboard.

TIP

To follow a site, click the Follow button in the upper-right corner of the site. If the Follow button isn't present, then the Following Content feature has not been activated for the site. After the Following Content feature has been activated, the Follow functionality is enabled for the site.

There comes a time when you might want to put together your own site for a particular reason. If your organization has enabled the ability for self-service site creation, then you can create your very own SharePoint site that you and others can use for a particular purpose. For example, you might create a site for everyone carpooling from your neighborhood.

You can create your own SharePoint sites by following these steps:

1. **Navigate to the Sites dashboard by clicking the Sites app in the waffle menu (app launcher) at the top-left corner of SharePoint.**

   Your Sites dashboard is displayed.

2. **Click the New button in the top-left corner of the page.**

   A dialog box pops up, asking for a name for the site and the location where you would like to save the site.

TIP

If you don't find the New button to create a new site, then you need to request it. This illustrates the point that the SharePoint user interface adds or removes components based on a number of different criteria. For example, in the case of the New site button, your SharePoint farm administrator needs to configure Self-Service Site Creation (SSSC) for the My Site host in order for the New Site button to appear. If you really want to impress your SharePoint administrator, just ask them to go to Application Management in Central Administration. There they will find a link called Manage Web Applications. Then they just click on the My Site host web application and then click the Self-Service Site Creation button in the Ribbon. On the dialog box, they need to select something other than the Be Hidden from Users option in the Start a Site section.

3. **Enter a name for the new site and remember the URL that is displayed, as shown in Figure 15-9.**

4. **Click Create to create the site.**

   The new site is displayed.

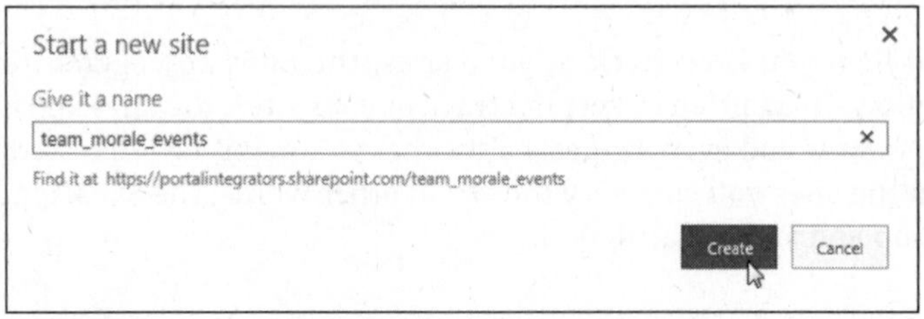

FIGURE 15-9:
The Start a New
Site dialog box.

Expressing Yourself with Your Profile

In addition to OneDrive, Newsfeed, and Sites you can also configure your personal profile. Your personal profile includes the usual boring data such as your name, phone number, department, title, and manager. In addition, you can upload your picture and enter information about yourself, such as things people should ask you about, your past projects, skills, schools you attended, your birthday, and your interests. Finally, your profile is where you set up your specific language and region information.

People are central to any business, no matter how big or small. Without people, a business wouldn't run. How people interact with each other creates the culture of a business, and part of that culture is how people figure out who does what job, who knows who, who knows what, and how someone might be able to help you do your job better. That culture, to some extent, can be reflected in SharePoint user profiles, and the better the user profile, the more likely you're going to get your job done more effectively. And, the more likely others are going to be able to find you easily when they need to.

Creating a holistic profile experience

The first part of creating your profile is to take a look at what properties are there by default. Many of the basic properties come from Active Directory (AD), but depending on how SharePoint was set up, you could also see information from other systems as well. The AD properties that typically show up in user profiles include your name, title, department, manager, and some contact information such as your work phone.

You can update other properties on your profile page, such as About Me, your picture, your location, your home phone, your skills, interests, and projects you've worked on in the past. All this extra information creates a much better sense of who you are than just the basic information about who you work for and where you are.

These properties can be edited by clicking your name in the upper-right corner of the screen and selecting About Me. When you're on your profile page, click the Edit Your Profile link to add in your information.

TIP

After browsing around your profile and the different sections of it, you may think of properties in the Outlook address book that should be in SharePoint profiles. Ask your SharePoint administrator to get those properties into SharePoint. This task is done in SharePoint Central Administration for SharePoint On-Premises or in the SharePoint Online administration area of Office 365.

Filling in your profile information

It seems like practically everyone in the world is familiar with social networking sites such as Facebook, Twitter, and LinkedIn, and Microsoft has taken some cues to extend that social networking functionality into SharePoint. It all starts with sharing some information about yourself so that other people in your organization can find you and read a little about you. That's where the basic profile information comes into play.

Along with the really basic information that comes from Active Directory (AD), you also see About Me, Picture, and Ask Me About fields when editing your profile, as shown in Figure 15-10. These items are shared with everyone, unlike some of the extra information we cover next.

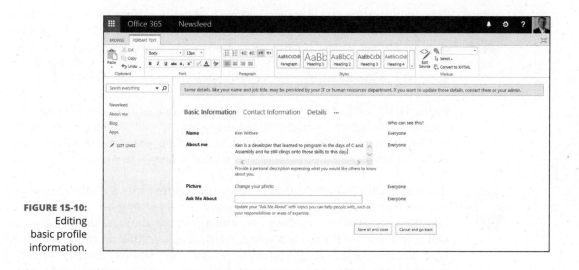

FIGURE 15-10:
Editing basic profile information.

The information you share in the About Me and Ask Me About fields should be what you want people to know about you as it relates to what you do at your company. There's really no need to share your love of pet rats (unless your business caters to owners of pet rats). Rather, share a little bit about where you came from, what you like to work on, and when you started at the company — keep it simple and useful for others.

In the Ask Me About section, put in what you're really good at, work-wise, and things that people might want to know more about you if they knew you had the same interests or a particular knowledge of something they need to know more about. But again, keep it business-related, because this information is shared with everyone.

For your picture, we recommend one of you in business attire rather than the one of you sunburned and on the beach. Remember, the picture you share here shows up in SharePoint, attached to documents you've created, or when you show up in search results. A picture is really helpful, for example, if you work in a large organization, and even a small- to medium-sized organization where people don't work in the same location. Maybe all the employees of your company are so distributed that they don't all get together but once every year or two, so being able to place a face with a name can help bridge that gap of unfamiliarity. (We've been in many situations where the voice doesn't go at all with the eventual face when we met them in person — a profile picture helps to alleviate some of that awkwardness.)

For administrators and managers, remember that if one person in the organization updates their profile, it's a start but it's really not that useful. But if everyone does, it becomes a great place to get to know who you work with, what motivates people, and what they're good at. Your challenge is to come up with a contest or some type of incentive program for getting employees to fill out their profiles.

Filling in the rest of your profile is up to you. One of the cool features of the Contact Information, Details, Newsfeed Settings, and Language and Region sections of your profile is that you can choose who you share that information with. You can choose to share it with everyone or keep it to yourself.

If you are using SharePoint Online, then you will find that the About Me page is actually part of a new app called Delve. Delve is an exciting new app that is built into SharePoint Online. It is designed to help you take control of the digital mountain that overloads the modern world. Rosemarie is writing an entire book called *Office 365 Apps For Dummies,* in which Delve is a major feature. There are actually a number of these new, and very powerful Office 365 Apps and thus why Rosemarie took on writing an entire book about them!

IN THIS CHAPTER

Using the Ribbon to share and track sites

Talking on blogs, wikis, and discussion boards

Getting familiar with feeds

Subscribing and managing alerts

Using Skype for Business to reach out and connect

Chapter 16

Getting Social

The folks at Microsoft got to thinking about how SharePoint is a lot like social networking communities on the web. *Social networking* services build online communities of people who share interests and/or activities and consist of services and sites such as instant messaging (IM), discussion boards, blogs, wikis, bookmarking sites, Facebook, LinkedIn, Flickr, Twitter, and so on (and on).

Some people use them all. We just can't. And neither should you feel like you have to use all the social networking options in SharePoint. Focus on picking the right tool(s) for you and your team. You can still be cool (and productive) using just a few. There are good and specific reasons for using discussion boards, blogs, and wikis, and even more reasons for using alerts and feeds. And SharePoint even has a What's Happening feature similar to the on-the-fly updates of Twitter.

SharePoint offers other social networking features that all site visitors can use and some features (such as wikis and discussion boards) that a site owner must set up for a team to use. SharePoint also offers social networking features with Newsfeed (see Chapter 15).

In this chapter, we discuss social networking tools that let individuals and groups communicate, collaborate, share, and connect. Depending on the culture of your organization and the projects you work on, these tools may find greater or lesser use; we encourage you to experiment with them all. Organizations generally experience some anxiety and growing pains around the less structured communications that social networking facilitates, but after a period of adjustment, we often find that those who were initially most reluctant become social networking advocates as they discover the value these tools can bring to productivity, collaboration, and morale.

Sharing and Tracking Using the Ribbon

The Ribbon in SharePoint 2016 features a Share & Track group that consolidates several common tasks for keeping track of useful SharePoint resources and sharing them with others. The Share & Track group is found on both the Files and the Library / List tabs. The components in the group depend on the tab you are viewing. There is no Share & Track group on the Items tab.

Figure 16-1 shows the Share & Track group for a document (on the Files tab of the Ribbon).

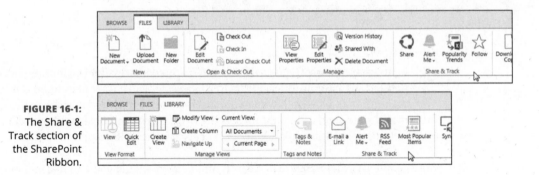

FIGURE 16-1: The Share & Track section of the SharePoint Ribbon.

The Share & Track group for a document has four buttons:

» **Share** opens a dialog box that lets you share the document with other people. You can invite people to view or edit the document, and you can also see who the document is currently shared with. If you are using SharePoint Online, you can also get a link that you can give to others so they can get to the document even if they are not part of your SharePoint environment.

» **Alert Me** allows you to set and manage your alerts to apps so that an email is sent to you when changes are made. Note that this is only visible when outgoing email is configured for your SharePoint environment.

» **Popularity Trends** allows you to export data into Excel and view trends about the document. This is a very handy feature to learn about data trends in content. Note that this is only visible when outgoing email is configured and the reporting feature is active for your SharePoint environment.

>> **Follow** lets you follow a particular document so you can keep up to date with any changes.

The Share & Track group for a List or Library has four buttons:

>> **E-Mail a Link** uses Outlook to send a link to a page to someone.

>> **Alert Me** allows you to set and manage your alerts to apps so that an email is sent to you when changes are made.

>> **RSS Feed** enables you to subscribe to an RSS feed. Each app in SharePoint 2016 publishes an RSS feed that you can subscribe to and view in your favorite RSS viewer.

>> **Most Popular Items** provides a report showing how many edits and views have been made to the document recently and during the life of the documents. It also ranks the documents in the list and allows you to sort to see the highest and lowest documents in terms of popularity.

Tagging for Yourself and Others

Tags are keywords that you assign to content. Tagging pages to share with others is *social bookmarking*, and it's very popular on the web. If you've ever used a site like Pinterest (https://www.pinterest.com), you already know how social book-marking works.

As more people assign the same tags, tags become a way to navigate to similar content. The Tags and Notes group on the Ribbon lets you type your own tag keywords, so you can mark content with terms that are meaningful to you. This button also lets you access the *Note Board*, which you can use to leave publicly viewable comments on a document or page.

Although you can still use tags and notes in SharePoint Server 2016, Microsoft has openly declared these features as deprecated. *Deprecated* means it is not getting any love or any new functionality from Microsoft, and you should expect it to go away in future versions of SharePoint. In fact, if you use SharePoint Online, then you won't be able to use tags and notes. If you are using SharePoint On-Premises, however, then you can still use tags and notes. To learn about this announcement, type the following keywords into your favorite search engine: *SharePoint Online Tags & Notes feature retired*.

The emphasis is on *keyword* in tagging. SharePoint doesn't prevent you from typing longer tags, but we recommend you use, and train others to use, single words or very short phrases as tags. Otherwise, you defeat the purpose in using tagging as a fast, concise way to categorize information. If you need to make longer remarks, use the Note Board.

To tag content in SharePoint, follow these steps:

1. **Browse to the page you want to tag.**

   To tag individual items or documents, you must browse to the app and click the row you want to tag. The Tags and Notes for individual items or documents is on the Items tab of the Ribbon.

2. **Locate the Tags and Notes group on the List or Library tab of the Ribbon to see your tagging options.**

3. **Click the Tags and Notes button.**

   The Tags and Note Board window appear, populated with recent tags you've applied.

4. **In the My Tags text area, click an existing tag and/or type the tags you want to apply to the content.**

   Use a semicolon to separate tags.

5. **(Optional) To mark your tags as private so others can't see them, select the Private check box.**

6. **Click the Save button to save your tags.**

   When you save your tags, they appear in the Suggested Tags section of the page. You can click any of the tags in this section to view the Tags Profile page.

To add a note to an item, follow these steps:

1. **Click the Note Board tab and type your note in the text box.**

   Unlike tags, notes entered with the Note Board can't be marked private and so are viewable by anyone else with the same access. Choose your words carefully.

2. **Click the Post button to post the note.**

The note appears in the window, along with any other notes that have been entered. You can scroll through all the posts entered for this content using the Next and Previous buttons.

3. **To close the window, click the X in the upper-right corner of the window.**

Information Sharing with Blogs and Wikis

Blogs are intended to be mainly one-way communication: An individual or group with an opinion or expertise creates posts that others read and subscribe to. Readers can comment, like, and email a link to the post, but the blog posts themselves aren't collaborative. You often see executives in an organization maintaining blogs to communicate to employees, or IT departments creating a blog with helpful posts that address FAQs.

Wikis, on the other hand, are specifically collaborative efforts: Information is added to, and maintained by, a network of users. Perhaps the most well-known wiki is *Wikipedia* (www.wikipedia.org), a web encyclopedia of information about any topic imaginable, editable by anyone in the Wikipedia community. A wiki is a very flexible and democratic way for individuals to work together to share, refine, and collect information.

TIP

Good candidates for wikis include corporate encyclopedias, dictionaries, and training manuals so that many individuals can add their knowledge and examples.

Creating a blog site

To create a blog in SharePoint, you create a new site or subsite using the Blog template. Take the time to consider where this blog will be located in your site hierarchy.

TIP

Your Newsfeed app has an integrated blog specifically for you. You access the blog in the left navigation of the Newsfeed site. For more about the blog in Newsfeed, see Chapter 15.

Although you can change permissions at any level, it may make more sense to have your president's blog on the main site of your SharePoint intranet (and open to all users of the site hierarchy), but perhaps your manager's blog should be created as a subsite of your team site (so that permissions can be inherited from the team site). See Figure 16-2 for an example of a blog site.

FIGURE 16-2:
A SharePoint
blog site.

To create a blog site:

1. **Navigate to the Site Contents page by clicking the Settings gear icon and choosing Site Contents.**

   The Site Contents page appears, showing all the apps in the site.

2. **Scroll down to the bottom of the page to the Subsites section and click New Subsite.**

3. **Type a name, description, and a URL for the site in the Name, Description, and URL text boxes, respectively.**

4. **In the Template Selection section, choose the Blog template located under the Collaboration tab.**

   Notice that there are different site templates to choose from. In Chapter 4, you used the Team Site template to create a team site.

5. **Keep the default to use the same permissions as the parent site.**

   You can also choose unique permissions if you want to break the inheritance of permissions for the blog site. (To find out more about permissions and inheritance, see Chapter 14.)

6. **In the Navigation Inheritance section, you can choose to use the same Top Link bar from the parent site or use a unique Top Link bar.**

   If you use the same Top Link bar of the parent, then you can navigate back to the parent site from within the blog. If you do not use the same Top Link bar, then the blog will appear isolated. You can always manually add navigation to the Top Link bar as well. (See Chapter 11 for more about SharePoint navigation.)

7. **Click the Create button.**

   You see a message that SharePoint is working, and then your new blog appears.

8. **Click the Create a Post button (under Blog Tools on the right side) to add a new entry to your blog.**

   The home page of the blog site shows a Welcome to Your Blog default post, a list of Blog tools for posting, a place for your picture, and RSS Feed and Alert Me buttons.

   The site content includes a Photos app, Categories app, Posts app, and Comments app.

Posting to a blog

Creating a blog post, commenting on a post, and liking a post are pretty straightforward. A user with permissions to post can click the Create a Post link under Blog Tools and type his post (or copy and paste text from a text editor or Word). The dialog box where the post is typed also allows for adding one or more category labels to the posts.

Comments and likes (if any) are displayed below the blog post to which they apply. The Comments link and the Add Comment field allow users to comment on a post by titling their comment (optional) and adding body text. The Comments link also shows the current number of comments. The Like button creates a smiley face and shows the number of likes, along with an Unlike button if you change your mind. You can also click the E-mail a Link to send a link to the post, or you can click the ellipsis to edit the post (assuming you're the author).

Other features of the Blog Site template are predefined links on the Quick Launch menu for post categories and archives, making it easy to see a filtered list of posts in one category or review older archived posts.

Using wikis to collaborate and coauthor

A *wiki* app is a library of pages that can be edited by any member (Contributor) of your site. As we describe earlier, encyclopedias, dictionaries, and training manuals are all good examples of wikis for an organization. These examples are entities that provide structure to what is being accomplished but benefit by input of a group.

One of the marketing mantras of SharePoint is *wikis everywhere*. A SharePoint 2016 team site is essentially a wiki with the capabilities to add additional kinds of apps. SharePoint 2016 includes the Enterprise Wiki site template, which is intended for collaborative content creation among larger groups of people, such as a division. The steps discussed in this section apply to wikis anywhere — that is, it doesn't matter where you encounter wikis in SharePoint.

Creating a wiki app

A wiki app in SharePoint is a library of wiki pages. Create the wiki the way you would any other app, which we describe in Chapter 7, by selecting Wiki Page Library app.

Adding pages to a wiki

Two pages are created by default in your new wiki app, Home and How to Use This Wiki Library. Both provide predefined instructions that may be helpful when you first create the wiki. Most users change the home page content before launching the wiki, but you can keep the How to Use This Wiki Library page or delete it, depending on its usefulness.

To add other pages to your wiki, follow these steps:

1. **Navigate to the home page of the wiki app by using the link on the Quick Launch menu, if available.**

   You can also navigate to the Site Contents page and open the app.

2. **Click the Page tab of the Ribbon and click the View All Pages button located in the Page Library section.**

   You see the list of pages.

   The Files and Library tabs appear on the Ribbon.

3. **Click the Files tab and click the New button.**

   The New Item dialog box appears.

4. **Type your new page name in the New Page Name text box, and then click the Create button.**

   The new page appears, ready for editing. Just click in the page, and then the Format Text tab appears.

   You can now edit the page, or repeat the steps to create multiple pages before editing.

Alternatively, you can click the Settings gear icon and choose Add a Page from an existing wiki page to add a new page to the same wiki library.

TIP

Another easy way to create pages is to create a link to them first in a wiki page and then click that link. The new page is created automatically with the name found in the link. For example, type **[[My New Page]]** to create a link to the My New Page page. The link to an uncreated page appears underlined with dashes. If users click the link, the page is created for editing and the link turns into a normal hyperlink. To create a link to a page and have the name be different than the wording of the link, type a pipe character (|) after the page name and type the display text. For example, type **[[Resources|Resources for You]]** to create the Resources link that points to the Resources for You page.

Editing a wiki page

When you first create a wiki page, the page appears in Edit mode, as shown in Figure 16-3. When you want to come back to a wiki page and edit later, follow these steps:

1. **Access the page from the Quick Launch menu or Wiki Library Page list.**

2. **Click the Page tab of the Ribbon and click the Edit button located in the Edit section.**

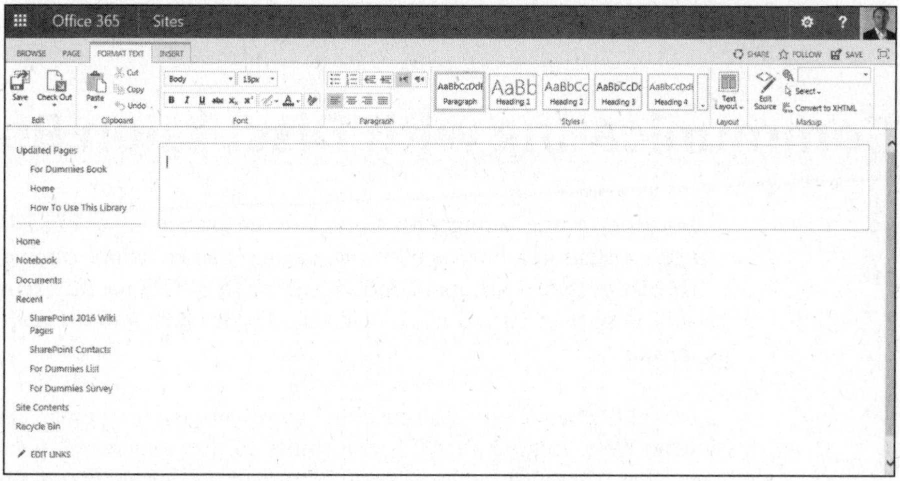

FIGURE 16-3:
A wiki page
in Edit mode.

TIP

Like other documents, check out the page if you don't want others to be able to edit at the same time and perhaps overwrite your work. See Chapter 18 for details.

Editing a wiki page is similar to working in a word processor. You can type or copy text, indent, make bullets, apply bold and italics, and insert all other types of content such as tables and images. To stop editing, click the Save button on the Format Text tab of the Ribbon. You need to check in your wiki as a separate step if you checked it out.

TIP

You can also find an Edit link in the upper-right corner of the wiki page. Clicking it moves you into Edit mode for the page.

You can also define your text layout. By default, text layout is one column (full page width), but you can change the layout by choosing one you like from the Text Layout drop-down list on the Format Text tab. (*Note:* You must be in Edit mode to see the Format Text tab.) Now you may have multiple text containers to work with.

WARNING

You can switch layouts at any point. But be careful — if you switch to a layout with fewer containers than your current layout, SharePoint combines content in one container with content in another. You won't lose the content, but you'll probably have to make some edits to fix the combined content.

TECHNICAL STUFF

Changing the text layout of a wiki page isn't the same as changing the layout on a Web Part page or the page layout on a publishing page. Wiki pages, Web Part pages, and publishing pages all behave slightly different and have different purposes. See Chapter 5 for a more thorough discussion on SharePoint's web pages. By the way, if you can articulate the differences among these three kinds of SharePoint pages, consider a career as a SharePoint consultant.

Communicating with Discussion Boards

Discussion boards, along with alerts, are the granddaddies of social networking services. Discussion boards have been around since before the World Wide Web and consist of text postings by individuals with others posting replies to the original subject or to other replies. A discussion board post and the responses to it are one *thread.*

One of the benefits of a discussion board (versus a long email chain, and you know what we're talking about) is the ability to find and search posts easily for information. Threads provide a useful history of the comments on a topic. Users generally have various levels of expertise in organizing and searching their email, but SharePoint discussion views and search make it easy for users to both find and read posts.

TIP

One of the benefits of a team discussion board is (should be) the less formal approach in posting questions and answers — a discussion board exchange resembles a true discussion. Blogs and wikis are more formal, so discussion boards are generally where team members can ask questions and share thoughts. Share-Point 2016 also includes the approach of *microblogging,* which is blogging in just a couple of sentences at a time. Microblogging is discussed later in this chapter in the "Staying connected with feeds and microblogs" section.

Creating a Discussion Board app

Adding a Discussion Board app is a very straightforward process. You simply choose the Discussion Board app from the Apps You Can Add page.

You can add as many discussion boards to your site as you like. You might find it beneficial to create a discussion board for each functional area to keep the discussions on topic. On the other hand, you might find that it is better to just have a single discussion board for the team and to get people using it and interacting with their ideas. As with most things in SharePoint, the way you work with the functionality is up to you. SharePoint just provides the platform, and it's up to you and your SharePoint consultant to determine the best way to use it.

To create a new Discussion Board app, follow these steps:

1. **Click the Settings gear icon and choose Add an App.**

   The Your Apps page appears.

2. **Scroll down and click the Discussion Board App button.**

3. **Type a name for the discussion board in the Name text box.**

4. **Click the Create button.**

   The new discussion board is added to your site and is accessible in the Quick Launch navigation on the left side. Congratulations! You're ready to start a discussion.

Posting and replying to a subject

To create a new subject in a discussion board, follow these steps:

1. **Browse to your discussion board.**

2. **Click the New Discussion button.**

   The New Discussion dialog box appears.

3. **Type a subject for the new discussion in the Subject text box.**

   This needs to be a short phrase that teammates can relate to as a topic.

4. **Type the detail of your post in the Body text area.**

   You have all the editing options of Rich HTML in this area. Use the Editing tools to format your text with the toolbar and styles, as well as insert tables, images, and links. You can upload files using the Insert tab.

   You also have spell checker in this dialog box!

5. **Select the Question check box if you're asking a question.**

6. **When you're finished with your post, click the Save button.**

   Your new post appears and shows the subject title, who created it, the amount of replies, and when it was updated last. Note that the amount of replies shows on the details of the discussion page.

The Discussion Board app shows a number of different views into the discussions: Recent, Unanswered Questions, Answered Questions, and Featured.

To reply to a subject or another reply, follow these steps:

1. **Click the Subject Title link for the discussion.**

   The subject appears in Flat view with a Reply button. If you're the owner of the discussion posting, you also see an Edit button. You can also click the ellipsis to be alerted to additional replies, mark the discussion as Featured, or delete the discussion.

2. **Click the Reply button or click in the Add a Reply text box.**

   The Reply dialog box activates, and you can type your reply. By default, the Reply dialog box shows only a Body field.

3. **Type your reply; if desired, use the Rich HTML features (as we describe in the preceding step list).**

   Remember that you can attach files, upload files, and add all sorts of text formatting.

4. **When you're finished with your reply, click the Reply button.**

Connecting with Others Using Feeds, Microblogs, and RSS

You can follow SharePoint feeds in your Newsfeed app. A *feed* is a stream of content that you follow. For example, whenever a user posts a status update on her Newsfeed page, she generates an item for the Everyone feed. You can also tune in to specific sites and documents by clicking the Follow button. The Follow button is in the upper-right corner of a site and in the drop-down list when you click the ellipsis next to a document.

The Newsfeed page includes the following feeds:

>> **Following:** The updates of documents, sites, and people you follow.

>> **Everyone:** All the updates from every person using SharePoint.

>> **Activities:** All your activities within SharePoint.

>> **Likes:** All the things you have liked. As the community rates content by clicking the Like button, you can begin to find the best content without having to go looking in every nook and corner.

>> **Mentions:** All the posts where you were mentioned. Mentions are accomplished using the @ symbol and your username.

A different type of feed is called an RSS feed. An *RSS feed* is a feed formatted in a special way to be read by an RSS reader. As you can explore later in the "Viewing RSS feeds" section, every app has the ability to display its data using an RSS feed.

TIP

A feed in your Newsfeed and an RSS feed are different. Both are feeds of data, but an RSS feed is designed for external applications to view SharePoint data, and the Newsfeed is a place for you to aggregate and view communication happening within SharePoint.

We cover the Newsfeed app further in Chapter 15.

Staying connected with feeds and microblogs

Microblogging was made famous by Twitter. Using Twitter, you post a short message (140 characters or less) out to the world. You can follow other people and attract your own followers. You mention other people using the @ symbol followed by their name and can tag a topic using the # symbol (called a hashtag).

SharePoint 2016 provides microblogging to the corporate world. Twitter is great, but do you really want to post your company secrets and ideas to the world? SharePoint provides the same functionality as Twitter, but in a controlled environment that is only accessible by other SharePoint users at your organization.

In SharePoint, you post microblog updates from your Newsfeed app. To post a microblog update, follow these steps:

1. Navigate to your Newsfeed app by clicking the waffle menu in the upper-left corner of the screen (also called the *app launcher*) and clicking Newsfeed.

The Newsfeed page is displayed. If you do not see the waffle menu, then SharePoint has not been configured to include your personal space.

2. **Click in the Start a Conversation text box, and type your message.**

   If you want to mention someone, type the **@** symbol and choose the person from the drop-down list. If you want to provide a hashtag topic, type the **#** symbol followed by a topic name (without spaces).

3. **At the top of the message box, click the drop-down list to decide who you want to share the message with.**

   By default, a message is shared with everyone. You can select the drop-down list and choose to share the message with a particular site.

4. **Click the Post button to publish your message.**

You can see trending hashtag topics in the lower-right corner of your Newsfeed page. A *trending topic* is the most popular hashtag at the time. For example, if a bunch of people use the tag #CompanyMovieNight, then the tag will show up in the trending list. You can click the tag to see the related posts for that topic. You can also choose to follow the tag so that you will be updated whenever someone makes a new post about the topic. (The Newsfeed app is discussed further in Chapter 15.)

TIP

If you are not able to add a hashtag (#cool_topic) to your feed, then your administrator will need to create a Managed Metadata Service application. This can be done in Central Administration by clicking on the Application Management page, clicking the Manage Service Applications link, and then choosing Managed Metadata Service from the New drop-down menu on the left side of the Ribbon.

Viewing RSS feeds

Nowadays, virtually all web sites publish a syndication feed, or *RSS feed*, of their site's content. SharePoint 2016 sites are no different. In fact, every app in SharePoint can publish an RSS feed. You can even create RSS feeds based on views, which means you can filter what gets published to the RSS feed. If you subscribe to the feed, you're *pulling* the information. However, you can also subscribe to alerts to make SharePoint *push* updates to you.

RSS feeds are a popular way for people to keep track of updates to a website without visiting that site.

To use RSS feeds, they must be enabled for the app. If you see the standard RSS button in the app's Ribbon as shown in Figure 16-4, RSS feeds are enabled. If RSS feeds are disabled, the button appears in the Ribbon but is disabled.

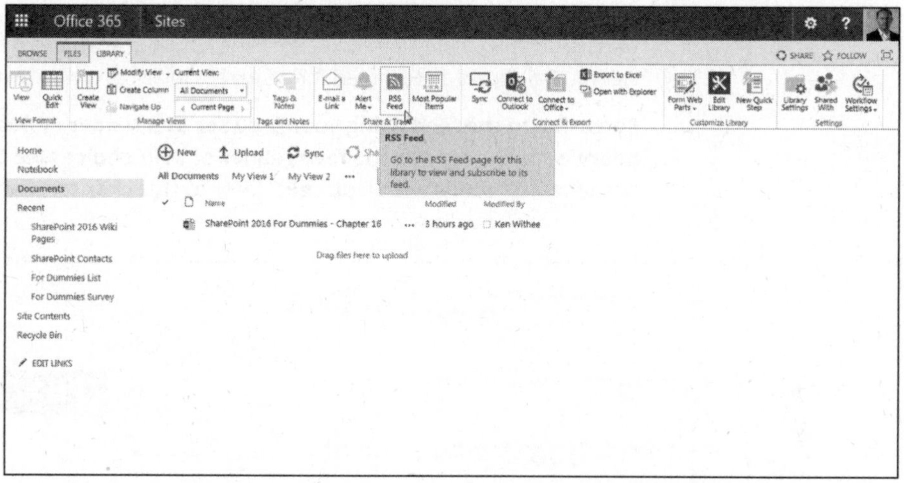

The RSS Feed screenshot shows the Office 365 Sites interface with the RSS Feed button highlighted.

FIGURE 16-4:
The RSS Feed button.

To enable RSS feeds for your List (or Library) app, follow these steps:

1. In your app, click the List tab of the Ribbon, and in the Settings group, click the List Settings button.

The List Settings page appears.

If you're in a Library app, click the Library tab of the Ribbon and click the Library Settings button.

2. In the Communications section, click the RSS Settings link.

If you don't see the RSS Settings link, RSS isn't enabled for your site. You can enable RSS settings for your site by clicking the RSS link in the Site Administration section of the Site Settings page. RSS must also be enabled for your web application by the SharePoint farm administrator.

3. On the Modify RSS Settings page, select the Yes radio button under the Allow RSS for This List option.

You can also use this page to configure the settings for the apps default RSS feed, such as the feed's title, columns, and item limit.

4. After you finish configuring the default settings for your app's RSS feed, click OK to save your changes.

Each list and app has its own RSS feed. Therefore, you must configure RSS for each app where you want to use RSS.

REMEMBER

After you enable RSS feeds for your app, you can view the RSS feed as follows:

1. Browse to the app where you want to view the RSS feed, click the List tab of the Ribbon, and click RSS Feed button on the Share & Track section.

Most browsers display the RSS feed using a built-in style sheet for formatting. Figure 16-5 shows an RSS feed for a SharePoint list in a web browser.

2. **Subscribe to the feed using your browser as a reader or paste the web address for the feed in the feed reader of your choice (see the section, "Reading RSS feeds with Outlook," later in this chapter, for instructions).**

You've successfully subscribed to this feed!
Updated content can be viewed in Internet Explorer and other programs that use the Common Feed List.

⭐ View my feeds

SharePoint 2016 For Dummies: Documents
Today, April 07, 2016, 1 minute ago

SharePoint 2016 For Dummies - Chapter 16
Thursday, March 24, 2016, 11:29:27 AM | Ken Withee →

Show all items

Displaying	1 / 1
All	1
● New	1

Sort by:
▾ Date
  Title
  Author

✓ Mark feed as read
View feed properties...

You can also view the RSS feed for a specific view in an app. (See Chapter 9 for details on creating a view.)

TIP

RSS must be enabled for the farm, site, and app. In other words, you can't use RSS feeds if they aren't turned on. You can also turn off RSS feeds for a given app or site if you don't want people to use them. The default option is to allow RSS feeds. At the site level, RSS feeds are enabled in the Site Settings page. The RSS settings for an individual app are managed in the List Settings or Library Settings page for that app, respectively.

Reading RSS feeds with Outlook

Your email application, and specifically in terms of SharePoint integration, Microsoft Outlook, is still the bedrock of online communication for most business users. As in the past, you can still integrate Outlook with SharePoint calendars, contacts, and tasks using the Sync with Outlook button in the Ribbon of an app. You might prefer following a SharePoint app using RSS.

To add a SharePoint 2016 RSS feed to Outlook 2016, follow these steps:

1. **Open Outlook 2016 and on the Ribbon, click File, then Info, and then select Account Settings from the Account Settings drop-down menu.**

2. **On the RSS Feeds tab, click New.**

    The New RSS Feed dialog box appears.

3. **Type the URL of the RSS feed (or press Ctrl+V to paste it).**

    You get the SharePoint app's RSS feed URL by clicking the RSS Feed button in the Ribbon of your app.

4. **Click the Add button.**

    The feed is added to the list of subscribed feeds on the RSS Feeds tab.

Displaying RSS feeds of other sites

SharePoint 2016 includes an RSS Viewer Web Part that allows you to display RSS feeds from SharePoint apps and public websites in your site. To use this Web Part, follow these steps:

1. **Browse to the page where you want to add the RSS feed, click the Page tab of the Ribbon, and then click the Edit Page button.**

    The page is in Edit mode.

2. **Click Add a Web Part in the layout zone in the page where you want the Web Part to appear.**

    The Insert tab appears on the Ribbon.

3. **In the Categories section of the Insert tab, click the Content Rollup category.**

    A list of Web Parts appears.

4. **Click the RSS Viewer Web Part.**

    A description of the Web Part appears.

    The SharePoint Server Standard Site Collection feature must be activated to see the RSS Viewer Web Part. If you don't see the Web Part, activate this feature. (See Chapter 12 for details on activating features.)

5. **Click the Add button to add the Web Part to the page, as shown in Figure 16-6.**

    The Web Part appears on the page, awaiting configuration.

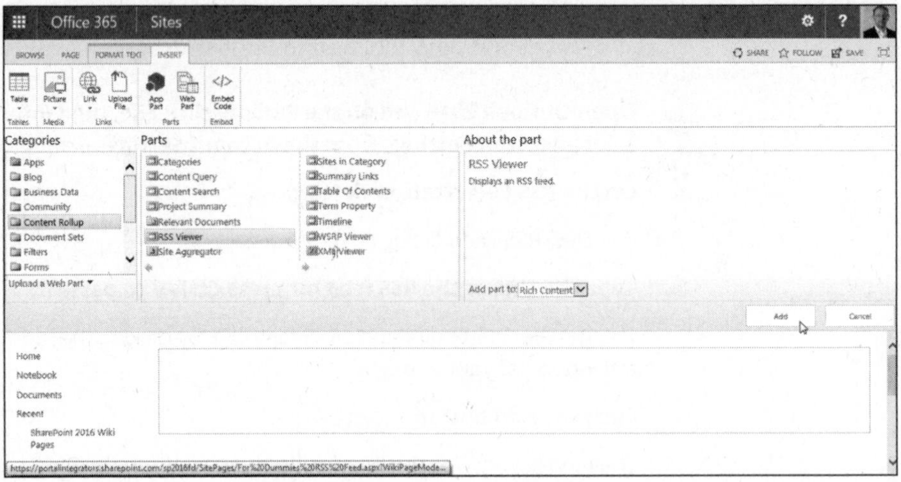

FIGURE 16-6:
Add the RSS Viewer Web Part to your page.

To complete the configuration of the Web Part, you need to have the web address or URL for a feed you want to display in the Web Part. To add an RSS feed web address, follow these steps:

1. **With your Web Part on the page, place a check mark in the upper-right corner of the Web Part.**

2. **Click the Web Part tab of the Ribbon, and then click the Web Part Properties button.**

   The Web Part's properties appear as a tool pane on the right side of the screen.

3. **In the RSS Properties tab of the tool pane, enter the web address of the RSS feed you want to display in the RSS Feed URL text box, as shown in Figure 16-7.**

   In this example, we pasted in the BBC News Top Stories RSS feed web address.

4. **Click OK, and your RSS feed appears in the web page.**

You can click a headline in your Web Part to display the item's details, as shown in Figure 16-8. You can also click the More link to open the items from the RSS feed.

You can use the RSS Viewer Web Part to display RSS feeds from SharePoint apps; however, your SharePoint farm must be configured to use Kerberos authentication. If you receive an authentication error while attempting to use the Web Part, it is most likely a Kerberos problem. You will have to engage your IT folks for help.

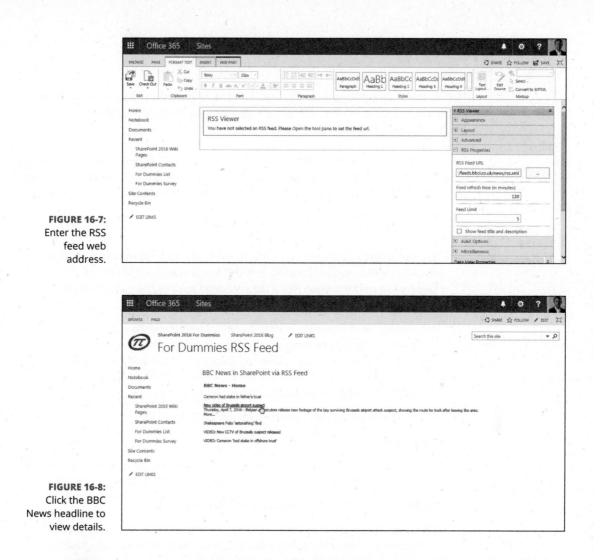

FIGURE 16-7:
Enter the RSS feed web address.

FIGURE 16-8:
Click the BBC News headline to view details.

TECHNICAL
STUFF

You can modify the default XSLT (Extensible Stylesheet Language Transformations) template that the RSS Viewer Web Part uses if you want to change the output display. The XSLT template can be accessed from the Web Part's properties pane. For example, you can change the template so that the headline links to the article instead of displaying the item's details. You can use any XSLT programming or text editor to modify the XSLT template.

Alert Me

If RSS isn't your thing, you can opt to receive email notifications when apps change by creating an alert. *Alerts* are a great way to keep track of the changes your teammates make to documents and items.

You need the Create Alerts permission to create alerts. This permission is granted usually with the out-of-the-box configuration of the *Site* Members SharePoint group. (See Chapter 14 for details on working with permissions.)

To create an alert to an app, follow these steps:

1. **Browse to the app where you want to subscribe to an alert and then click the Alert Me drop-down button in the Share & Track section of the Library tab of the Ribbon (for a library-based app) or the List tab of the Ribbon (for a list-based app).**

   If you don't see the Alert Me button, chances are your administrator has not configured outgoing email settings. If outgoing email settings are not configured in Central Administration, then the Alert Me button simply will not appear to users. If you are using SharePoint Online, however, then outgoing email has already been configured by Microsoft and you are good to go.

2. **Choose Set Alert on this Library from the drop-down list.**

   The New Alert window appears.

   You can subscribe to an alert for an item or document by selecting the item or document and choosing Alert Me on the Items tab of the Ribbon.

3. **In the Alert Title text box, enter a name for the alert.**

   We suggest making the name something meaningful to you in your inbox, such as **Documents Modified Today – Budget Team Site**. Otherwise, you have no meaningful way to tell one alert from another.

4. **In the Send Alerts To text box, enter the names of people in addition to you who should receive the alert.**

   That's right, you can subscribe other people to an alert! You must have the Manage Alerts permission, which is granted by default to Site Owners.

TIP

   Organizations and site owners may want to subscribe multiple users to an alert to make sure they get important updates, as well as encourage them to contribute to a discussion board, blog, or wiki. Users can still opt out by modifying settings in their Alert settings.

5. **In the Delivery Method section, select whether to receive alerts via email or text message to your cellular phone.**

   Text messaging requires that your SharePoint administrator configures this service through a third party, so you may not be able to send alerts to your phone.

6. **In the Change Type section, select the option that matches the type of notifications you want to receive — All Changes, New Items Are Added, Existing Items Are Modified, or Items Are Deleted.**

   If you're responsible for managing an app, we recommend receiving an alert any time items are deleted.

7. **In the Send Alerts for These Changes section, choose when to receive alerts.**

   The options you see here vary based on the kind of app you're working with. For example, a Tasks app allows you to receive an alert when a task is marked Complete or any time a high-priority task changes.

8. **In the When to Send Alerts section, choose the frequency of your alert delivery.**

   You can receive them immediately, once a day, or once a week. We like to receive a daily summary; otherwise, we get too many emails.

9. **Click OK to create your alert.**

Figure 16-9 shows an example of configuring an alert.

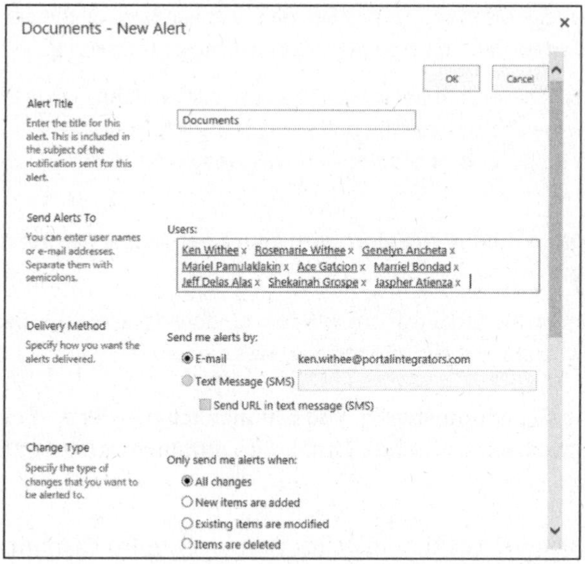

FIGURE 16-9:
Receive an email when a list or library changes.

TIP

Any time users say they need a workflow to receive notification, try an alert first. You'd be surprised at how often alerts provide the options that are needed.

TIP

If your app has a personal or public view that includes a filter, you can subscribe to changes to just that view. For example, say you want to be notified via text message when an item in an Issue Tracking app has its priority set to High. You would create a view that filters the app for high-priority issues. Select the filtered view in the Send Alerts for These Changes section when you create your alert, and you will receive alerts when items meet the filter criteria.

You must have an email address configured in your SharePoint profile in order to receive alerts. If your SharePoint server is located in your network, that's usually not an issue. However, Office 365 may not be integrated with your network and email information. In those situations, your administrator can either manually configure your email address or grant you permission to do so.

You can manage all your alerts from a single page instead of navigating to each list. To manage all the alerts you have on a given site and modify or delete them, follow these steps:

1. **Browse to an app where you currently subscribe to an alert.**

2. **On the List tab of the Ribbon, in the Share & Track section, choose Alert Me ⇨ Manage My Alerts.**

3. **Select the proper alert name link.**

   The Manage My Alerts on this Site page appears with all the options you viewed when you first created the alert. Change the settings as desired.

   Didn't set the alert to begin with? You can still read through the settings and change the choices (see the preceding steps list). Your changes don't affect the Alert settings for others if the alert was created for multiple users at the same time.

4. **Click OK to modify the alert with your new settings or Delete to delete the alert.**

   Deleting an alert that was created for you doesn't delete the alert from other users who are in the group the alert was created for.

TIP

If you're the site administrator, you can manage the alerts of everyone on the site by clicking the User Alerts link on the Site Administration section of the Site Settings page.

When the event occurs that matches your alert — for example, the time or location of a calendar event change — you receive an email in your inbox. The email notification you receive is based on a template. These templates can be modified by your administrator, so they can provide for more detail.

Staying in Sync with Skype for Business

Skype for Business is an application that instantly connects with others in your organization. When Skype for Business is integrated with SharePoint, you have access to a user just by hovering the mouse cursor over his or her name in Share-Point, as shown in Figure 16-10.

FIGURE 16-10:
Hovering over a
user in Share-
Point provides a
Skype for
Business pop-up
window.

Skype for Business shows the status of the person and if he or she is available. For example, if a user is available, a green bar appears next to the user's picture. Using Skype for Business, you can send an email, chat, call, schedule a meeting, or view the person's profile.

TIP

Skype for Business is included with Office 365; however, if you're using Share-Point On-Premises, then it is only available if the IT team configured it when setting up SharePoint.

Chapter 17

Taking SharePoint Mobile

Mobile devices quickly took the world by storm. We have grown so attached to our smartphones that we can barely remember what it was to not have it with us. We check email, text, browse the web, view status updates, and generally stay connected whenever and wherever we choose. We no longer get that nagging feeling that we need to remember to do something when we get back to the office. When something comes up, we deal with it and then carry on with what we were doing. And of course, there are always those times when we choose to just turn off our smartphones and revert to the past.

In this chapter, you explore the mobile aspects of SharePoint. SharePoint 2016 has been particularly designed to work with mobile devices such as smartphones and tablets. You see how to create special views in your apps for mobile devices and how to target channels toward specific devices such as a tablet or smartphone. This chapter also shows you how to push content to devices and set items in lists with location information. Finally, you see how you can view Office documents such as Word, Excel, OneNote, and PowerPoint on your mobile device.

Viewing SharePoint on a Mobile Device

Every SharePoint site has the ability to be viewed by a mobile device. A SharePoint feature called Mobile Browser View makes it possible. When you activate the feature, three different site views become available to mobile devices:

>> **Classic** view shows the site with HTML links to the different navigation components.

>> **Contemporary** view shows the navigation components of the site using tiles that you click on to navigate.

>> **Full Screen UI** is the same view of SharePoint you would see on a regular desktop computer, only rendered in your smaller mobile browser.

The three different mobile browser views are represented in Figure 17-1, which is published on Microsoft's TechNet site.

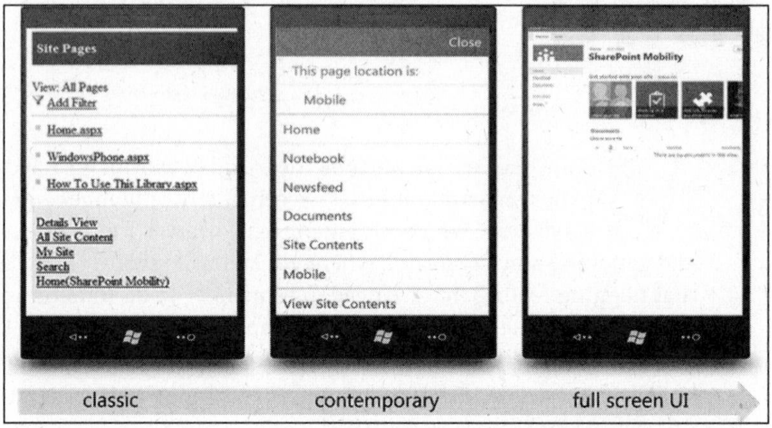

FIGURE 17-1: Three mobile browser views.

classic   contemporary   full screen UI

Image courtesy of Microsoft's TechNet site:
http://technet.microsoft.com/en-us/library/fp161351.aspx

Creating Views for Small Screens

When you create a view for your app data, you select whether it should be available on a mobile device. You can even select if the view should be the default view for a mobile device. Chapter 9 walks you through creating a new view and discusses the Mobile section on the Create View page.

The bottom of the app settings page (such as List Settings or Library Settings) shows the views available for the app. A column shows whether the view is available for mobile devices and if it is the default view. Figure 17-2 shows these columns on the List Settings page for an app.

Views

A view of a list allows you to see a particular selection of items or to see the items sorted in a particular order. Views currently configured for this list:

View (click to edit)	Show In	Default View	Mobile View	Default Mobile View
All Items	All	✓	✓	✓

▪ Create view

Targeting Devices Using Channels

If you have a complex SharePoint site, you might want to render it depending on the device being used to view it. You can do this using the Device Channels functionality of SharePoint. Using Device Channels, you can dictate that certain devices should use certain master pages and style sheets. When a particular device, such as an iPad, Android tablet, or Windows Phone, browses the site, it displays in a customized way for that type of device.

WARNING

Creating custom master pages and style sheets is a very technical task and should be done by experienced web developers.

Note: Device Channels are only available for sites with the SharePoint Server Publishing Infrastructure feature activated.

Click the Device Channels link in the Look and Feel section of the Site Settings page to create and configure channels. When you create a new channel, you provide a name, an alias for reference in website design code, a description, and inclusion rules. A web designer can then build the SharePoint master page to display differently based on the channels available. Developing master pages and referencing Device Channels in code is beyond the scope of this book, but you should know that the option is available when you need to customize SharePoint. The result is that SharePoint displays differently, depending on different channels of devices.

Pushing Content to a Smartphone

Push technology was made famous by the addictive Blackberry devices of the early 2000s. When an email was sent, it would push the message to the mobile Blackberry device. Push technology has become standard and is available with the Microsoft Exchange email server (part of Office 365).

SharePoint 2016 brings push technology to the next level by pushing alerts to your smartphone from a SharePoint site. For example, after you register a smartphone with a SharePoint site, you can receive instant updates on your phone when events occur. For example, SharePoint can push a notification email to your smartphone when a new item is added to an app. Alerts and tracking of content are covered in Chapters 15 and 16.

Keeping Track of Locations

SharePoint 2016 includes a column type specifically designed for keeping track of a geographic location. Have you ever browsed a mapping service such as Bing Maps or Google Maps and seen the pushpins marking specific locations? This is exactly the type of data the new column type is designed to store.

A scenario where this would be valuable would be when a field worker needs to track location information along with other data. For Ken's graduate thesis (more than a decade ago), he developed a field biology application that collected data using a handheld GPS. At the time, SharePoint was not yet available, so he uploaded the data to an Excel spreadsheet. That same application today could store the data directly, and instantly, to a SharePoint list using a mobile device. (On one field trip with a biologist in the San Francisco wetlands, he nearly lost his leg to a muddy sinkhole and can remember dipping the device underwater. Having saved his leg, he didn't really care much about the data until he made it back to campus.)

Ken spent months developing his application to collect data and store it. Share-Point, along with modern cellular technology and powerful smartphones, makes a similar scenario available right out of the box.

Viewing Office Documents on Your Phone or Tablet

Opening an Office document on a mobile phone is still an amazing feature for us. We met with a colleague the other day who had a question about a Word document we had been working on. We weren't anywhere near our work computers and didn't have a laptop with us, so we pulled out our iPhones and were able to open the document directly from our SharePoint Online site. As long as you have a device that is capable of contacting the Internet, you can view documents right in the browser.

This goes for laptop and desktop computers, too. If you happen to be at a computer that doesn't have Office installed on it, you can still open and edit Office documents right in the web browser. This capability is made possible through Office Online, which can be configured to provide this capability to SharePoint 2016 sites.

TIP

Microsoft has embraced the fact that people use all types of devices including iPhones, iPads, Android tablets and phones, Macs, and PCs. You can find mobile versions of your favorite office apps, such as Word, Excel, PowerPoint, OneNote, and Exchange for each of these devices. Going into detail about these Office 365 Mobile Apps is beyond the scope of this book — which is why Rosemarie is currently writing another book called *Office 365 Apps For Dummies*. Look for it in stores soon!

Viewing a Word document in the web browser is shown in Figure 17-3.

The important thing to remember about SharePoint 2016 and mobile devices is that there isn't a lot to remember. You can access and work with your SharePoint content using a mobile device in much the same way you would from your desktop. The experience is different, but your content is the same.

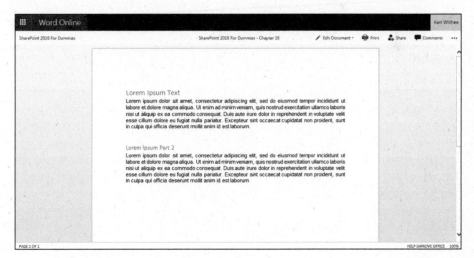

FIGURE 17-3:
Viewing a Word document in the web browser.

5
Managing Enterprise Content

Chapter 18

Sharing and Approving Content

You may remember Bill Gates proclaiming that "content is king" back in the mid-1990s. Nearly two decades since, it still couldn't be more true. The rate at which modern organizations are generating digital content is staggering. One of SharePoint's sweet spots is managing content, which is why many organizations adopt the platform in the first place.

In this chapter, you delve into dealing with documents in SharePoint. You find out how to get documents into SharePoint and share them with others. You discover SharePoint apps based on libraries and how they are used to manage documents. Finally, you see how to approve and publish content that you want to display on web pages.

Sharing Your Documents

You're probably familiar with *network file shares:* the file systems that enable people to upload files to a shared network drive so that other people can access and use them. File shares, when they were invented, revolutionized the ability of organizations to keep files in relatively secure locations and manage who had access. But SharePoint has done the file sharing one (okay, a whole bunch) better.

SharePoint apps based on libraries let you store and share files securely, and they also add features that help you manage things such as *document workflow* (the processes that let people edit, comment on, and approve documents) and *version histories* (what happened to a file, and who did what). And although file shares give you one path through folders to your document, SharePoint Library apps give you other paths to expose content. You can access documents directly through the browser, you can display them up in Web Parts, and you can sort and filter them with their metadata and content types. And with Library apps, you can expose files by their title, not just their filename.

Library apps give you multiple choices about how the documents get into them, too. You can save a document to a Library app using a Microsoft Office client such as Word or Excel, or you can email documents to Library apps or drag and drop from Windows Explorer. And you can create documents directly in the app.

No matter how you get your documents into SharePoint's Library apps, just get them there — it's so much easier to share documents with your coworkers in an app than it is to use file shares or email attachments.

REMEMBER

SharePoint apps can be confusing. An app based on a list is designed to store data in columns. An app based on a library is designed to store documents and data about those documents in columns. SharePoint 2016 tries to simplify the whole discussion of list and library and just calls everything an app. When you create the app, you give it a name and choose an app template. From that point on, you just call your app by its name. For example, you might create the Sales Pitch app. The app is designed to hold sales pitch documents. Because the app holds documents, it uses the Document Library app template. After your app is created, you wouldn't call it the "Sales Pitch app based on the Document Library App template." That would be a mouthful! If you're a seasoned SharePoint user, this new app stuff might take you a while to get your head around. It did us! But when you realize that most users don't think in terms of lists and libraries, and instead think about what a list or library does, it really is much easier to just call everything an app.

TECHNICAL STUFF

An app can also be built from scratch by a web developer as a standalone app, so such an app isn't based on a list or a library.

Getting Your Documents into an App

SharePoint 2016 gives you many ways to get your files into an app. In this section, we show you how to upload your documents. You can upload them one at a time or a whole bunch in one swoop. You can drag and drop them right into the web browser window or save them to an app directly from your Office applications. You can even upload documents using the familiar Windows Explorer window. With all these options, you have no excuse to keep your files on your hard drive!

TIP

A Library app isn't restricted to only Microsoft Word files. Library apps can contain many file types, including Excel, PDF, and Visio files. Even web pages are stored in Library apps.

Uploading a single document

When you have a single document to upload to an app, you can do so easily through the browser. The easiest way is to simply drag the file onto the app and drop it, as shown in Figure 18-1.

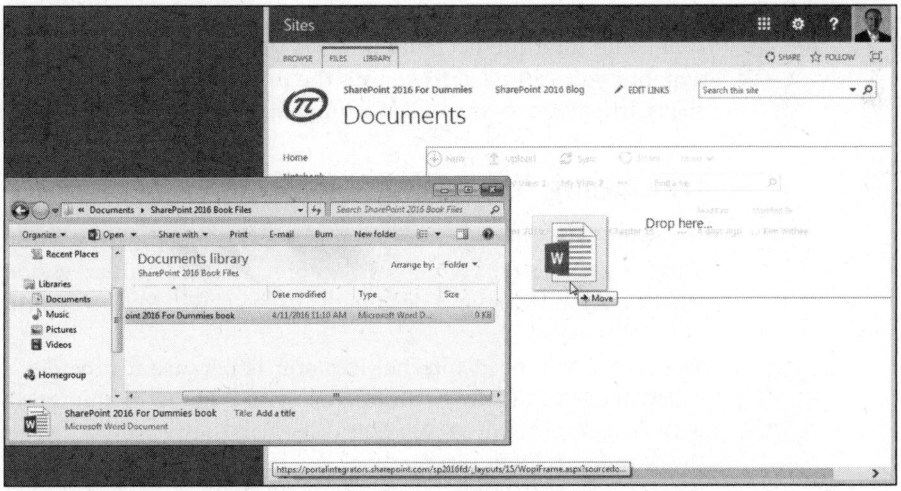

FIGURE 18-1: Dragging and dropping a document into an app.

WARNING

Drag and drop doesn't always work with all browsers. Since the last version of SharePoint, Microsoft has made big strides in adapting to the quirks of various browsers, but if drag and drop doesn't work as expected, you might need to try a different browser or an alternative way of uploading your files. One way to know if your browser will work is to look for the words *Drag Files Here.* When you have the app open, you should see the text *+ New Document or Drag Files Here.* If your browser doesn't have the ability to drag and drop files, you'll see only the *+ New Document* link.

In addition to dragging and dropping files into an app, you can also click the Upload Document button on the Files tab or click the + New Document link at the top of the app.

You can also send documents to an app via email. If your SharePoint farm administrator has configured SharePoint 2016 to accept incoming email, individual apps can be given their own email address. When someone sends a document as an attachment to that email address, it's uploaded to the app. This approach works well when you need to allow people outside your organization to place documents in an app. We recommend creating a workflow to move the incoming documents out of the Collection app and into an Approved Documents app after they have been approved and to delete them if they are rejected. This creates a process for ensuring the apps your users see have been reviewed and are acceptable.

Uploading multiple documents

There may be times when you have multiple documents to upload. You can drag and drop multiple documents into an app in the same way as a single document. To select multiple documents, hold down the Ctrl key as you click documents to select as many as you want.

Uploading multiple documents saves you time getting the documents into your app, but you still need to go into the properties for each document and set it for that particular document. Unfortunately, you can't batch-upload for properties.

Uploading files using Windows Explorer

If you use Internet Explorer, you can also upload documents to your app using Windows Explorer. (Windows Explorer is the familiar window that you open whenever you work with documents on your Windows computer.)

The reason you need Internet Explorer is because it provides special technology called ActiveX that allows interaction with Windows Explorer. If you have an issue with dragging and dropping files directly into the browser, then you can try using the Windows Explorer method. As long as you are using Internet Explorer (32-bit), that is. If you don't use Internet Explorer (32-bit), the link to upload using Windows Explorer won't appear. However, when we tried dragging and dropping files directly into the browser using non-Microsoft browsers, we had no problems and didn't feel sad that the Windows Explorer method was not available. Welcome to the wonderful world of SharePoint!

To upload multiple documents to an app using Windows Explorer, follow these steps:

1. **Open Internet Explorer (32-bit) and browse to the app where you want to upload your files.**

   For example, click the Documents link on the Quick Launch to go to the Documents app.

2. **Click the Files tab in the Ribbon and click the Upload Document button.**

   The Add a Document window appears.

3. **Click the Upload Files Using Windows Explorer Instead link, as shown in Figure 18-2.**

   A Windows Explorer window appears with a network path to the SharePoint app.

   Alternatively, click the Browse button to browse for a single file on your computer.

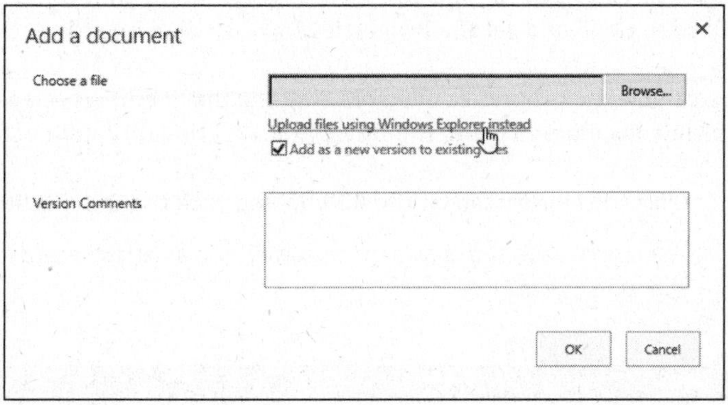

FIGURE 18-2:
The Add
a Document
dialog box.

Add a document   ×

Choose a file

[   ] Browse...

Upload files using Windows Explorer instead
☑ Add as a new version to existing files

Version Comments

[   ]

[OK]   [Cancel]

4. **Drag documents into the app just like you would drag documents into a shared folder.**

   The documents are uploaded to your app in SharePoint. You can now browse the documents in the web interface and set the properties for each document. If you already have the app open, then simply refresh the browser window to see the documents.

TECHNICAL STUFF

SharePoint 2016 uses a number of protocols to allow you to access libraries as folders with Windows Explorer. In our experience, this feature either works or it doesn't. If it doesn't, most organizations aren't willing to spend any energy to figure out why.

A green icon appears in the app next to the name of each of the files you just uploaded, letting you know it is a new document. By default, this icon appears on all newly uploaded files for a period of three days.

REMEMBER

Your SharePoint farm administrator can block certain file types, such as executable (.exe) files. The reason is to prevent a malicious person from uploading a virus to SharePoint, because any user that clicked the virus file would run the virus. If you try to upload a blocked file type, you see a message letting you know that the file has been blocked from uploading by the administrator.

Updating document properties using Quick Edit view

You may have noticed that SharePoint didn't prompt you to enter the properties for the files that you uploaded. When you upload a single document using the Browse button, you're prompted to enter the properties for the document. When you perform a multiple upload or drag and drop files, you aren't prompted to enter the properties for the documents. This is true even for properties that are required. The result is that you have documents in your SharePoint app, but you still need to go and set the properties for each document.

You can update properties quickly using the Quick Edit view. To edit properties for multiple documents using the Quick Edit functionality, follow these steps:

1. **Click the Library tab on the Ribbon and click the Quick Edit button.**

The app reloads and shows the documents in an editable grid format, as shown in Figure 18-3.

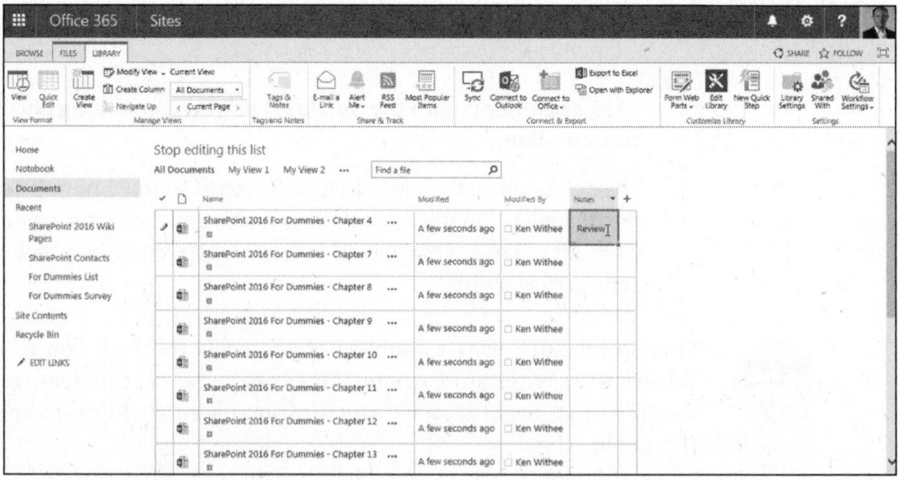

FIGURE 18-3: Editing documents in an app using Quick Edit.

MOVING DOCUMENTS IN AND AROUND SHAREPOINT

Just because you uploaded your document into one app doesn't mean it's stuck there forever. Sometimes you want to move documents to a different app. You can use the Open with Explorer button located on the Library tab of the Ribbon to quickly move documents from one app into another. But unfortunately, Windows Explorer moves the files only, and not any associated metadata. So for that reason, investigate the Save Document Library as Template link on the Library Settings page and the copy and move function of the Site Content and Structure tool. The Site Content and Structure tool is located under the Site Administration section of the Site Settings page. However, the tool is only available if the SharePoint Server Publishing Infrastructure feature is activated for the site collection.

Windows Explorer is great if you need to upload a lot of documents into an app. But resist the urge to take all the files from your shared drives and to copy them into apps with Windows Explorer. That's usually a recipe for disaster because most people store files in folders and re-creating that folder structure in a SharePoint app makes it very hard to find files. (Although folders have some uses in SharePoint, navigation isn't one of them.) Instead, consider putting many files at the top level of an app and creating views based on metadata. The views can be added to different pages so that different people or groups of people see the app in a different way, but the documents are all in the same location.

2. **Place your cursor in the field you want to update and make the changes.**

You can also add new columns on the fly by clicking the + button in the right-most column.

3. **Move your cursor off the cell you updated, and your changes are saved.**

See Chapter 9 for more details on working with Quick Edit.

Uploading documents into a folder

You can use folders within your apps as a means to organize your documents. We show you how to create a folder and upload files into it, but we urge you to first read the sidebar, "Why folders in SharePoint are evil."

Perhaps you have an app and you have a subset of files that only supervisors should see. You could put those files in a separate app and set the permissions on it. But say you already have one app set up the way you like and it seems silly to create another one. Instead, you can use a folder to separate the restricted files from the rest of the files in the app.

WARNING

WHY FOLDERS IN SHAREPOINT ARE EVIL

Resist the urge to use folders in your apps; this file share paradigm generally causes nothing but problems. One reason to use SharePoint instead of a file share to begin with is so that you can add properties to describe your documents. Properties allow you to view your documents in different ways. If you dump your files in folders just like they were arranged on the file share, ignoring properties, you probably won't be very satisfied with your SharePoint experience.

As well, nested folders in SharePoint are just as hard to navigate as nested folders in file shares (and nested URLs in folders inside apps get unwieldy quickly). Instead of replicating your file structure in SharePoint, we recommend that you flatten the folder hierarchies by replacing them with views. If you decide to use folders and find yourself going more than two layers deep, stop and ask yourself if you should create another app instead.

The only reason to use a folder in an app is to separate a group of documents to give them separate permissions. For pretty much everything else, we recommend that you use properties to organize your documents.

To create a folder within an app:

1. **Browse to the app where you want to create the folder.**

2. **Click the Files tab in the Ribbon and click the New Folder button.**

   The Create a New Folder dialog box appears. If you don't see the New Folder button, folders are disabled for the library. Use the Advanced Settings option in Library Settings to enable or disable folders in your app.

3. **Type the name of the folder in the Name text box and click the Save button.**

   The folder appears in the app.

To upload files into the folder, follow these steps:

1. **Click the folder name to navigate inside it and click the Upload Document button on the Files tab of the Ribbon.**

   The Upload Document window appears.

2. **Browse to the document you want to upload to the folder.**

3. **Make sure the Destination Folder text box lists the folder where you want to upload the document, as shown in Figure 18-4.**

   If the folder is incorrect, click the Choose Folder button to select the right folder.

4. **Click OK to upload your document to the folder.**

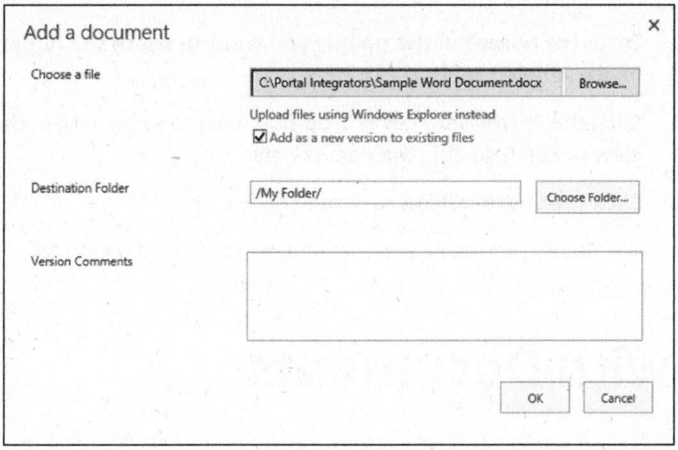

Add a document

Choose a file	C:\Portal Integrators\Sample Word Document.docx	Browse...

Upload files using Windows Explorer instead

☑ Add as a new version to existing files

Destination Folder	/My Folder/	Choose Folder...

Version Comments

OK	Cancel

FIGURE 18-4:
Uploading a document to a folder in an app.

TIP

You can work with folders the same way as you work with documents. That is, the rules about working with properties and the Ribbon also apply to folders.

Follow these steps to restrict access to your folder so that only certain groups can access it:

1. **Click the ellipsis next to the folder and choose Share, as shown in Figure 18-5.**

The Permissions page appears. Note that the ability to share folders must be enabled. If it is not enabled, then you must manually disable the limited access lockdown mode feature for the site.

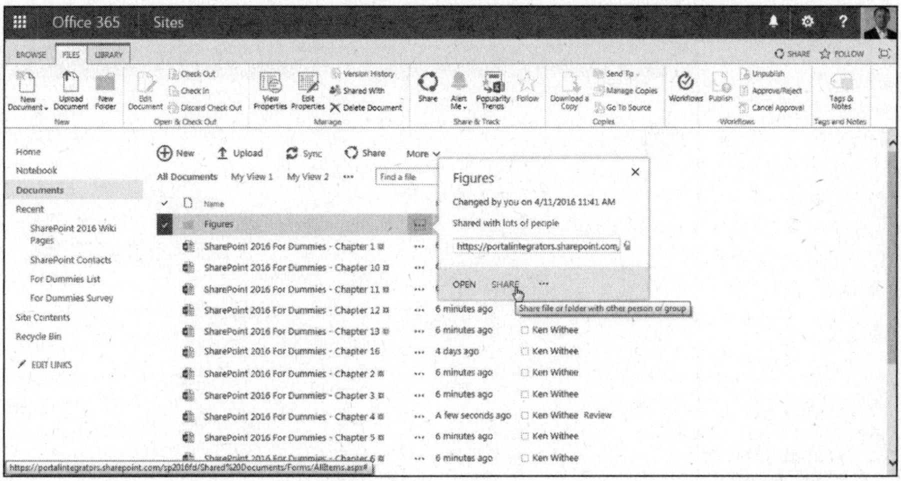

FIGURE 18-5:
Sharing a folder in an app.

2. **Enter the names of the people you want to share the folder with in the Invite People text box.**

3. **Click the Permission Level drop-down list to set whether they can only view or can also edit the documents.**

4. **Click the Share button to share the folder.**

   We discuss permissions management in detail in Chapter 14.

Working with Documents

After you upload your documents to an app, you need to be able to work with them. This includes adding descriptive properties and letting other teammates know where the documents are stored.

SharePoint 2016 provides two methods for working with documents. Each document has a set of actions contained in the Ribbon that can be targeted to the document. In addition, you can click the ellipsis next to the document to see a menu of actions for the document. For example, you can check out a document, edit it, and check it back in.

Using the ellipsis

Accessing the menu for a specific document is accomplished by clicking the ellipsis next to the document, as shown in Figure 18-6.

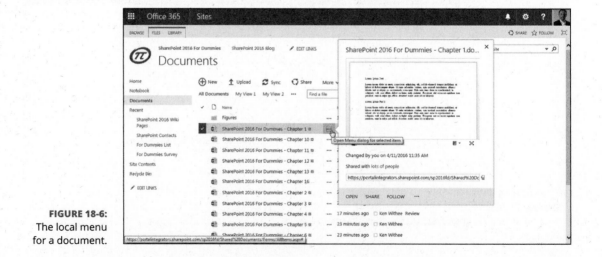

FIGURE 18-6:
The local menu for a document.

With the ellipsis menu, you can see key information about the document, such as who it is shared with and the URL. You can also open the document to edit it, share it with others, or follow that particular document. You can use another ellipsis to open the Edit menu for the document. The second ellipsis is shown in Figure 18-7.

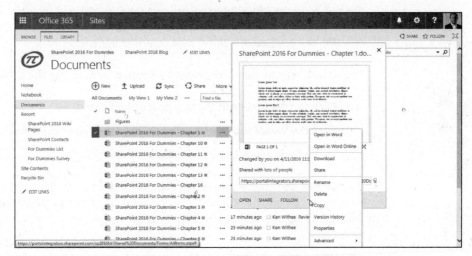

FIGURE 18-7:
The second
ellipsis contains
the Edit menu for
the document.

Using the Edit menu (second ellipsis), you can view and edit properties, check out the file, view compliance details, manage workflows, download a copy, view the sharing information, manage versioning, and delete the document. Some options in the Edit menu depend on how your app has been configured. For example, if versioning is enabled for the app, you see a Version History option in the Edit menu. If versioning is not enabled, then you won't see the Version History option. All items and documents in apps follow this same paradigm. The actual options depend on the type of app you're using and how you configured it.

TIP

Your organization can add custom menu items to the menus, so don't be surprised if your menus look different than the one shown in Figure 18-7. The point is that you can use the ellipsis menus to access a list of actions that you can take on the selected document.

Editing a document's properties

You can use a document ellipsis menu or the Ribbon to view and edit a document's properties. By default, SharePoint 2016 asks only for these two properties:

>> **Name:** The filename. For example, if you upload a myspreadsheet.xlsx file, that's the value you see as the filename.

>> **Title:** A caption that describes the document. If a title already exists in the document, SharePoint uses that. Otherwise, you can enter your own descriptive title.

The app owner can add more properties to describe the document. For example, the owner might add a Category property that allows you to apply a category to the document. Properties are actually just new columns that you add to your app. We describe the process of adding new columns in Chapter 8.

The easiest way to view a document's properties is to use the Ribbon:

1. **Click the document in the app so it's highlighted.**

2. **Click the View Properties button on the Files tab of the Ribbon.**

   The document's properties are displayed.

Figure 18-8 shows the properties page for a document. This window includes its own View tab on the Ribbon. The View tab includes buttons for managing the document and actions for working with the document.

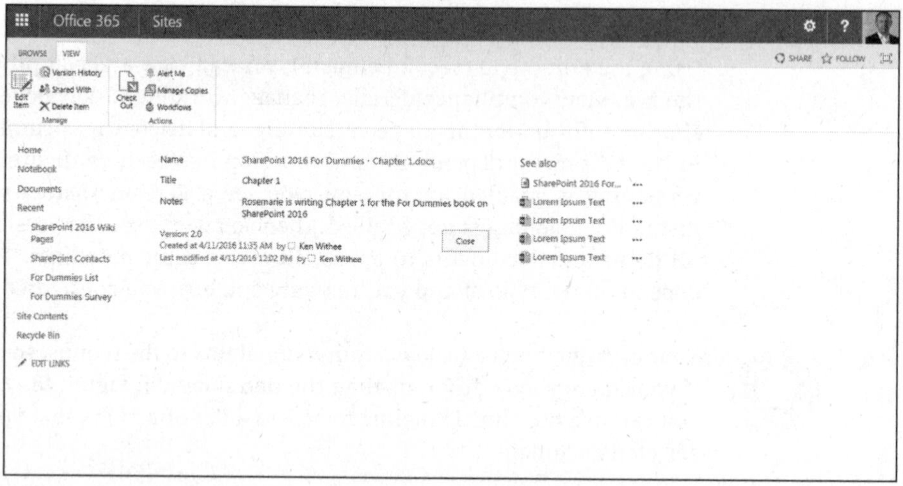

FIGURE 18-8:
The properties
page for a
document.

Checking documents in and out

The Ribbon displays many of the same document actions as the ellipsis menu. One of the advantages of using the Ribbon is that you can use it to take actions on multiple documents at the same time. For example, say you want to check out three documents at one time. Here's how you can do it with the Ribbon:

1. **In your app, select the check box (left most column) next to each document that you want to check out.**

2. **Click the Files tab of the Ribbon and click the Check Out button.**

3. **Click OK at the confirmation prompt.**

   The documents are checked out, and a small green checked-out arrow appears on the document icons.

Alternatively, you can use a document's ellipsis menu to access the Check Out menu command.

You may be thinking, "That's great, but why would I want to check out a document?" To us, checking out — and its counterpart, checking in — is just good document editing etiquette. What better way to let others know that you're making changes to a document than by checking it out? Checking out a document sets the Checked Out flag to Yes and stores the name of the person who checked out the document. Of course, always remember to check in documents when your edits are complete.

An app can be configured to force a person to check out a document before it can be edited. This is achieved on the Versioning Settings page located in the Library Settings.

You can check out a single document at a time in SharePoint 2016. To check out a document, follow these steps:

1. **In an app, click the ellipsis next to a document, and then click the second ellipsis that appears on the new window to display the Edit menu. Then scroll down to the Advanced fly-out.**

2. **Click the Check Out option to check out the document, as shown in Figure 18-9.**

   SharePoint returns to the listing of documents, and a green check-out icon is displayed next to the document to let everyone know you have checked it out.

3. **You can now edit the document in Word Online or open it in Word on your local computer and edit it from there. When you are done, check the document back in using the same process but click the Check In option instead of Check Out.**

Documents that are checked out show an arrow in the document type icon. As shown in Figure 18-10, the top item is checked out, whereas the next two aren't.

If you want to see who has a document checked out, you have to look at the Checked Out To column in the app view. This column is displayed by default. You can customize views and rearrange columns. (We discuss working with views in Chapter 9.)

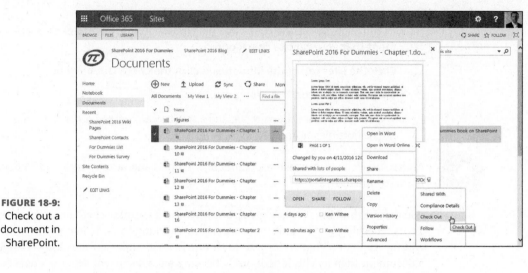

	Name		Modified	Modified By	Notes
🗔	Figures	...	29 minutes ago	☐ Ken Withee	
📄	SharePoint 2016 For Dummies - Chapter 1 ⊠	...	8 minutes ago	☐ Ken Withee	Rosemarie is writing Chapter 1 for the For Dummies book on SharePoint 2016
📄	SharePoint 2016 For Dummies - Chapter 10 ⊠	...	35 minutes ago	☐ Ken Withee	
📄	SharePoint 2016 For Dummies - Chapter 11 ⊠	...	35 minutes ago	☐ Ken Withee	

To check in a document after you're done making your changes, you can repeat the steps you followed earlier in this section to check out the document, only in Step 2, choose the Check In option from the menu. You are asked to provide a comment and choose if you want to retain the check out after you check in the document. This is because you might want to check in a document as you are working on it and pass a milestone. Think of a check-in as a snapshot of the document at that state. You can use the Files tab of the Ribbon to check in documents as well.

If you change your mind and want to pretend that the check-out never happened, you can click the Discard Check Out button instead of checking in the document. This can be useful if you accidentally checked out the wrong document or made changes that you wish you wouldn't have made. When you discard the check out, the document reverts back to the state it was in before you checked it out.

Sending a link to your document

To share your document with others, they must know where to find the document. One way to do so is to send them the web address of the team site or the app. You can also send them a link directly to the document itself.

To obtain the URL to a document, follow these steps:

1. **Click the ellipsis next to the document to view the pop-up window.**

   The document information is displayed, including the URL.

2. **Highlight the URL and press Ctrl+C to copy it.**

3. **Paste the URL by pressing Ctrl+P.**

Alternatively, if you want to email a link, click the ellipsis and click the Share button and then choose Shared With. The dialog box shows you who has access to the document. From here, you can choose to email a link to the people that have access to the document.

As long as your team members have network access and permissions to the document, they can click the link and open the file.

Viewing documents in the browser

Office Online Server is a sister product to SharePoint that enables you to view and edit documents in the browser. Office Online Server is installed separately from SharePoint, and then configured to provide the in-browser document capability to SharePoint.

TIP

Office Online Server is preconfigured with Office 365 so you don't even really need to know it exists. If you are using SharePoint Online, part of Office 365, then you already have Office Online and can edit documents right from your browser. This magic happens because Office Online Server is already configured to work with SharePoint Online (because Microsoft engineers did this for you).

If Office Online Server is installed and properly activated in your team site, Microsoft Office documents such as Word and PowerPoint files open in the browser. The experience happens automatically, so you just have to click the filename in the app to open the file. Figure 18-11 shows a Word document displayed using the Word Online.

Office Online Server is especially useful when you don't want to install the Office 2016 clients on your local computer. It also makes quickly browsing document contents a breeze because the file opens right in the browser.

TIP

Office Online Server is also available in the consumer version of OneDrive as well as Dropbox. Using OneDrive or Dropbox, you can open your Office documents right in the browser. And each has a free version available!

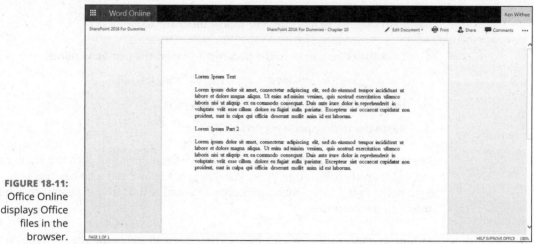

FIGURE 18-11:
Office Online
displays Office
files in the
browser.

Using Office 2016

You can access many of the commands mentioned in this chapter directly within Office 2016 clients, such as Word and Excel. For example, if you click the File Ribbon in any Office 2016 application and click Save or Save As, you see your SharePoint Library apps and OneDrive as options where you can save the document. This is a shift from previous versions of Office where you were prompted to save your document locally and had to dig to find the cloud-based storage locations. Now, cloud-based storage is the primary option, and you have to dig to save the document locally! Which you can do, by the way, by choosing This PC down at the bottom of the save locations list.

The Info tab on the File menu in Office 2016 clients provides a wealth of information regarding the file's status, properties, and history in SharePoint.

Recovering Deleted Documents

It is often said that SharePoint delivers on the promise of making people more productive through software. Although that's not always true, one feature of SharePoint that truly delivers is the Recycle Bin. When you delete a document from an app, it isn't gone forever. Nope. The document just moves to a holding place in your site — the Recycle Bin.

Go ahead and try it. Go to an app and delete a document. You can use the ellipsis menu or the Manage group on the Ribbon to access the Delete command. Either way, you're prompted to confirm the deletion, and then your document appears in the Recycle Bin.

TIP

The Recycle Bin works for items in apps that use the Custom List app template as well.

Follow these steps to restore a document from the Recycle Bin to its original location:

1. **Go to the Recycle Bin by clicking the Settings gear icon and choosing Site Contents.**

   The Site Contents page is displayed.

2. **Click the Recycle Bin button in the upper-right corner to display the Recycle Bin.**

3. **Select the deleted document, and then click the Restore Selection link, as shown in Figure 18-12. Click OK to confirm the restoration.**

   The file is restored to the app.

You can click the Delete Selection link in the Recycle Bin to remove the file from your Recycle Bin. Doing so, however, doesn't permanently delete the file. Instead, the file is moved to another Recycle Bin that can be accessed by the site collection administrator.

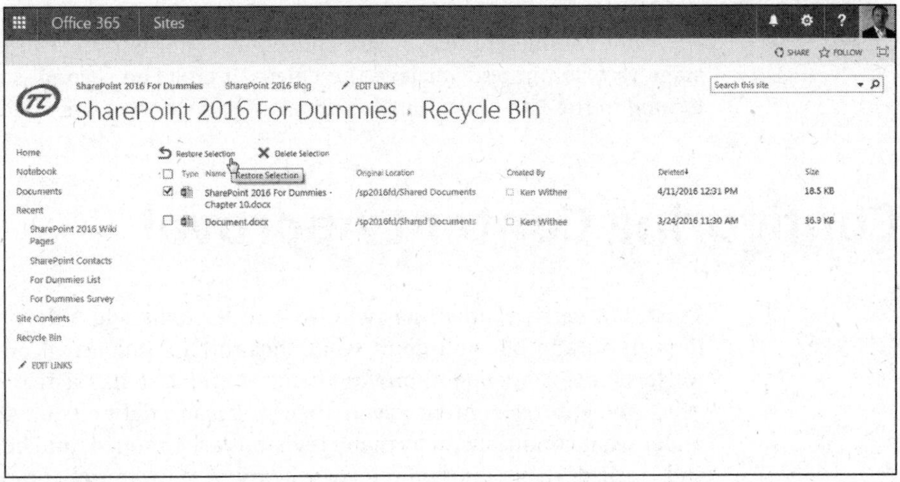

FIGURE 18-12:
Restoring a document from the Recycle Bin.

If you're the site collection administrator, you can follow these steps to access the administrator's Recycle Bin:

1. **Log in to the site as the site collection administrator.**

   Your SharePoint administrator in IT can look up this account information.

2. **Click the Settings gear icon and choose Site Settings.**

   The Site Settings page appears.

3. **In the Site Collection Administration section, click the Recycle Bin link.**

   Because you are the Site Collection Administrator, you can see items deleted from all sites within the site collection. If you don't find what you are looking for, you can also check the second-stage recycle bin. Yes, there is a second stage to deleting a document forever, which means you can no longer use the digital equivalent of the dog-ate-my-homework excuse!

4. **Click the items you want to restore and click Restore Selection.**

   The items are restored.

Files remain in the site collection Recycle Bin for a period of 30 days or until they're deleted by the administrator, whichever comes first. When removed from the Recycle Bin, the fate of your documents depends on your company's business continuity management plan. That's a fancy way to say, how does your IT team back up data? SharePoint stores your documents in databases. An administrator can connect to a backed-up copy of the database and select individual documents to restore.

TIP

A second-stage recycle bin is at the site collection level. If a user deletes a document or item and goes directly into the Recycle Bin and also deletes it from there, all is not completely lost. A site collection administrator can go to the second-stage recycle bin and retrieve the deleted item. The second-stage recycle bin is located in the Site Collection Administration section of the Site Settings page.

Configuring Content Approval

Trust, but verify: Sometimes you want to let folks add a document or create an item in an app but you don't want those items unleashed on an unsuspecting world before someone approves them. SharePoint has a few ways to help you enact and enforce content governance policies to define what gets published and under what conditions, how many revisions are retained, and how they're secured and tracked. Depending on the complexity of your approval process, you can use the standard content approval option, or you can create a more sophisticated — and custom — approval workflow. Using workflow to approve documents and items is discussed in Chapter 21.

Content approval is approval-light; it's a publishing function that you turn on or off at the app level, and it has just a handful of configuration settings. Content approval — also called *moderation* — doesn't include item routing or notifications, and it doesn't facilitate reviews and commenting. Content approval just ensures that drafts and new uploaded content don't get published to your app until someone with some authority says it's okay. The content approval process controls who can see those documents until they're approved.

Content approval also can specify (in the case of documents) whether items must be checked out before they can be edited. And content approval can hide draft documents from everyone except the item author and those users with approve permissions on the app. (Contrast this with draft item security on apps without content approval enabled in which you can limit views only to users with app-level Read permissions or users with app-level Edit permissions.)

This is a subtle distinction, but specifying that only the item author and users with approve permissions can view items means that the author can check in an item without exposing it to the view of other readers or editors until it's formally published and approved. We find this useful in cases when we have multiple authorized contributors to an app and we want to keep them from seeing each other's work until someone (the approver) says it's okay. This also gives me a way to let authors work on drafts without readers looking over their shoulders (few things are more frustrating than editorial feedback on something you're still working on!).

Turning on content approval

By default, content approval is turned off and (usually) any user with Read access can see Draft items in most apps. Sites created with the publishing site template, however, already have content approval turned on in the Pages app.

To turn on and configure content approval, follow these steps:

1. **Navigate to your app's Settings Page (Library Settings or List Settings) and click the Versioning Settings link.**

   The Versioning Settings page appears.

2. **Select the Yes radio button below Require Content Approval for Submitted Items.**

   You see options to retain versions, specify who can see drafts, and in library-based apps — document check-out options.

   Notice that the options below Who Should See Draft Items in This Document Library switches to the Only Users Who Can Approve Items (And the Author of the Item) option as soon as you select the Yes radio button to require content approval for submitted items, as shown in Figure 18-13.

You need to decide whether readers, editors, or only authors and approvers can see drafts. We usually enable content approval partly because we don't want to expose items to just anyone before they meet some level of credibility or *done-ness*. So we select the Only Users Who Can Approve Items (And the Author of the Item) option.

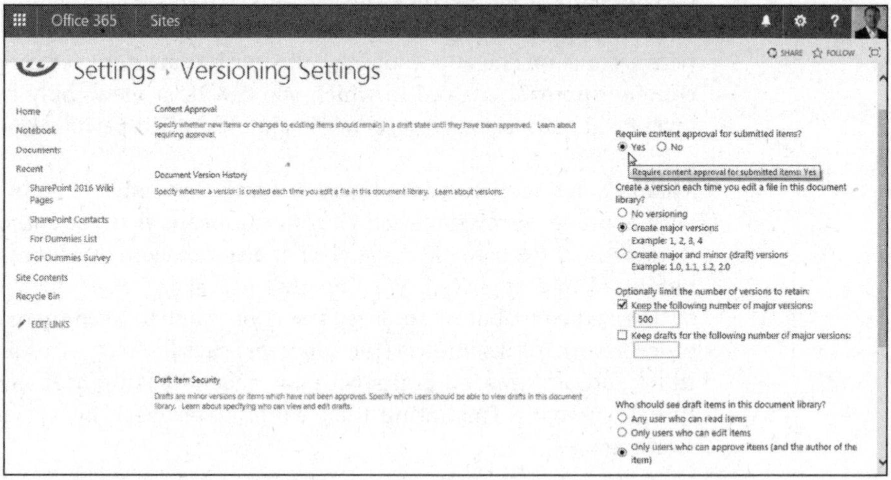

FIGURE 18-13:
The Draft Item Security settings change after you select Yes under Require Content Approval for Submitted Items.

3. **Verify the Document Version History settings in the Document Version History section.**

   You can specify versions *without* turning on content approval. A major version is created when you publish a document and a minor version is created when you save a document. You can configure which level of detail you want to set in versioning by choosing None, Major, or Major and Minor.

4. **Click a Draft Item Security option in the Draft Item Security section.**

   TIP

   The security referred to by draft item security — Read, Edit, and Approve — maps to SharePoint's Visitors, Members, and Approvers groups. (See Chapter 14 for details on managing security groups.)

5. **Click a check-out option in the Require Check Out section.**

6. **Click OK to save your changes.**

   You return to the Library or List Settings page from whence you came. The items created in (or changed in) the app are subject to approval (unless you disable content approval later).

   REMEMBER

   If content approval is active, when users add an item to the app, they see a note that items require content approval in the item properties window. After the item is added, it appears in Pending status in the app view until it is approved.

Identifying approvers

You need to specify who the approvers include, generally by adding users to the created Approvers group. (See Chapter 14 for information about groups and permissions.)

Oh, and by the way, content approval isn't just about Big Brother checking someone else's work. You may want to ensure that documents can be checked in and versioned, but that they aren't displayed to readers until they're formally approved. In these cases, you set the same person or people both to create and to approve items. That way, all people in the group can see the item's current version, but the rest of the organization can't see it until it has been approved by someone in the group.

Casting an approving eye

In an app that has approval turned on, when a new document is created and a major version is published, the approval status is marked Pending and designated approvers can approve, pend, or reject the item either from the List view by choosing Files ⇨ Approve/Reject or by using the View Properties window. In either case, when you select Approve/Reject, you're presented with the aptly named Approve/Reject page, as shown in Figure 18-14, with the Pending option selected by default. At this point, you can leave a comment in the Comment text box but leave the item as Pending or you can select the Approved or the Rejected option to approve or reject the item with or without comment. (Rejecting without comment is pretty poor form, though.) The action, name of the person who took the action, and timestamp are recorded in the item's version history.

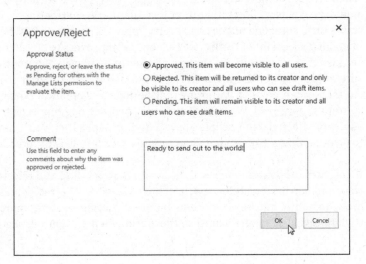

FIGURE 18-14:
The Approve/
Reject window.

You can get a quick view of all your items that are in a pending status using the Site Content and Structure tool. You access the tool from the Site Administration section of the Site Settings page. When in the tool, click the View: Default View drop-down list in the upper-right corner and select Pending Approval. If you are using SharePoint Online, then this option won't be available on the Site Settings page. However, you might still be able to access it by typing `http://<site_url>/_layouts/15/sitemanager.aspx` into your web browser. Content and Structure is the exact link text.

Unless alerts are enabled on the app or the item itself, the item originator won't know you've taken an action until the next time that person is in the app and checks the approval status on the item. We recommend using alerts with content approval unless you have some alternative process where approvers make it part of their daily routine to check for pending items.

Disapproving: Not just for stern parents

Everyone wants approval, but sometimes you don't get it. Sometimes an approver rejects an item. When this happens, the item is changed to Rejected status, and then it's visible only to the author and anyone with permission to manage the app.

When you first enable content approval on an app, all existing items are approved automatically.

Getting alerts on approval/rejection status

When an item is marked Pending with content approval turned on (and no associated approval workflow), that item just sits there, marinating in its own pending status until someone notices and either approves or rejects it. When the app we're managing sees a lot of traffic, we rely on the approvers to check for pending items because they're working in the app all the time anyway. But another way to make sure approvers get the heads-up is to set alerts (see Chapter 16). In addition to alerts, you can create a workflow that periodically emails a person or group until an item is approved. We have found this constant nagging type behavior is actually very effective, and people appreciate it because they don't have to remember to do something. (Approving content with a workflow is covered in Chapter 21.)

If you turn off content approval, be aware that pending and rejected items, which were hidden from public view, are now viewable. We recommend resolving all draft, pending, and rejected items before disabling content approval; it's a dirty trick to reveal someone's draft to the world when she isn't expecting it!

Chapter 19

Finding What You Need with Search

S harePoint search provides a powerful and intuitive mechanism for finding content. Right out of the box, SharePoint lets users search for content and narrow down results. SharePoint search can be configured and fine-tuned to meet the needs of your organization. In this manner, you can think of search as a platform instead of a feature that is either on or off.

In this chapter, we walk you through how search works in SharePoint. You find out how to search for content and refine results. You then explore some of the configuration options available for search and discover how to create your own Search Center site.

Understanding How SharePoint Search Works

Search is an often misunderstood feature in SharePoint. Many users simply think that search is either on or off. In fact, search can be configured and is very robust. For example, the results of a SharePoint search can be tweaked using query rules in order to provide the best possible results for users. Maybe a user searches for *marketing*, but what she is really looking for is the Marketing app, which contains all the official marketing documents for the organization. Using query rules, you can make the Marketing app show up at the top of the search results.

TECHNICAL STUFF

One of the biggest improvements in search in SharePoint is the integration of FAST search. FAST was an Oslo, Norway–based company that Microsoft acquired. In previous versions of SharePoint, FAST search was a separate product. In Share-Point 2016, the FAST technology is baked right into SharePoint. So when you search in SharePoint, you're using FAST technology even if you don't realize it.

Under the covers, SharePoint search is provided through the Search Service application. The Search Service application crawls through content and creates an index. The index is then used to provide results for a search query. (Service applications are administered in Central Administration.)

When a user types a term in the Search text box and presses Enter, the Search Service application consults the index and returns the results in a web page.

If you add a new document or item but can't find it in a search result, then the search service has not yet crawled and indexed the content. The frequency of crawling is set by a farm administrator in Central Administration.

Searching for Content

Searching for content in SharePoint is straightforward. Every site contains a Search text box in the upper-right corner, as shown in Figure 19-1.

To search for content, you simply type your term in the text box and click the magnifying glass to the right of the Search text box. The SharePoint search engine performs a query using your terms and displays the results.

Aside from simply typing in search terms, you can instruct the search engine to do special things in a number of ways when it performs the query. For example, you can use special characters and limit the search results based on properties in SharePoint.

Searching for a string using quotation marks

When you enter multiple terms in the Search text box, the SharePoint search engine looks through the content and returns instances that contain any of those words. If you want a phrase of two or more words (called a *string*), then you need to surround the phrase in quotation marks. For example, the following search query returns any content that contains either the word *Annual* or the word *Report*.

```
Annual Report
```

Search text box

FIGURE 19-1:
The Search text box on a SharePoint site.

If you're looking for content where the words are found together, then you would type the search string in quotation marks.

```
"Annual Report"
```

The search engine takes anything within the quotation marks and looks for that entire string in the content.

Wildcard searches

The asterisk character (*) can be used to represent a wildcard in a search. For example, maybe you need to find a document that you know begins with *Quarter*, but you can't remember if it is *Quarters* or *Quarterly*. You could use the wildcard character to search for everything that begins with the word *Quarter* as follows:

```
Quarter*
```

This search would return everything that begins with the term *Quarter*, including *Quarterly* and *Quarters*.

Along the same lines, you might know that the first word is *Quarterly*, but you don't know if the second word is *Reports* or *Results*. You would then use the quotation marks along with the wildcard character to tell the search engine that you want all content that contains the word *Quarterly* followed by any word that starts with the letter *R*. The query would be as follows:

```
"Quarterly R*"
```

The wildcard character is a very powerful way to expand your search results when you know only a piece of the puzzle instead of an exact term.

Including and excluding terms

You can instruct the search engine to only return results that include a certain word by using the + symbol. For example, you could write your search as:

```
Annual Reports +Marketing
```

The plus symbol says that any content that is returned must have the word *Marketing* in it, in addition to either the word *Annual* or the word *Reports*.

One problem with search is that you often get many more results than you can sift through. You can also exclude specific words to trim your search results. For example, you might be searching for product marketing content, but want to exclude any content that contains the word *internal*. You could write your search as follows:

```
"Product Marketing" -internal
```

The search engine then returns all content that contains either the words *Product* or *Marketing* and removes any content that also contains the word *internal*.

Building compound search queries using Boolean operators

Building compound search queries involves multiple search expressions. You use the Boolean operators to string expressions together into compound queries.

The Boolean operators consist of the following:

>> **AND:** Only returns content when both statements are true.

>> **NOT:** Only returns content where the statement is not true. This is the same thing as using the minus sign, as described in the previous section.

>> **OR:** Returns content when one or more of the statements are true.

TIP

Typing two words in the Search text box is the same thing as typing the first word followed by OR and then typing the second word. Where Boolean operators become valuable is when they are used with parentheses. Boolean operators are often used in combination with parentheses in order to let the search engine know how to group the query statements, as described in the next section.

Getting fancy with the parentheses

The parentheses characters, (and), are used to build compound search queries that use multiple expressions. For example, you might want to search for two key words and narrow the results down by one type of property or another. How would you write all this together in a search term? Wouldn't the search engine get confused? Well, you use parentheses to tell the search engine exactly what you want it to do and when. For example, say you want to search for any content that has the string *For Dummies* or contains the word *Reports*. You would write this query as:

```
"For Dummies" OR Reports
```

Now say you also want the query to also only show content where the location property of the content is *Pacific Northwest* or the author is *Rosemarie Withee*. You use parentheses to combine these two aspects:

```
("For Dummies" OR Reports) AND (location:"Pacific
Northwest" OR author:"Rosemarie Withee")
```

TIP

Note that when you actually type a long query, it will all be on one line in the Search text box. (The margins in this book required a line break.) When you enter a query into the Search text box, don't press Enter until you're ready to execute your search. Hitting the Enter key is the same as clicking the magnifying glass.

Finding terms in proximity

You sometimes may need to find content where you know two words are near each other but not necessarily right next to each other. For example, take a look at the following sentence:

The sales figures for China are excellent.

This sentence contains the words *sales* and *China* in close proximity. If you were just to type *sales China* in the Search text box, you would surely get this content, but you also might get a ton of other, irrelevant content. You could find the result you're looking for using the NEAR operator as follows:

```
"sales" NEAR(5) "China"
```

The number in the parentheses lets the NEAR operator know that you want to only turn results where the words are within five words of each other. The number is not required, however. You could just as easily write the query:

```
"sales" NEAR "China"
```

When you do not specify the number of words, the search engine uses eight words as a default. That is, the words are considered near if they are within eight words of each other.

You might come across a scenario where it isn't enough if two terms are near each other, but they should also appear in a particular order. For example, you might want to only return results were the word *sales* is followed by the word *China* within a certain number of words. The Boolean operator that makes this possible is ONEAR.

The ONEAR operator works just like the NEAR operator; however, it assumes an order. The following query tells the search engine to only return content where the word *sales* is followed by the word *China* within five words.

```
"sales" ONEAR(5) "China"
```

Same meaning, different terms

Did you watch the TV, tele, or television? Did you go to the theater or theatre? Well, you could watch or attend either and it would all mean the same thing. Synonyms are easy for humans to understand. So easy, in fact, that we don't pay many of the blatant ones much thought. Have you ever heard someone answer the question by saying he doesn't watch television but watches TV? If only computers could be so smart.

The WORDS operator is used to let the search engine know when two words mean the same thing. For example, if you're looking for all content that references *California*, you could write the query as follows:

```
WORDS(CA, California)
```

The result is that the search engine knows *CA* and *California* mean the same thing and returns the results accordingly. This begs the question, why not just type the two words in the Search text box? The answer is in the ranking of the results. If the search engine knows these words mean the same thing, then it will return results accordingly. If it doesn't know this, then it might return content that contains both terms *California* and *CA* at the top of the list but have more relevant content that only contains the word *CA* farther down the list. If you use the WORDS operator, the search engine knows that these words mean the same and will provide you the best matches in the results.

Viewing and Refining Search Results

After a query is run, you are presented with the results page, as shown in Figure 19-2.

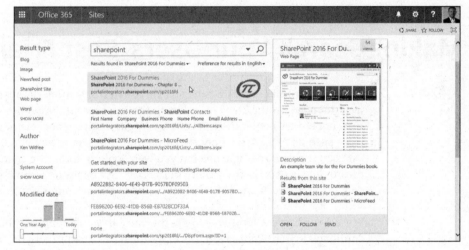

FIGURE 19-2:
The search results page.

The results page has a lot going on, but it's mostly intuitive. When you hover the mouse cursor over a search result, you see a preview of the content and relevant information about the type of content. In Figure 19-2, you can see that the result is a SharePoint site, while in Figure 19-3 the result is an Office Word document.

The left side of the page includes refiners for narrowing down the results. You can click a particular type of content, click a particular author, or narrow the results based on the date the content was modified.

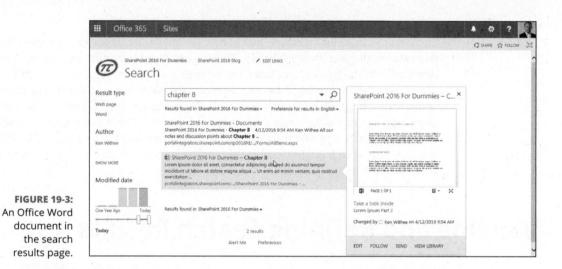

FIGURE 19-3:
An Office Word
document in
the search
results page.

TIP

We find narrowing down content based on the last modified date to be an extremely useful feature because stale content can be a real problem in search results.

Making Search Your Users' Best Friend

Finding the right content can be an exercise in frustration. Companies like Google were founded on the basis of indexing the Internet and providing access through search. Before Google, the Internet was organized into pockets of content on services such as AOL. After Google roared onto the scene, you could just browse to www.google.com and type in what you were looking for in the Search text box, and presto, it was usually right there in the first few pages of results. How did Google do it? It used specialized algorithms to index all the content on the Internet.

Search has come a long way since the early days of Google (though Google still dominates). SharePoint search is a platform designed to let your users find content in, and outside, of your SharePoint environment. Right out of the box, SharePoint indexes content in your SharePoint sites and returns the results. Many organizations don't take search any further than the out-of-box experience, but they should.

As a site administrator, you can tweak the SharePoint search results based on the nuances of your company. For example, maybe you have a site for call center representatives. You know they're always searching for product documentation, so you don't want the official product documentation sites to appear mixed down in with the rest of the content that just happens to mention the products. You can configure SharePoint search to promote the official pages above other pages.

You can even create related searches that will show up right next to the search results that users see. All of this is made possible using query rules.

A *query rule* is a rule that SharePoint search uses when processing a search query. Well, that seems fairly obvious by the name. In other words, a query rule allows you, as a site administrator, the ability to instruct the search engine how to respond to certain queries.

TIP

The search query functionality provides the same result as the Best Bets functionality of previous SharePoint versions. The Best Bets functionality has been extended to include related search blocks and result ranking. The entire feature set is now made possible in search queries.

Here's an example to help you understand how a query rule works. This example consists of two parts. The first is that you want a Marketing app to show up whenever someone searches for the words *marketing* or *sales*. In this example, the Marketing app is a library that contains all the sanctioned sales and marketing material of the organization. The second part is that you want a result block added to the results whenever someone searches for *marketing* or *sales*. A *results block* is just a parallel query of your choosing that will show up in the search results.

To promote the Marketing app whenever a person searches for the words *marketing* or *sales*, follow these steps:

1. **Navigate to the Site Settings page by clicking the Settings gear icon and choosing Site Settings.**

   The Site Settings page appears.

2. **In the Search section, click the Query Rules link.**

   The Manage Query Rules page appears.

   If you're a site collection administrator, you also see the Search Query Rules link in the Site Collection Administration section of the Site Settings page. The difference between these two Query Rules settings is that one affects only the site, and the other affects every site in the entire site collection. Because in this example, you only want to build the query for your particular site, click the Query Rules link in the Search section of the Site Settings page.

3. **Click the Result Source drop-down list and select Local SharePoint Results (System), as shown in Figure 19-4.**

   The Query Rules load for the Local SharePoint Results source.

   The Result Source drop-down list enables you to set the context of the query rule you're creating. Notice that there are many different result source options. These allow you to create finely tuned query rules. For example, you might want to create a rule for people search or conversations. In this example, you want only results for the local SharePoint site, so you choose Local SharePoint Results (System).

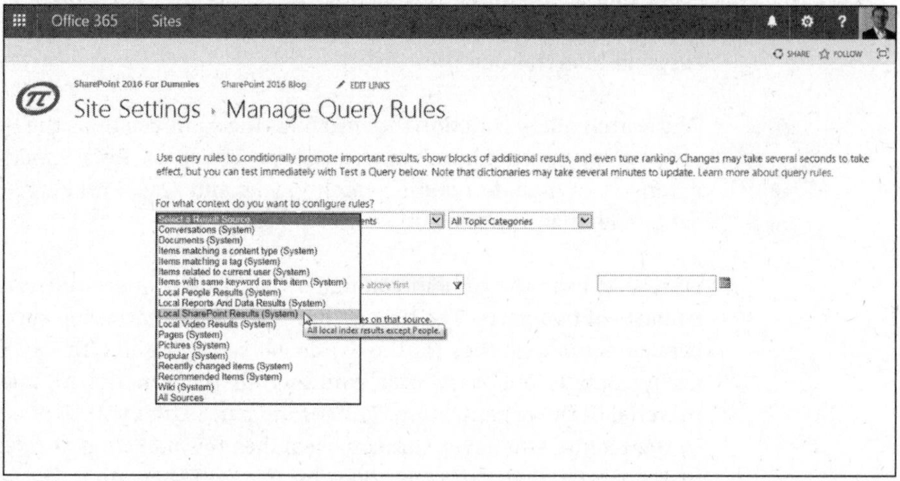

FIGURE 19-4:
Selecting Local SharePoint Results from the Manage Query Rules page.

4. **Click the New Query Rule button.**

   The Add Query Rule page is displayed.

5. **Enter a name for the rule in the Name text box, and then provide the search terms *marketing* and *sales* with a semicolon as a separator in the Search Term text box.**

   The exact text you should type is

   ```
   marketing; sales
   ```

6. **Click the Add Promoted Result link.**

   The Add Promoted Result dialog box is displayed, as shown in Figure 19-5.

   A *promoted result* is the same as a Best Bet in previous versions of SharePoint. When someone searches for the exact words *marketing* or *sales*, the promoted result appears at the top of the results page.

7. **Enter a title for your promoted result in the Title text box, provide the URL to the desired content in the URL text box, and type a description of the promoted result in the Description text box.**

   In this example, we typed Promoted Result for Marketing Example in the Title text box. The Marketing app is an app created from the Document Library App template with the name Marketing.

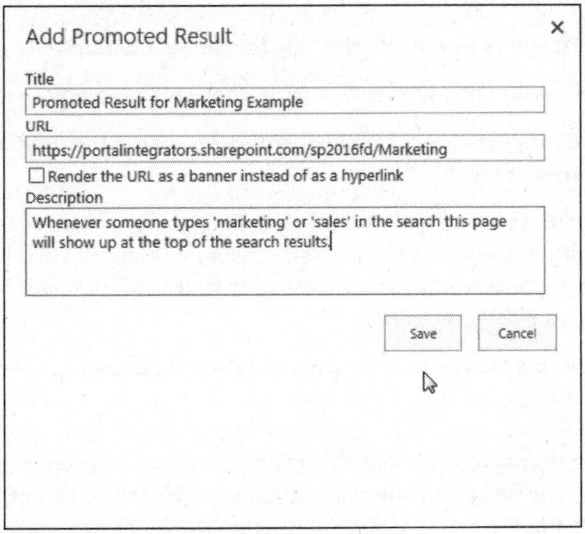

FIGURE 19-5:
The Add
Promoted Result
dialog box.

8. **Click Save to save the promoted result to the query rule.**

9. **Click the Add Result Block link to add a related search to the results of a search that uses the specified words (*marketing* or *sales* in this example).**

   The Add Result Block is displayed, as shown in Figure 19-6.

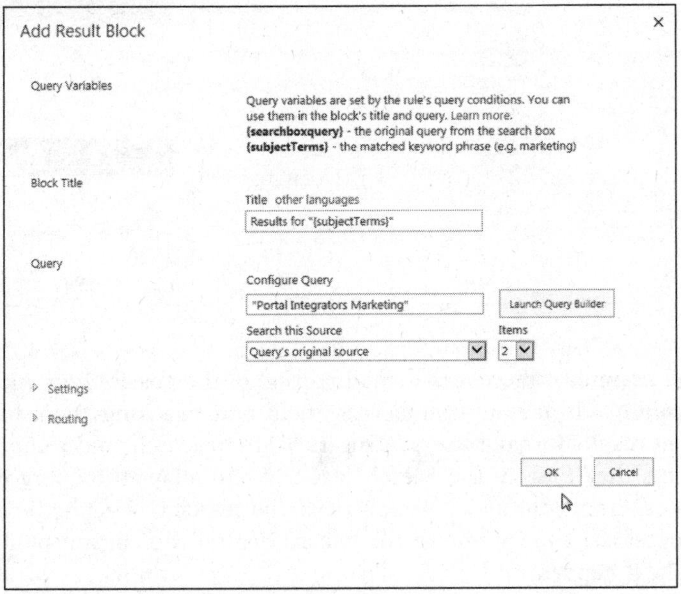

FIGURE 19-6:
The Add Result
Block dialog box.

10. In the Title text box, enter the title for the result block.

The default is to show the search terms that were used for the result block.

11. In the Configure Query text box, enter the search terms you want to use for the result block.

Think of these terms as if you were searching the SharePoint site and wanted to include this second search in a search for *marketing* or *sales*. In this example, we use the search query *Portal Integrators Marketing*, which will return all content with this exact string.

12. Click OK to save the result block, and then click Save to save the query rule.

Now when a user types the search term *marketing* or *sales* into the Search text box for the site, she sees a promoted Marketing app at the top of the page and the result block for a parallel search with the words "*Portal Integrators Marketing.*" Figure 19-7 shows the result.

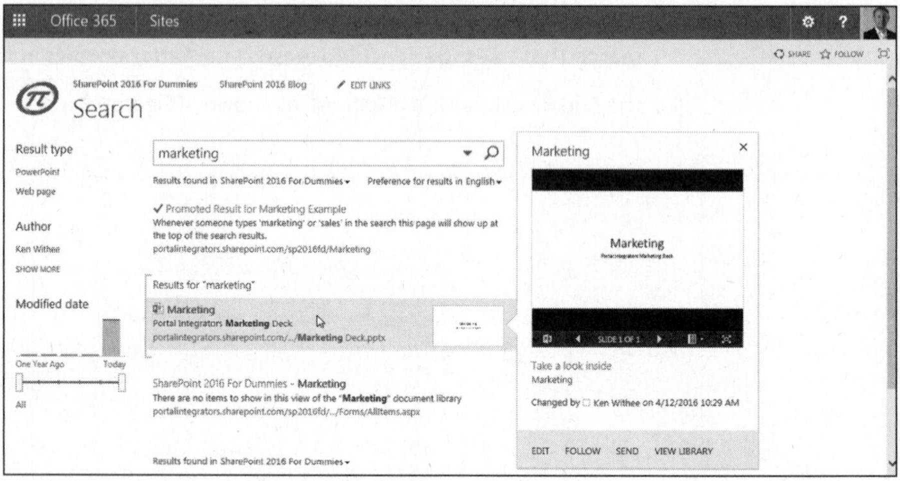

FIGURE 19-7:
The search results page with a marketing/sales query rule.

TIP

The example only covers a small portion of the possibilities with query rules. We recommend playing around with them and tweaking them to provide just the right results for your users. As users begin to search on the site, you can see what terms they type in the Search text box and adapt the query rules to suit their needs. From your users' perspectives, the search will get better and better as time progresses, even if you're the wizard behind the curtain pulling the strings to make it happen.

TIP

Search results don't appear immediately after you make a change. In order to see the change, you need to wait for the search engine to reindex the content in the site. *Indexing* just means looking through all the content and prepping it for search results accordingly. You can force the site to start reindexing by going to Site Settings, opening the Search and Offline Availability page, and then clicking the Reindex Site button.

Removing Content from Search Results

By default, items and documents in apps appear in search results. You may not want these items to appear in search results. To keep items and documents in apps out of search results, follow these steps:

1. **Navigate to the app that you want to remove from search by clicking the Settings gear icon and choosing Site Contents.**

   You see a list of all apps.

2. **Open the app settings page by clicking the List or Library tab of the Ribbon and then clicking List Settings or Library Settings.**

   The app settings page appears.

3. **Click the Advanced Settings link in the General Settings section.**

   The Advanced Settings page appears.

4. **In the Search section, select the No radio button, as shown in Figure 19-8.**

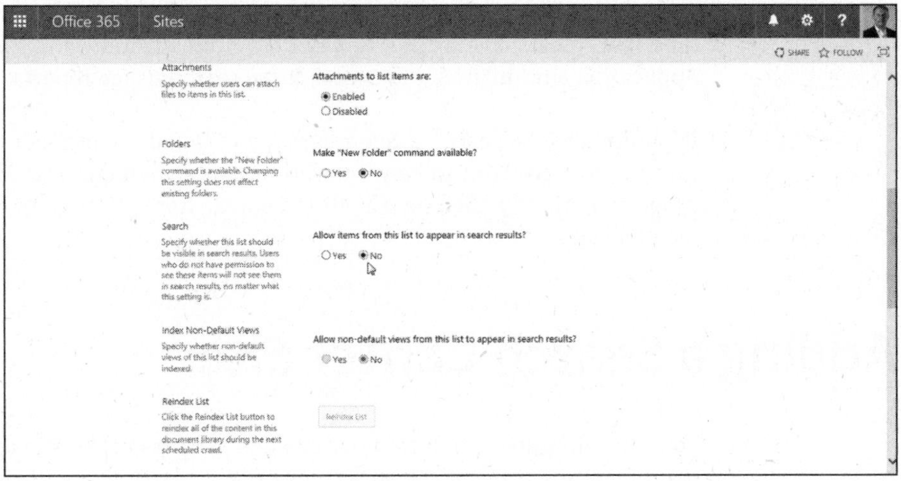

FIGURE 19-8:
Removing the contents of an app from SharePoint search results.

5. **Click OK to save the settings.**

The content of the app will not be indexed the next time the search engine indexes content.

You can view which properties are searched by clicking the Schema link in the Search section of the Site Settings page. The Search column shows whether the property is used in building the search index.

TIP

The Search Service Application administrator can also remove specific results from the search index or results. This is accomplished in the Search Service Application Management page. Click the Crawl Log, find the result to remove, click the ellipsis button for the item, and choose Remove the Item from the Index. Likewise, a URL can be removed from the results by clicking the Search Result Removal page in the Queries and Results section of the Search Service Application management page in Central Administration and entering the URL that should be removed from the search result. You can find the result to remove by clicking the URL view and then clicking the arrow to choose the Remove the Item from the Index link.

Reviewing Search Analytics

SharePoint provides a number of usage reports for search. These include reports such as Number of Queries, Top Queries, Abandoned Queries, No Result Queries, and Query Rule Usage. The good news is that the reports are based in Excel, so you can download them, open them in Excel, and use the data to present in nice graphs for executives. The reports can be found in the Search Service Application in Central Administration. Click the Usage Reports link in the Diagnostics section.

Note: You must have access to Central Administration and be a Search Service Application administrator to access these search usage reports.

In addition to the search usage reports, you can also check out the view usage for content in SharePoint to help you refine your search queries. You access the view usage statistics by clicking the Most Popular Items button on the List or Library tab of an app.

Adding a Search Center Site

You can configure search for your site and settings at the site collection level and point results to a specific Search Center site. A *Search Center site* is a SharePoint site that has been created using a search template. By creating a Search Center site, you have the ability to customize it for your particular needs.

SharePoint 2016 provides two site templates that are built for delivering search results. You can use these templates to create a branded search experience or to customize how results appear. The Search Center site templates are:

>> **Basic Search Center:** This template delivers a stripped-down search experience in one page. This site template uses Web Part pages and is essentially a team site specialized for search.

>> **Enterprise Search Center:** This template provides multiple pages for displaying search results. This site template uses publishing pages, which makes it easier to brand and customize than a page based on the Basic Search Center template.

Follow the steps in Chapter 4 to create a new site using one of the Search Center templates.

To configure your site collection to use your Search Center site:

1. **Click the Settings gear icon and choose Site Settings.**

   The Site Settings page appears.

2. **In the Site Collection Administration section, click the Search Settings link.**

   The Search Settings page appears, as shown in Figure 19-9.

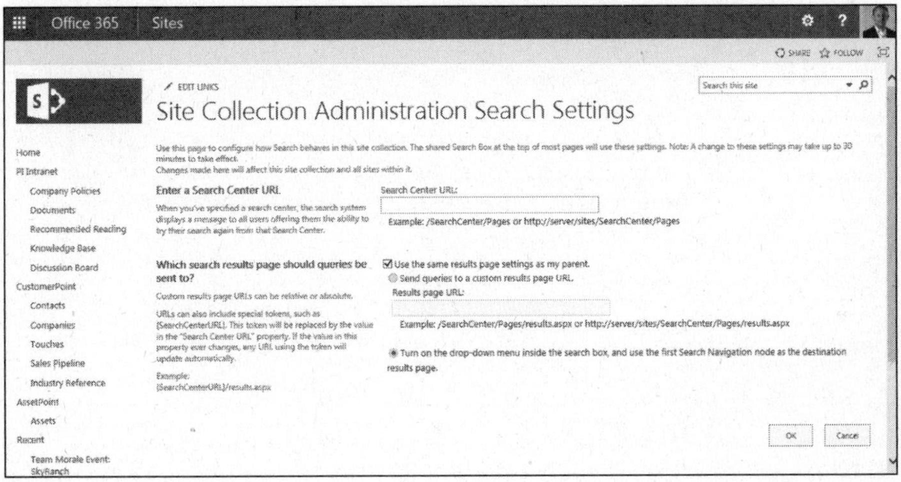

FIGURE 19-9:
Configure search settings.

3. **Enter the URL of the Search Center site in the Search Center URL text box.**

   Your search center doesn't have to be in the same site collection as the sites that are using it for search. You can create a new site collection using one of the Search Center templates and configure multiple site collections to use that same search center.

4. **Click OK to save the settings.**

   After making the change, you need to wait up to 30 minutes before the change is reflected in search.

After the Search Center site is in place and configured in Search Settings, all results are directed to the search site. It takes some time for the changes to take effect, however, because a SharePoint scheduled process has to update the configuration for the site. If you don't see your changes right away, check back an hour later. You can then develop the search site to meet the specific needs of your organization.

REMEMBER

The settings we describe in this section set the default experience for all Search text boxes in your site. Individual Search text boxes found on the master page, in page layouts, or placed directly on web pages can be configured to use the default settings or have their own custom settings.

TIP

You aren't restricted to using the Search Web Parts in the search center. You can create your own search results page and add the Search Web Parts to the page.

Chapter 20

Archiving Documents and Records

I n SharePoint 2016, the Records Center is a useful and powerful tool for declaring holds and managing records. First, it's *metadata-driven,* which means that all policies for automatic declaration, retention, and disposition can be based on metadata. Second, it's capable of *hierarchical archiving,* meaning that each level or folder where documents are routed, based on their metadata, can inherit from its parent or have separate policies. Third, you can manage the entire lifecycle of the document in a single policy, from declaration through disposition. Fourth, administrators can allow users to declare records outside of the official Records Center, allowing records to be kept where they are actively being accessed and updated.

In this chapter, you explore the records management functionality in SharePoint 2016. You discover how to define terms, create information management policies, and set up a site based on the Records Center template. Finally, this chapter covers some of the finer points of records management, such as using the Content Organizer tool and placing holds on content.

Defining the Terms

SharePoint 2016 provides many records management features, including the Managed Metadata Service, Content Types, Content Organizer, Policies, Document Sets, and the Records Management site template. The following list is a quick guide to these terms and what functionality they provide:

>> **Managed Metadata** ensures a common vocabulary and a central place for terminology used in your company, which can be managed centrally or by departments.

>> **Content Types** scale across the enterprise with SharePoint 2016 and are not limited to each site collection. This means you have a much more scalable way of controlling and managing the types of content people can create, the metadata on those content types, and the information policies associated with them.

>> **Content Organizer** enables you to take routing documents and content beyond content types. You can create rules based on one or more pieces of metadata on the content. Essentially, this simplifies routing from the user's perspective, and content gets routed to the right place without too much forethought.

>> **Information Management Policies** can be applied to the content type or the location of the content, which can become part of the policy. You can expire record and non-record content in the same policy.

>> **Document Sets** allow you to group together multiple documents into a single set. This helps keep track of all the documents you might use for a particular idea or task. For example, you might want to group all of the documents for a proposal that multiple people are working on.

>> **Records Management Site Template** is a SharePoint site template that has most of the records management capabilities of SharePoint already included and ready to use. You can use this site template to get up and running with managing records in SharePoint with very little configuration overhead.

With these features, declaring records, holds, and policies is scalable and powerful in SharePoint 2016.

Creating Information Management Policies

Here are four different types of policies that you can set up in a single information management policy:

>> A **Retention** policy enables you to manage how items, documents, team mailboxes, and sites are stored on the server and what happens to them after the retention stage expires. A simple example of this would be that if a document has not been modified in one year, its version history is deleted.

>> An **Auditing** policy enables you to track what happens to an item at particular stages as an item is being moved or copied, opened, downloaded, viewed, checked in and out, and deleted and restored, so you have a full history of who has done what to an item.

>> A **Barcodes** policy assigns a barcode to each item, allowing you to incorporate the barcode into your tracking of the item. You can optionally specify that you want users to insert a barcode before saving or printing.

>> A **Labels** policy allows you to insert important and contextual information about the document when it is printed.

As shown in Figure 20-1, all these policies can be part of a single information management policy.

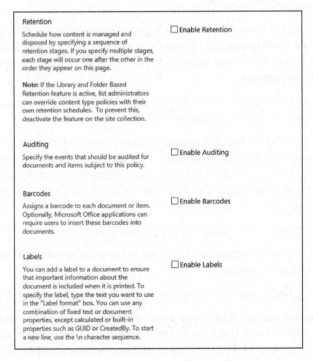

FIGURE 20-1: Creating a new information management policy.

To create a new information management policy, you can start from an app or content type. Content type retention policies are the most powerful because they scale across the farm, but for the purposes of this example, we stick to a retention policy in a Library app. (If you want to follow along with a content type, simply browse to that content type in the site collection's Site Content Types gallery.)

TIP

Site collection administrators can turn off this feature of allowing app-based retention policies.

Follow these steps to create a new information management policy:

1. **From the app settings page (Library Settings or List Settings), or from the content type's properties, click the Information Management Policy Settings link.**

2. **Click either the item or the folder; if you're on the content type, you don't have to do anything.**

    For Document Library apps, you can have the policy inherit from the content type, or you can choose to create a new policy just for the app.

TIP

    These policy pages look a bit different if you're using a list-based app or a list content type because you don't have as much to manage, but they have the same essential functionality.

3. **After you're on the policy settings page (refer to Figure 20-1), give the policy a description and a statement by typing in the Administrative Description and Policy Statement text boxes, respectively, and then click Enable Retention.**

    We just talk about retention here because it's the most interesting, and the other policy settings are straightforward.

    After you click on Enable Retention, you see some extra information, a link, and some options. For Document Library apps, you can treat non-records and records the same way if you choose, or different stages for handling records. Whichever you choose, you should define at least one retention stage for either records, non-records, or both.

TIP

    If you don't define a stage, the retention policy will not do anything.

4. **Click the Add a Retention Stage link in the new section that appears after you enable retention.**

    A dialog box appears, shown in Figure 20-2, that has a couple of different options.

5. **Choose the Event that triggers the retention by selecting the This Stage Is Based Off a Date Property on the Item radio button, select an option from the Time Period drop-down list, and enter a number and select Years, Months, or Days from the drop-down list.**

    From the Time Period drop-down list, you can select Created, Modified, or Declared Record. This determines the amount of time the stage lasts.

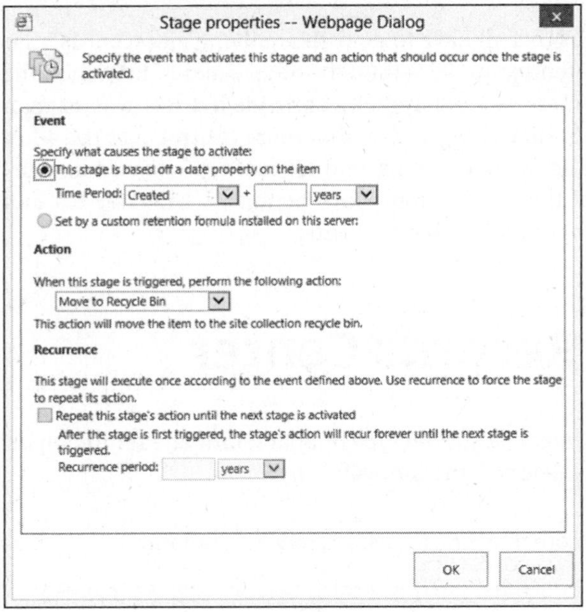

FIGURE 20-2:
Adding a
retention stage.

6. **In the Action section, select an option from the When This Stage Is Triggered, Perform the Following Action drop-down list.**

You can choose from a variety of actions:

- Move to Recycle Bin
- Permanently Delete
- Transfer to Another Location
- Start a Workflow
- Skip to the Next Stage
- Declare Record
- Delete Previous Drafts
- Delete all Previous Versions

You can also set the action to recur, but this depends on the action you've specified previously. You can't, for example, keep deleting the same document over and over again, but you can keep purging previous drafts or all previous versions until the next stage is active.

7. **Click OK to close the dialog box, and then click OK again to save the policy.**

So what does this all have to do with archiving and records management, you may wonder? Retention policies (and the other types of information management policies you can create in SharePoint) provide a direct way of managing records and non-records alike and give you a lot more control over the who, what, when, why, and how of documents, items, and content types stored in your SharePoint site. In fact, one of those retention policy actions is Transfer to Another Location, and that location can be a Records Center.

Setting Up a Records Center

A *Records Center* is a special type of SharePoint site template. Using a site based on the Records Center template, you can

>> Have more than one Records Center in your farm

>> Move a document to the Records Center instead of creating a copy, and put a link in the old location that points to the new location in the Records Center

>> Route more intelligently based on content or item properties

>> Have better control over the naming of the folders when items are routed to the Records Center.

>> Allow users to create records in place and not have to use the Records Center at all

With all these improvements, it's time to create a Records Center and start setting it up. Because a Records Center is a site template, you simply create a new site based on that template. (Refer to Chapter 4 for more information on how to create a new site.)

After you have created a Records Center, your home page looks like Figure 20-3.

Click the Settings gear icon and choose Manage Records Center. On this new page, you see a lot of information to help you set up your Records Center. Read the steps about tasks and file plans because those are much like standard SharePoint functionality, such as creating Library apps, looking at and/or creating content types, and designing the home page. We talk about Content Organizer rules in the next section.

TIP

You can set up Send To links in Central Administration for users to send documents to a Records Center. In the Action section of the Stage Properties dialog box, you specify three options: Copy, Move, and Move and Leave a Link.

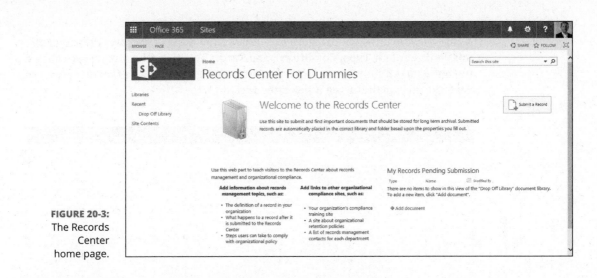

FIGURE 20-3:
The Records
Center
home page.

Using the Content Organizer

The Content Organizer, and specifically the rules that it manages, is where all the intelligence happens in the Records Center. Rules allow you to control where records go after they are submitted to the Records Center and what properties those items have. The absolute best thing about the Content Organizer is that it allows users not to have to think about their own content — they just declare it a record and their job is done.

Figure 20-4 shows a new, blank Content Organizer rule. You get to this page by clicking the Add Item link in the Content Organizer Rules list. (You navigate to this page by clicking the Settings gear icon and choosing Manage Records Center.)

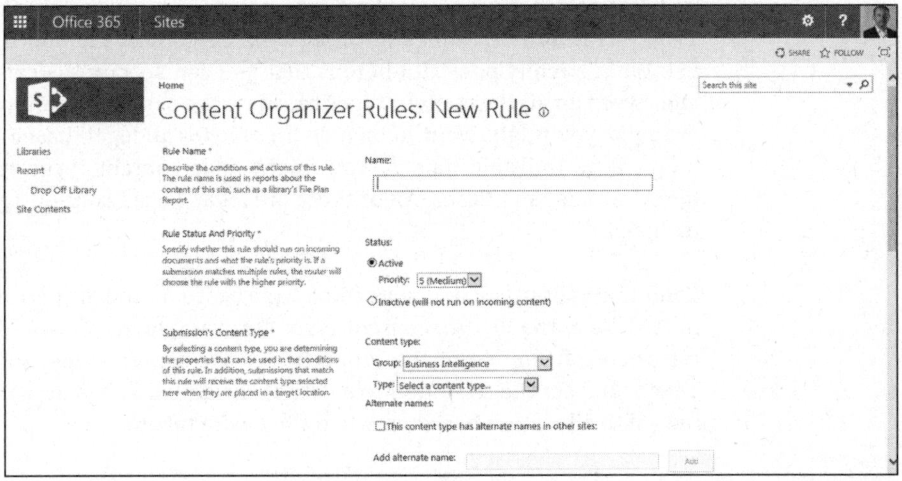

FIGURE 20-4:
Creating a new
Content
Organizer rule.

A rule has five different categories — Rule Name, Rule Status and Priority, Submission's Content Type, Conditions, and Target Location (the last two are shown in Figure 20-5). Rule Name and Rule Status and Priority are self-explanatory, so we focus on explaining the other categories.

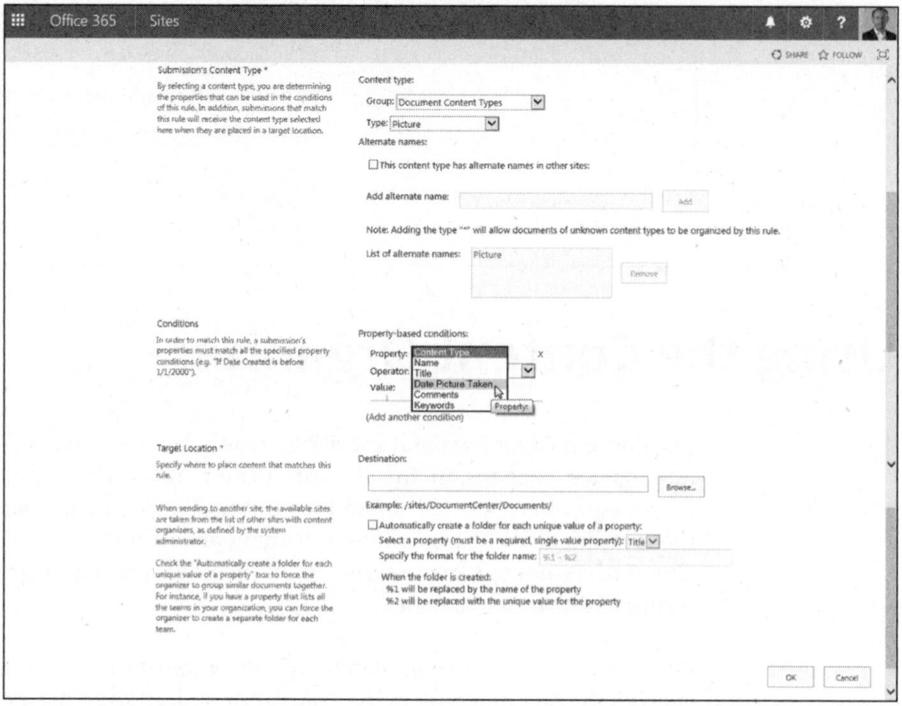

FIGURE 20-5:
Adding a
condition
based on a
property value.

Submission's Content Type may seem simple, but it has the ability to make matches across multiple content type names, so you can check the This Content Type Has Alternate Names in Other Sites check box and add those names to the list. What's really powerful here is that you can specify the catch-all asterisk (*) and sweep up all the content types based on the base content type for this rule. For example, you might want to include the rule for all legal-based content types that might have multiple names. You might have content types called Legal Documents, Briefs, and Cases. All of these are legal-based content types and should be included.

Conditions allow you to devise some logic based on the properties of the item submitted. Take the Picture content type, for example. As shown in Figure 20-5, you can choose from one of the properties of the content type, such as Date Picture Taken, and set the condition to a date at the end of last year, so all pictures can be moved to a location based on when they were taken.

Also notice in Figure 20-5 that you can have multiple conditions by clicking the Add Another Condition link. So you could have a rule that routes pictures taken during the 2016 or 2017 calendar year.

Target Location, the last item for your new rule, is where you want to send these items. Remember that these rules are run on items that are submitted to the Records Center. So items are held in the Drop Off Library until the Content Organizer has a chance to evaluate the content based on the rules set up for the Records Center. That's a long-winded way of asking, where do you want these documents to go?

You can specify another site that has a Content Organizer configured, or you can route the items that meet the conditions to a Library app in the Records Center itself. You can also have the Content Organizer group items with the same properties together in the same folder, and you have control over the name of that folder. Based on a property of the content type, the folder name includes, by default, the name of the property and its value. So if, for example, you had a custom picture content type that included the employee's department name, and the column on the content type was called Dept, your folder would be named Dept –Claims Adjusters if the user worked in the Claims Adjusters department.

REMEMBER

Having (or creating) the right columns on the content types that you want to manage is critical for getting the rules to function the way you need them to. So spend some extra effort to identify and get the right content types in place for your important documents and files. Not only will it help you maintain some sort of control over how content is created, but it also helps you establish good policies for organizing your records.

Managing Records in Place

In the effort to make records management more flexible, SharePoint 2016 supports managing records outside the Records Center, on any document and on any site. The In Place Records Management feature must be activated at the site collection level. After it is, each list-based or library-based app gets a Record Declaration Settings link on the app settings page. As shown in Figure 20-6, the settings on this page enable you to control whether and how records are declared, and you can even declare records automatically as items are added to the Document Library app (not that it is used very often).

TIP

The Automatically Declare Items as Records When They Are Added to This List option is selected by default. This causes the Manual Record Declaration Activity option to be disabled until you change the selected option.

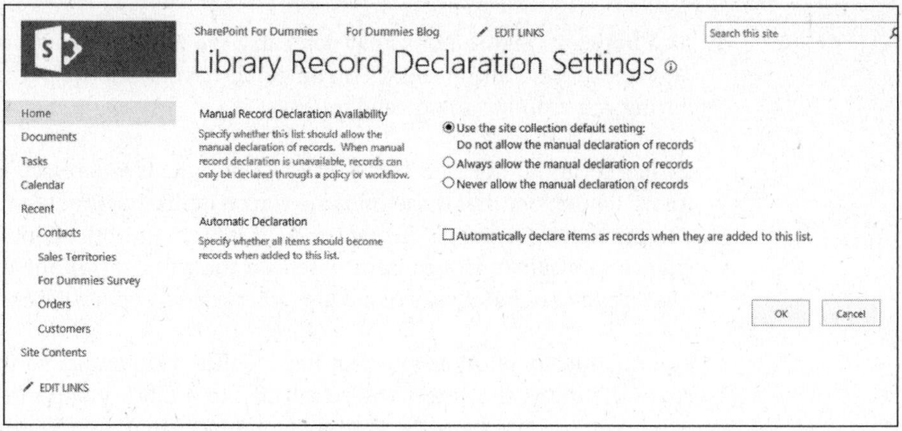

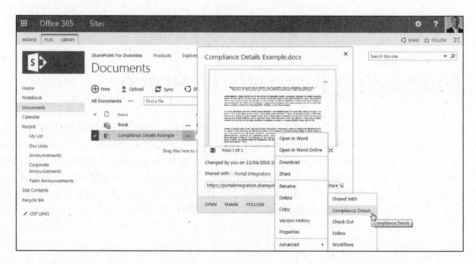

FIGURE 20-6:
Controlling
in-place records
declaration.

If records are allowed to be declared in the Library app, you click the ellipsis for the document, click the second ellipsis, and then select Compliance Details from the Advanced menu, as shown in Figure 20-7. The Compliance Details dialog box includes a link to declare the document as a record if records are allowed to be declared in the app. Clicking it shows a warning about locking down the item for editing. After you click OK, it makes it a record. Users can revert a record to a document from this same dialog box, and if anyone tries to edit the document while it's a record, they receive an error message saying that it's checked out by the system account.

FIGURE 20-7:
Declaring a
record in-place.

TIP

The powerful feature of in-place records management is that it keeps the documents available for users to reference without taking them out of the context of the app and site where they were originally created. But the record still shows up on records reports and can be managed centrally.

Placing Records on Litigation Hold

After you have all these retention policies and records being managed based on rules, you may have to temporarily suspend these policies. This is typically due to pending litigation where records matching certain criteria must be preserved until the litigation or court matter is settled.

The first thing you have to do is create the hold. You can do this in the Records Center, or you can do it at the site collection level. Figure 20-8 shows the Hold section of the Site Settings page for a Records Center site. Holds are easy to create and need a title, description, and an owner. Make sure to create at least one of these for each litigation or court matter that is required.

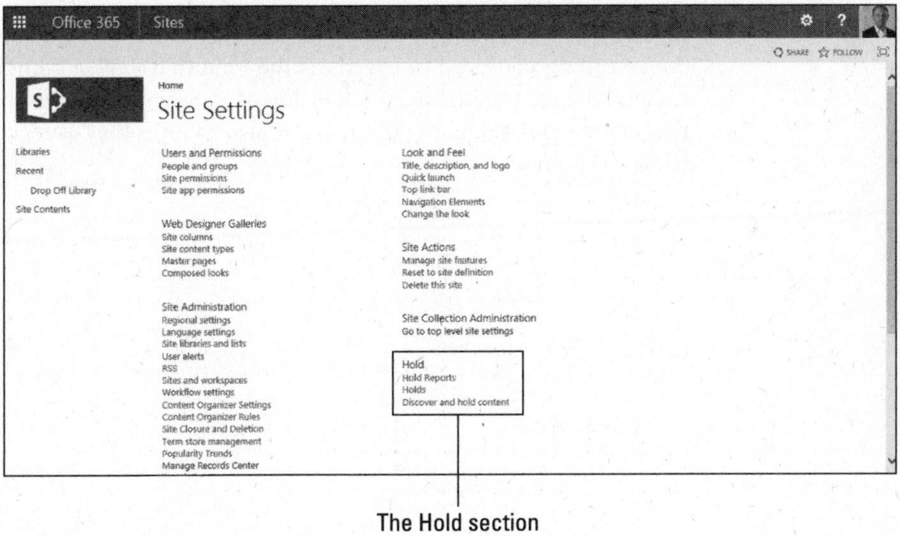

FIGURE 20-8: Managing holds and eDiscovery at the site collection level.

The Hold section

The more interesting part is the Discover and Hold Content link. As shown in Figure 20-9, there are a few different parts to discovering content to put on hold. The first one, Search Criteria, allows you to select a site and enter search terms much the same way that you regularly search for content in SharePoint. Click Preview Results after typing in one or more terms to see the results in a new window.

After you have your search terms down, you can choose whether you want the items that come back in the search results to be kept in place and added to a local hold or copied to another location. If you choose another location, most likely that will be the Records Center site, which might be the best way to put items on hold without alerting users.

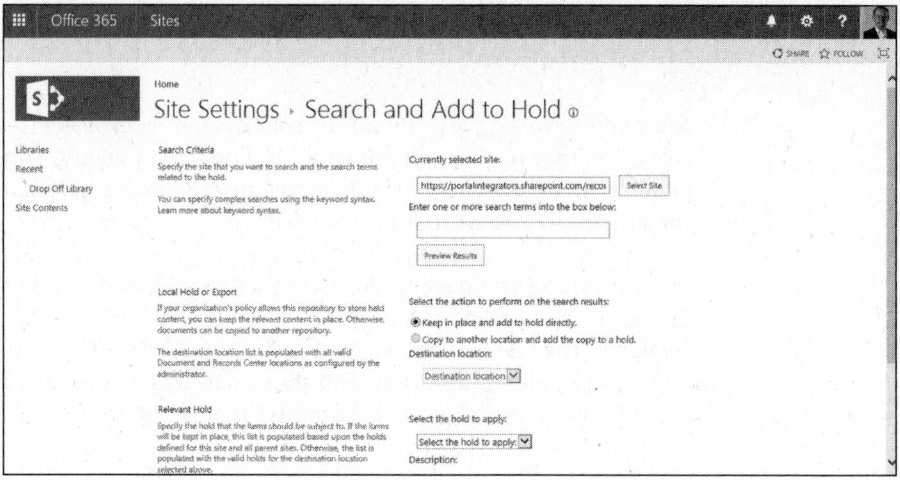

FIGURE 20-9: Configuring eDiscovery and placing items on hold.

The last thing you need to specify is the hold that you're going to put the records in. This ensures that the documents do not expire or are otherwise altered due to an information management policy, and it also ensures that users can't "accidentally" delete the items.

Chapter 21

Gaining Total Control with Workflow

A ny organization is made up of processes. Some processes might be very simple, such as checking an email, responding, and then filing it in a folder. Other processes are more complex and might involve multiple people and computer systems. In any case, processes are at the core of an organization. SharePoint has the capability to manage processes through workflow.

In this chapter, you explore workflow in SharePoint. You discover the two different workflow platforms in SharePoint 2016. You find out how they work and how to develop workflows. Finally, you see firsthand how a workflow can be used as an approval system for documents.

Getting Up to Speed with SharePoint Workflow

A SharePoint workflow can be used to manage a human-centric process or a computer-centric process. For example, you might have a process that involves five people working partly in parallel and partly in sequence. If these five people are all in the same room and accomplish the process in one sitting, then using a workflow to coordinate their activities wouldn't make much sense. If the people are dispersed in different offices or cubes or the process takes place over a period of time, then a workflow can be used to coordinate and keep the process on track.

In addition, a process might interact with other computer systems. For example, you might have a process that needs to pull customer data from a Customer Relationship Management (CRM) system. The CRM data might then need to be used by multiple people as the processes proceed. SharePoint workflow can handle both types of processes. Many workflows can be developed quickly without writing code, but other more advanced workflows require programmers.

TIP

The reason SharePoint workflow is so adaptable is that it is built on the Windows Workflow Foundation portion of the Microsoft .NET platform. What this means is that the possibilities are limitless because you can always have a programmer write workflow code to do just about anything you can imagine and interact with any system.

The primary tool used to develop a SharePoint workflow is called SharePoint Designer (SPD). SharePoint Designer includes a no-code interface for developing workflows using components such as actions, tasks, steps, loops, and goto statements. When you need more advanced capabilities, you use a tool called Visual Studio to extend workflows beyond what SharePoint Designer can handle.

SharePoint Designer has changed course dramatically from previous versions of the tool. Previous versions of SPD included functionality for visual design of Web Parts and conditional formatting. Those portions of SPD were removed, and the tool moved into a workflow development tool.

Microsoft focused on stability and backend improvements with SharePoint 2016 workflow and, as a result, maintained functionality with the version 2013 version of SPD.

REMEMBER

To build workflow in SharePoint Server 2016, you still use SharePoint Designer 2013.

You can build a workflow visually using the Visual Designer interface. The Visual Designer interface leverages Office Visio and allows you to drag and drop workflow shapes in order to create the workflow.

TIP

In order to use the Visual Designer, you must have Office Visio Professional installed on the same computer as SharePoint Designer. The Visual Designer is known as a *light-up feature*, which means that it only lights up (becomes available) when Visio is installed.

In addition to SPD, you can also use a tool called Visual Studio to develop a Share-Point workflow. Visual Studio is an Integrated Development Environment (IDE), and it's primarily used by programmers. Using Visual Studio, you can make a workflow do anything you can imagine. Be warned though, it isn't a tool for the faint of heart. You need a solid understanding of .NET programming to develop your own custom SharePoint workflow using Visual Studio.

Understanding Workflow in SharePoint 2016

As the march to the cloud continues, technologies are changing to accommodate this march; workflow is a prime example. SharePoint recently introduced a work-flow platform named SharePoint 2013 Workflow Platform. If your organization is using SharePoint On-Premises, then the workflow platform is a separate (but free!) product from SharePoint and requires its own download, installation, and configuration. The workflow product is called Workflow Manager, and when it's configured to work with a SharePoint 2016 farm, it provides the SharePoint 2013 Workflow Platform. Do all of these versions sound confusing? It is fairly simple: The "new" workflow platform was introduced in SharePoint 2013, so it was called the SharePoint 2013 Workflow Platform. SharePoint 2016 still uses this workflow platform that was introduced in the previous version of SharePoint. To get a better handle on it, see the sidebar, "Understanding the differences between workflow platforms," just ahead.

TIP

If you are using SharePoint Online, you don't have to worry about the various workflow platforms. Microsoft handles all of that for you. You just need to build your workflows. You can continue to use SharePoint Designer 2013; however, there are also a number of third-party workflow tools available for creating work-flows in SharePoint Online. In particular, check out the workflow creation tools made by Nintex (www.nintex.com) and K2 (www.k2.com).

In addition to the Workflow Manager-based workflow platform is a legacy work-flow platform. The legacy workflow platform is the same workflow engine that shipped with SharePoint 2010 so it is called the SharePoint 2010 Workflow Plat-form. The legacy platform continues to install in the same manner it did in the previous version of SharePoint. That is, when you install SharePoint, you are also installing the legacy workflow platform. Again, if you use SharePoint Online, though, you don't need to worry about this. If you use SharePoint On-Premises, then you will need to contact your administrators to get workflow configured (if it is not already).

UNDERSTANDING THE DIFFERENCES BETWEEN WORKFLOW PLATFORMS

The SharePoint 2010 platform is built on the Windows Workflow Foundation components of the .NET 3.5 framework. The SharePoint 2013 platform is built on the Windows Workflow Foundation components of the .NET 4.5 framework. The 2013 platform is built as a Windows service and is designed to handle massive workloads from multiple SharePoint environments. What this means is that it was designed specifically to work with the cloud.

In addition, because Workflow Manager (the service that provides workflow) is separate from SharePoint, it can sit at the center of an organization's ecosystem and provide workflow service to many different applications. In this sense, SharePoint is a customer of Workflow Manager, but it doesn't have to be the only customer. An organization might have third-party applications or in-house applications that also utilize the workflow capabilities of Workflow Manager.

When SharePoint Server 2016 was released, Microsoft did not change the terminology for the two workflow platforms. So we still use the terms *SharePoint 2010 Workflow Platform* and *SharePoint 2013 Workflow Platform*. Yes, even though we are using SharePoint 2016.

Confused by the two workflow platforms? Just remember that SharePoint has two workflow platforms: a platform called SharePoint 2013 Workflow and a legacy platform called SharePoint 2010 Workflow. The 2013 platform is made available by a product called Workflow Manager. The 2010 platform installs when you install SharePoint 2016, just like previous editions of SharePoint. Figure 21-1 outlines the two platforms.

TIP

If you install SharePoint 2016, install SharePoint Designer 2013, and go to create a workflow, you only see the SharePoint 2010 Workflow Platform as an option in the platform drop-down list. After you, or your administrator, install Workflow Manager and configure it to work with the SharePoint farm, you then see another option called SharePoint 2013 Workflow Platform. If you don't see the 2013 platform, then Workflow Manager has not been configured to work with your SharePoint 2016 farm.

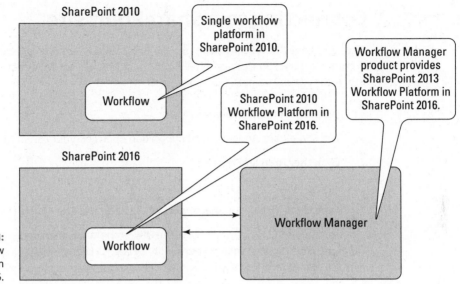

FIGURE 21-1:
Workflow
platforms in
SharePoint 2016.

Getting Up to Speed on SharePoint Designer

SharePoint Designer is a client application that you use to connect to your SharePoint site and build workflows (among other things). When you open a SharePoint site, you first open your web browser, and your web browser connects to the SharePoint site located on a server. SharePoint Designer works in the same manner. You download it, install it, and then open and connect it to a site.

REMEMBER

Microsoft did not change the SharePoint Designer client, so you still use SharePoint Designer 2013 to build workflows for SharePoint 2016.

You can download SharePoint Designer from the Microsoft Download Center located at `www.microsoft.com/download`. Make sure to search for *SharePoint Designer 2013* and download the latest version (and any relevant updates).

Microsoft has guidance on installing SharePoint Designer here: `http://msdn.microsoft.com/en-us/library/jj554671.aspx`.

Connecting to a SharePoint site

After you have SharePoint Designer 2013 installed on your computer, you're ready to connect it to a SharePoint site. To connect SharePoint Designer to a SharePoint site, follow these steps:

1. **Open SharePoint Designer 2013.**

The SharePoint Designer 2013 application opens on your computer.

2. **Click the Open Site button.**

The Open Site dialog box opens.

3. **Type the URL to your SharePoint 2013 site in the Site Name text box.**

Make sure to include `http://` in the URL of the site. For example, `http://intranet.portalintegrators.com/sites/site1` would be what you would type for a site called site1.

The dialog box refreshes and shows you all the contents of the site. This includes any subsites. This is useful if you can't remember the subsite URL. You could type the parent site, such as `http://intranet.portalintegrators.com`, and then browse to the subsite named site1.

TIP

After you have connected to a site once, you see the Site URL as a button to automatically connect again below the Open Site button in SharePoint Designer. You don't need to type the URL each time you want to connect.

4. **Click Open to open the site in SharePoint Designer.**

When you connect to a SharePoint site, you see the navigational components along the left side, as shown in Figure 21-2.

Creating a workflow

You can create three types of workflows in SharePoint:

>> **A List workflow** is attached to an app and works with only that app. For example, you might create a List workflow for a Documents app that is used for approval. Or you might create a List workflow for a Contacts app that emails you whenever a new contact is added.

>> **A Reusable workflow** is not associated with a single app but can be used by many apps.

>> **A Site workflow** is not associated with any app at all but is used by the website in general.

Navigation section

FIGURE 21-2:
The navigational
section of
SharePoint
Designer 2013.

The most common scenario is using a List workflow for a particular app.

REMEMBER

An app can be based on a SharePoint list or library. When you create an app, you choose the template it should use. A List workflow is tied to a specific app that has already been created.

TIP

The term *List workflow* might cause some confusion. SharePoint 2016 uses the term *app* instead of *list.* (This workflow type should really be called List Based App workflow to come in line with SharePoint 2016 naming conventions.)

To create a List workflow for a Documents app, follow these steps:

1. **Click Workflows in the left navigation of SharePoint Designer 2013.**

The current workflows in the site are displayed.

2. **In the New section of the Workflows tab, click the List Workflow drop-down list and choose the app that you want to associate with the workflow.**

In this example, we build a workflow for the Documents app, so we select Documents from the drop-down list, as shown in Figure 21-3.

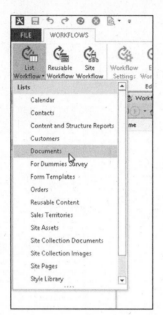

FIGURE 21-3:
Choosing the
Documents app
in the New
Workflow
drop-down list.

3. **In the Name and Description text boxes, type the workflow name and description.**

4. **Select SharePoint 2013 Workflow from the Platform Type drop-down list, as shown in Figure 21-4.**

   The workflow opens in SharePoint Designer.

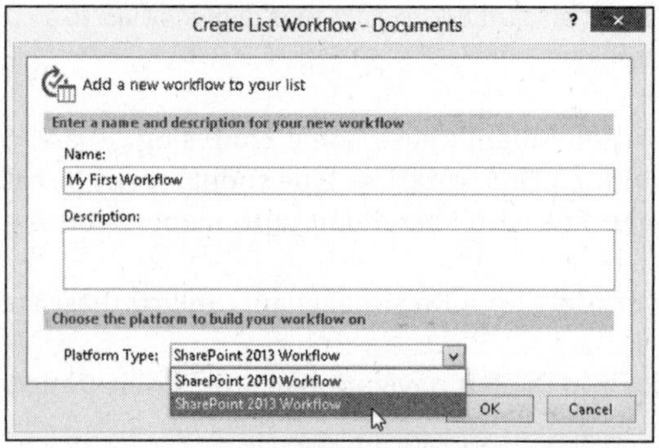

FIGURE 21-4:
Creating a new
workflow in
SharePoint
Designer 2013.

At this point, you're ready to add actions, conditions, steps, stages, and loops to your workflow. There are endless possibilities with workflow scenarios in Share-Point. Covering workflow development is beyond the scope of this book, but if you play around with the actions, you will start to get the hang of it quickly. In addition to building your own workflow from scratch, you can use the out-of-the-box workflows. To find out more about the out-of-the-box workflow for approval, see the later section, "Setting up an approval workflow."

Most business processes can be achieved with the out-of-the-box actions, conditions, steps, stages, and loops. Custom actions can also be created by a programmer using Visual Studio.

TIP

You can finding a detailed listing of the actions, conditions, steps, stages, loops, and other aspects of SharePoint workflow on MSDN at `https://msdn.microsoft.com/en-us/library/office/jj164026.aspx`.

Rediscovering the Out-of-the-Box Approval Workflow

If you're familiar with the out-of-the-box workflows from past versions of SharePoint, then you will be glad to know that they are still included in SharePoint 2016. They are now included as a site collection feature that is deactivated by default. To turn them on, you need to activate the Workflows feature for your site collection, as shown in Figure 21-5.

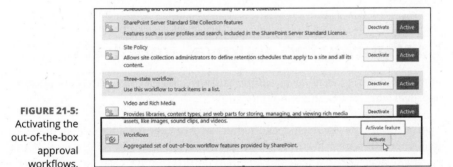

FIGURE 21-5:
Activating the out-of-the-box approval workflows.

To find out more about activating features in SharePoint, see Chapter 12.

The out-of-the-box approval workflows use the legacy SharePoint 2010 Workflow platform. They are turned off by default for performance reasons.

Deciding whether to use content approval or approval workflows

You might be wondering whether it's better to use the content approval mechanism in SharePoint (discussed in Chapter 18) or to use workflow for approval. Well, as we're sure you've discovered in SharePoint, the answer is, it depends.

Before you apply content approval or an approval workflow, make a few governance decisions:

>> **Which apps contain (or will contain) content that requires approval?** This isn't the time to turn loose your inner control freak; your goal is to apply the minimum level of content governance necessary to achieve your approval goals.

>> **What kind of approval process do you need?** Is the approval just a thumbs-up or thumbs-down process that approvers can track and manage? If so, content approval will probably make you happy. Or do you need a way for reviewers to provide feedback and a way to track tasks associated with the reviews? In that case, you need an approval workflow.

>> **Who needs to know about items that need approval?** Do you want approvers to be notified when something needs their approval? If so, you need an approval workflow, with or without content approval.

>> **Do you want the process to start automatically or do you want a manual trigger?** If you want a manual trigger, you need an approval workflow.

Configuring the approval workflows

Approval workflows can layer additional functions on top of content approval, or approval workflows can go it alone.

Approval workflow by itself doesn't affect who can see draft items and, unlike content approval, doesn't control item permissions. The out-of-the-box approval workflow does create a task and an email notification for each approver when the workflow is initiated; for example, it can be useful for getting the attention of people who review documents but who otherwise don't spend a lot of time in the app.

In fact, because the notification and task include a link to the pending item, the out-of-the-box approval workflow is a good way to get the input of users who otherwise won't go to SharePoint. And the approval workflow facilitates an exchange between the approver and the author of the content by allowing the approver to provide feedback on the document (better to have dubbed it review workflow).

There are three components of using the out-of-the-box approval workflow: configuring the workflow for the app, initiating the workflow for a document or item, and responding to the workflow.

Setting up an approval workflow

Approval workflow is one of several out-of-the-box workflow templates in Share-Point 2016. To set up an approval workflow, follow these steps:

1. **Access the Library Settings page using the Ribbon in your app.**

2. **In the Settings section, click the Workflow Settings link.**

   You need to activate the Workflows feature for the site collection before you see the out-of-the-box workflows.

TIP

3. **Click the Add a Workflow link.**

   The Add a Workflow page is displayed, as shown in Figure 21-6.

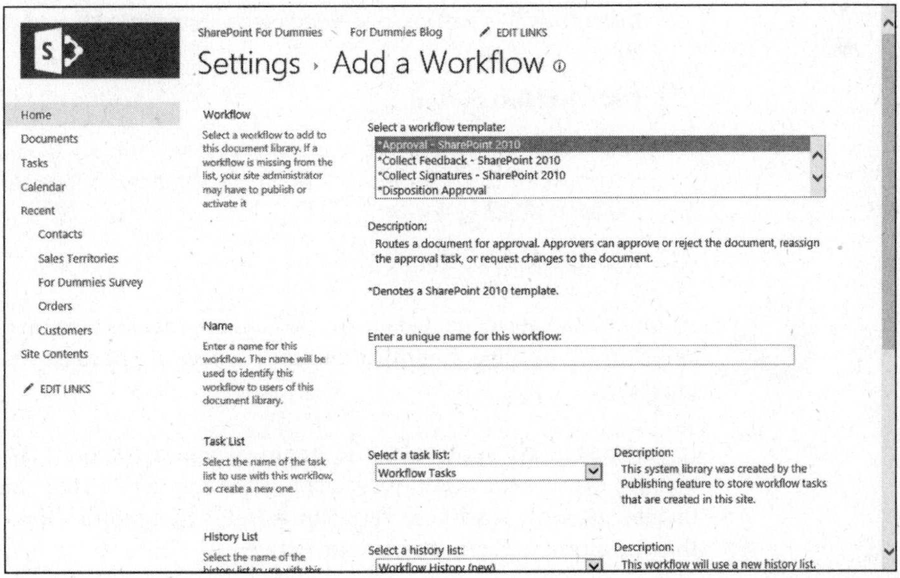

![The Add a Workflow page showing the Settings > Add a Workflow interface with a left navigation menu (Home, Documents, Tasks, Calendar, Recent, Contacts, Sales Territories, For Dummies Survey, Orders, Customers, Site Contents, Edit Links) and workflow configuration options including Workflow template selection, Name, Task List, and History List sections.]

FIGURE 21-6:
The Add a
Workflow page.

4. Click the Approval - SharePoint 2010 option in the Select a Workflow Template list.

5. Enter a name in the Type a Unique Name for This Workflow text box.

We recommend choosing a name that describes the step in your business process this workflow fulfills. In our experiences, most business processes can have several approval steps, so calling it "The Approval Workflow" isn't meaningful. For example, if your approval workflow is actually a review workflow, call it the "Author Review Workflow." If you need to add a second approval workflow, you could call it the "Regulatory Editorial Review Workflow."

6. Use the Select a Task List drop-down list to choose a task list.

We recommend going with the default — Workflow Tasks — unless you have a special reason for wanting to track this workflow in a list by itself.

7. Use the Select a History List drop-down list to choose a history list.

Again, we suggest accepting the default, which is Workflow History.

8. Select a Start option by selecting the appropriate check box.

Decide how you want the workflow to be triggered. If you want the workflow to start manually, select the Allow This Workflow to Be Manually Started by an Authenticated User with Edit Item Permissions check box.

Note: You can have only one workflow that's triggered by publishing in a library.

9. Click the Next button.

The Approval page appears, as shown in Figure 21-7. See the options we discuss in the following section, "Approval workflow options," and then specify the appropriate options.

10. Click the Save button.

TIP

If you have an alert enabled on an app, and approval is also turned on for that app, you may not receive a notification until a new or changed item is approved and published.

If you just need approvals, the approval workflow may be overkill. Consider turning off workflow and just keeping the approvals functionality discussed in Chapter 18, with or without versioning. Items that require approval will quietly sit there, waiting for someone to take notice.

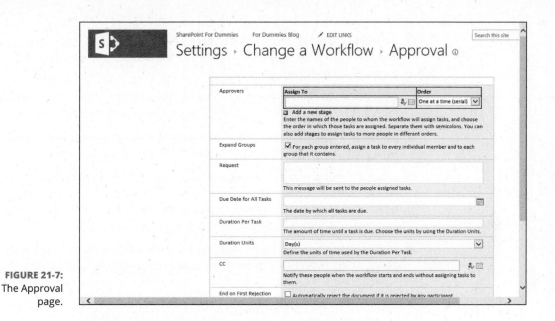

FIGURE 21-7:
The Approval
page.

Approval workflow options

Think of a workflow as the orchestrator, and potentially automator (yes, we made that word up), of a business process. Say you have a business process for reviewing and approving real estate contracts. This process may include someone drafting the contract, emailing a copy to someone who reviews it, and then emailing it to someone else for approval. The out-of-the-box approval workflows in SharePoint provide all these options so you can automate the routing of the document from the person drafting it to the document's reviewers and approvers.

You can select options for how you want the approval workflow to work when you associate the workflow with your app, which we describe how to do in the next section.

The following list describes the options available for approval workflows:

REMEMBER

>> **Approvers (Assign To):** Assigns individuals and groups to the approval tasks. If you have multiple approvers, you can also specify the order in which they're assigned the item. The approval status doesn't change from Pending to Approved until all approvers have approved the item.

Unless you have the Cancel on Rejection option enabled, if an approver rejects an item, the approval continues to the next approver.

>> **Approvers (Order):** Specifies whether the approvers will be assigned the approval tasks all at once or whether when one person approves, the next person is assigned the task, and so on.

Go with the standard — arrange approvers in ascending order of importance so, for example, you don't bother the director until the managers have approved.

>> **Add a New Stage:** Enables you to add a stage to the approval process. Don't get carried away here, because you have to manage all those stages.

>> **Expand Groups:** Assigns an approval task to each individual in each approver group, rather than assigning a single task to the entire group. If you've also specified an order, all approvers in the expanded group are treated as one approver, and they're assigned the approval when the group is.

>> **Notification Message:** Sends a message to each member of each approval group. All approvers get the same notification message. (We recommend saying, "Please.")

>> **Due Date for All Tasks:** Creates a date by which all tasks not completed are considered overdue; this overrides the Duration for Serial Tasks/Duration Units values.

>> **Duration Per Task:** Determines, with the Duration Units text box, how long each serial task can be active before being marked overdue.

>> **Duration Units:** Determines, with the Duration for Serial Tasks option, how long a serial task can be active before being marked overdue.

>> **CC:** Notifies specified people when the workflow is started but doesn't assign tasks to them (unless they're also in the approvers group).

>> **End on First Rejection:** Cancels the entire workflow if one approver marks the item as rejected. The item moves to rejected status, and the item author is notified.

In any case, if End on First Rejection is selected, when one approver rejects the item, this halts the approval workflow for this round, until the item is resubmitted. We recommend listing the tougher critics as earlier approvers to reduce the number of times you have to request approval from someone who's already given it.

>> **End on Document Change:** Cancels the workflow if the item is changed while the workflow is running.

If you work in a regulated industry and are requesting approval of regulated items, we highly recommend enabling this option.

>> **Enable Content Approval:** Updates the status of the approval when the workflow has completed. For the most reliable results, configure your approval workflow before turning on content approval.

TIP

Need more options? You can create your own workflows (either SharePoint 2010 platform or SharePoint 2013 platform–based) or customize the approval workflows provided by SharePoint using SharePoint Designer 2013 or Visual Studio.

Initiating a workflow

Configuring your app to use a workflow only solves part of the problem. If you don't have your workflow configured to kick off automatically, someone must manually start the workflow.

Manually initiate a workflow by following these steps:

1. **Browse to the item you want approved, click the ellipsis, and then click the inner ellipsis (see Figure 21-8), and choose Workflows from the Advanced menu.**

You see the Workflows page for that library or list.

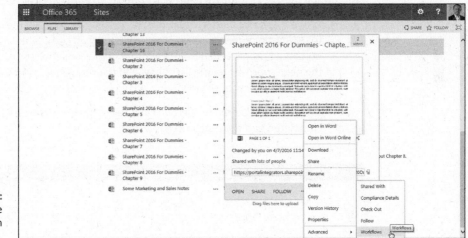

FIGURE 21-8:
Choose Workflows from the menu.

2. **Under Start a New Workflow, select the approval workflow you want to initiate.**

The form to initiate the workflow displays, populated with the default values specified during the workflow configuration; you can accept the defaults or change them.

3. **Click the Start button.**

A Workflow task is created in the specified task list app and is assigned to the first approver. If email alerts are enabled, an email is sent to that person with a link to the item, instructions, and a link to the associated task. The requestor also receives an email indicating that the task has been started, as well as a link to the item and the workflow status page.

Approving an item

If you're an approver on an item, follow these steps to respond to an approval request:

1. **Review the task by clicking the link in the email request or by accessing the item directly in the task list app.**

   You can review the task by clicking the Settings gear icon and choosing Site Contents to go to the Site Content page, and then clicking on the Tasks app. Click the task that was generated to approve the document.

2. **Enter comments in the Your Comments text box.**

3. **Click a button to indicate what you want to do with this item (see Figure 21-9):**

   - *Click the Approve button to approve the item.* If you approve the item and there are no other approvers, the task is marked completed and the outcome is approved. If there are other approvers, the task is assigned to the next approver on the list, if any, and the requestor is notified. The task version history is updated.

   - *Click the Reject button to reject it.* If you reject the item, the task is marked completed and the outcome is rejected.

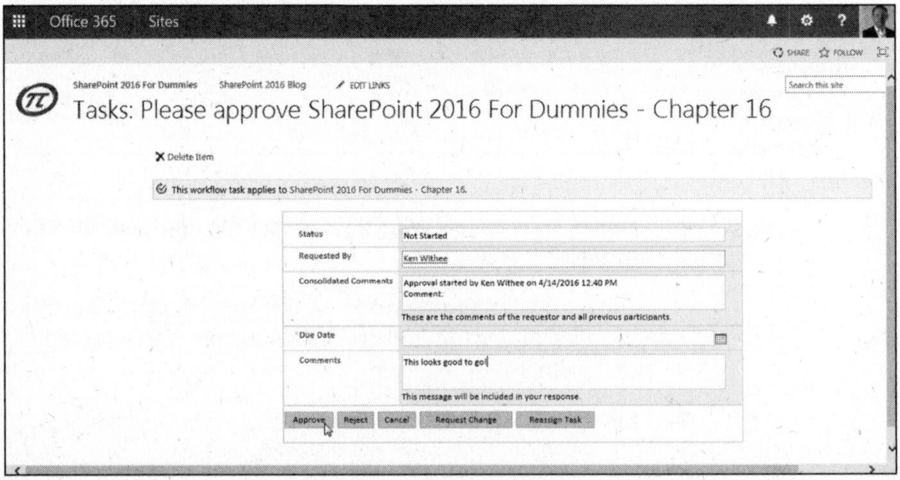

FIGURE 21-9: Task details for an approver.

- *Click the Cancel button to back out of this task.*

- *Click the Request Change button to indicate that further edits are needed.* The Workflow Task window displays, as shown in Figure 21-10. Enter the name of the person whom you want to make the change in the Request Change From text box, a description of your request in the Your Request text box, the task duration (if any) in the Duration for Serial Tasks, and select a time unit from the Duration Units drop-down list, and then click the Send button. A new task is created for the person you specified, and your task status is marked completed.

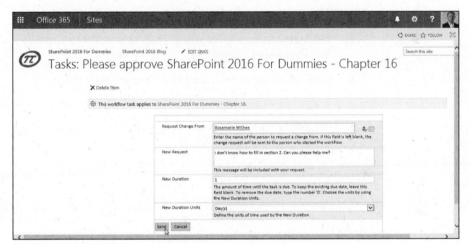

FIGURE 21-10:
Request the author to make changes.

- *Click the Reassign Task button to ask someone else to approve the item.* If you reassign the task, you're prompted to enter the name of the person to whom it should be reassigned. A new task is created, and your task is marked complete but the status is delegated.

The requestor is notified each time the task is updated.

REMEMBER

WARNING

Don't confuse status with outcome. *Status* merely indicates whether the workflow task is active or complete. *Outcome* is what tells you whether the item really passed muster and was approved. Whether the item was approved or rejected, the task status is marked as complete when the last approver has approved or rejected it. However, the task outcome indicates whether the item was approved or rejected.

You can also respond to an approval request by accessing the items using the Site Content and Structure tool. Use the tool to locate the item in the site hierarchy, and then use the item's context menu to select an approval option. Alternatively, you can also edit the task from Outlook.

Checking the status of workflows in an app

You can check the status of the workflows in your List- or Library-based app by looking at the Workflow Settings page. You access this page by clicking the Library or List tab in the app and then selecting Workflow Settings from the Settings section.

Checking the status of all workflows

Requestors and reviewers can check the status of an approval workflow as follows:

1. **Navigate to the site for which you want to check the status of one or more approval workflows.**

2. **Click the Settings gear icon and choose Site Settings.**

3. **In the Site Administration section, click the Content and Structure link.**

   The Site Content and Structure page appears, as shown in Figure 21-11.

FIGURE 21-11:
The Site Content and Structure page.

TIP

The Site Content and Structure tool is only available if the Publishing Server Infrastructure feature is active for the site collection. If the feature isn't active, the link won't appear in the Site Administration section of Site Settings. If you are using SharePoint Online, then this option won't be available on the Site Settings page. You might still be able to access it by typing http://<site_url>/_layouts/15/sitemanager.aspx into your web browser.

4. **To view the status of items specific to you, select an item from the View drop-down list:**

   - *For requestors,* choosing Pending Approval displays all items that you've submitted for approval and aren't completed yet.

   - *For approvers,* choosing My Tasks displays all tasks, including approval workflow tasks, assigned to you.

5. **To view all tasks (your own as well as those assigned to other people), click Workflow Tasks in the navigation pane on the left, and then choose All Tasks from the View drop-down list.**

   The Workflow Tasks – All Tasks page appears.

6. **Click any task to view its details.**

A light touch with content approval and approval workflow can help facilitate reviews, support governance policies, and help you track and retain information about whether content has passed the right checkpoints before being formalized. Experiment with them alone or in combination until you hit on the process that works.

6

Office 365 and SharePoint Online

Chapter 22

Creating a Public Website

Microsoft has discontinued the ability to create a public website using SharePoint Online. They did this because they recognized that their partners have a very strong solution. If you are new to Office 365 and SharePoint Online and you need a public-facing website, then you can use one of Microsoft's suggested partners, GoDaddy or Wix. If you already have an existing public-facing website built on SharePoint Online, however, then you will still be able to work with it.

In this chapter, you find out how to create a public-facing website using Microsoft's partner recommendations and how to use your existing SharePoint Online public-facing website if you already have one.

Creating a Public-Facing Website

If you have Office 365 and you need a public-facing website, then you are in luck. Microsoft has negotiated special deals with a couple of select partners: GoDaddy and Wix.

To create a public-facing website, the first thing you need to do is browse to the Office 365 Administration Center (`https://portal.office.com`) and then click Public Website in the left-hand navigation. You are presented with a page outlining the partners Microsoft decided to work with for public-facing websites, as shown in Figure 22-1.

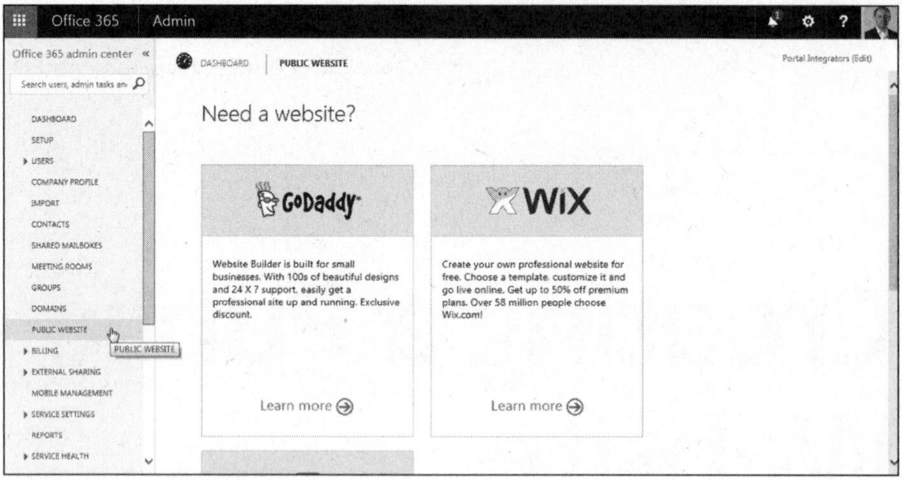

FIGURE 22-1: Navigating to the Public Website section of Office 365.

Choose GoDaddy and you can use a tool called Website Builder. Choose Wix and you can leverage their much-loved drag-and-drop functionality to create a website.

In our opinion, GoDaddy is a much more powerful platform, but Wix is much simpler to use and can help you get your site up and looking beautiful right away. One additional benefit to Wix is that getting started with it is free.

We will always choose GoDaddy just for the additional power features they offer such as their advanced hosting, premier DNS, and customization options. That said, though, Wix is easy to use if you just need a basic website.

GoDaddy

If you decide to go with GoDaddy, then click the Learn More link (see Figure 22-1) to start the process. You are redirected to a special GoDaddy site setup to give you the special Microsoft Office 365 discounted rate.

If you just want to set up a basic site using GoDaddy's Website Builder functionality, then click the Get Started link and follow through the process, as shown in Figure 22-2.

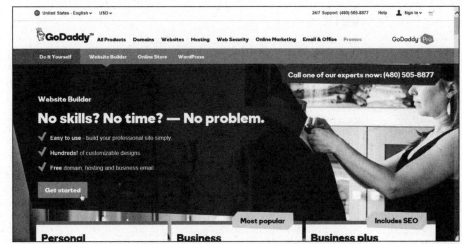

FIGURE 22-2:
Getting started
with a GoDaddy
website from
the Office 365
admin center.

You can then review the type of website plan you are interested in and walk through a GoDaddy wizard to set up your site. Figure 22-3 shows the available plans along with the special Microsoft Office 365 pricing as of this writing.

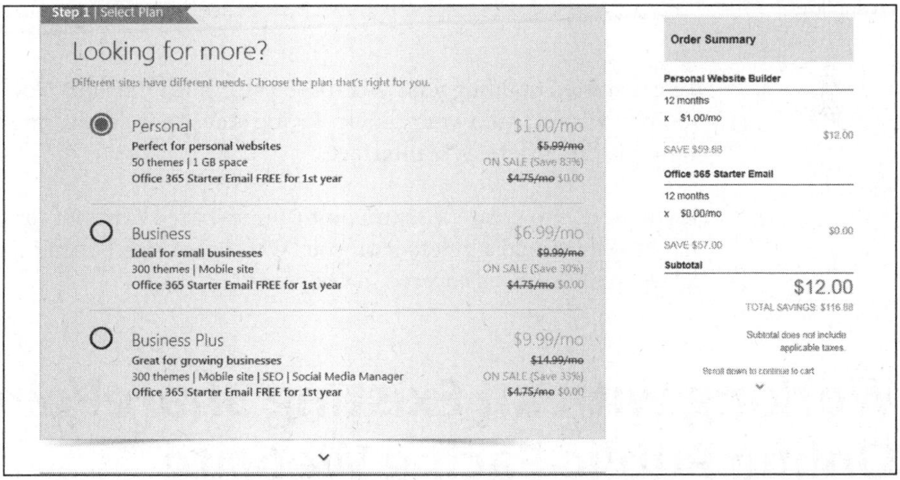

FIGURE 22-3:
Choosing a
website plan
from GoDaddy
with the
Microsoft Office
365 discounts.

As you continue through the process, you will be guided in setting up your public-facing website. You control your public-facing website and decide how you want to integrate it with SharePoint Online and Office 365. For example, you might want to have an Extranet link that takes people to your SharePoint Online-based extranet. (Setting up an extranet in SharePoint Online is covered in Chapter 23.)

Wix

If you decide to go with Wix, then click the Learn More link (see Figure 22-1) to start the process. You are redirected to a special Wix site set up to give you the special Microsoft Office 365 discounted rate on Premium Plans, as shown in Figure 22-4.

FIGURE 22-4:
Getting started with a Wix-based public website.

To get started building your Wix-based site, click the Start Now button and follow the Wix wizard. After your public-facing website is set up, you have control of its content through the Wix interface.

If you decide to create a SharePoint Online-based extranet for your partners, you might want to add a link to it on your Wix-based site. Setting up an extranet using SharePoint Online is covered in Chapter 23.

Working with an Existing SharePoint Online Public-Facing Website

A SharePoint-based public website site collection is still SharePoint behind the scenes, but it looks and behaves quite differently than your typical SharePoint site.

WARNING

The public-facing site was designed with the best intentions but Microsoft realized their partners provide a better solution and stopped allowing for the new creation of SharePoint-based public websites. However, if you already have an existing SharePoint Online-based public-facing site, you can continue to work with it and manage it, and we cover this subject in the next few sections.

Updating and Adding Web Pages

If you have some experience with updating and adding pages to a regular SharePoint site, you'll find yourself in familiar — but not exactly the same — territory when doing the same thing in your public website. If you've never done this stuff in SharePoint before, relax: It's pretty easy and straightforward.

Reviewing what you get with your site

Wondering what you get in your SharePoint Online public website? A number of apps are contained in the default site:

» Categories

» Documents

» Form Templates

» Pages

» Photos

» Posts

» Reusable Content

» Site Assets

» Site Elements

» Style Library

Most of these apps are empty, but some are pre-populated for the default site (see Figure 22-5). The Pages app is where all the web pages for your public site are located. It contains the pages that make up the default website. These are:

» About Us

» Archives

» Blog

» Contact Us

» Default

» Directions

» PageNotFoundError

>> Post

>> Posts

>> Search Results

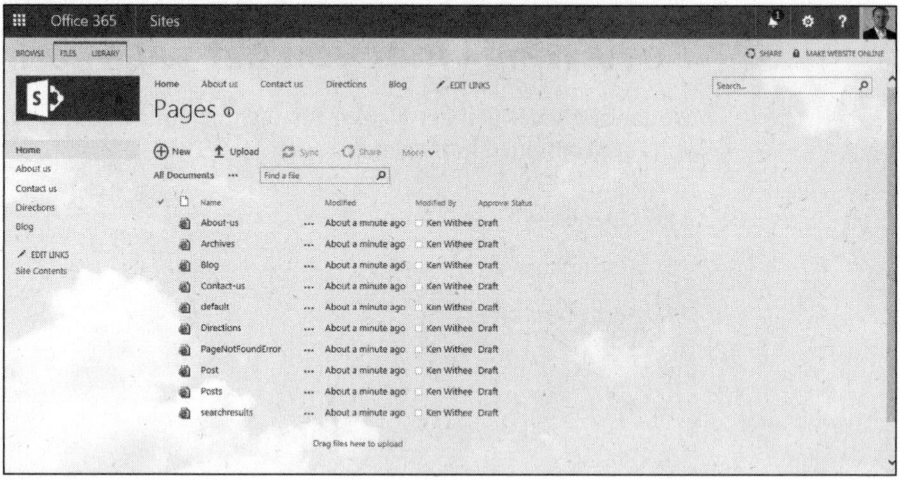

FIGURE 22-5:
The Pages app,
where all your
pages are stored.

Most of these pages are self-explanatory. As you customize your public site, you will add pages to and remove pages from the library. The pages that are there by default are the ones used as an example and make up the default website shown in Figure 22-5.

TIP

Your site is not available to the world until you publish it. This gives you time to work on it and perfect it before unleashing it on the world. You will see a Make Website Online link in the upper-right corner of the page. When you click that link, your website will be published for the world to see. When you want to take your website offline, you can click the Make Website Offline link, which appears in the same location.

Adding a new page

You get to the list of contents for the site by clicking the Settings gear icon and choosing Site Contents. This automatically takes you to the Site Contents page. Here, you can add new apps or click the Pages app and add new pages, as shown in Figure 22-5.

When you are in the Pages app, you can click the New Document drop-down list on the Files tab of the Ribbon. You have the option to add a new page to your site. When you add a new page, you choose a template from the drop-down list, as shown in Figure 22-6.

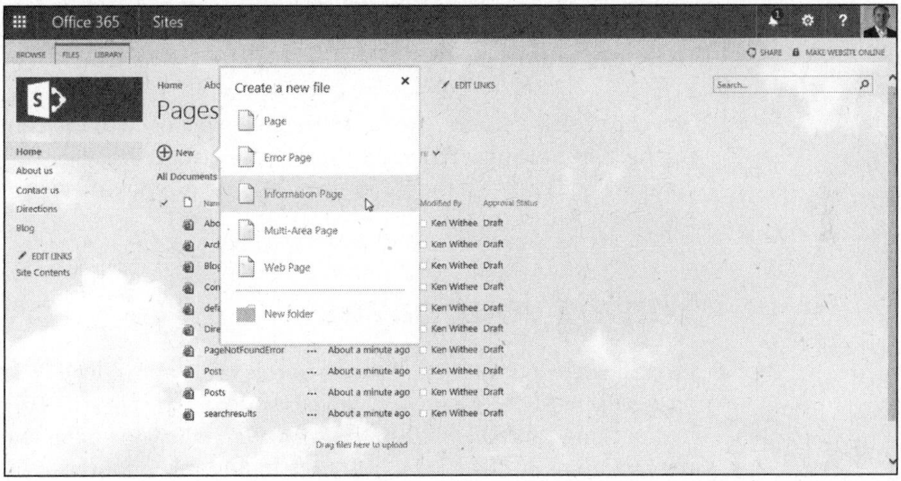

FIGURE 22-6:
Creating a new page in the Pages app of a public SharePoint Online site.

This is convenient for quickly getting the layout and design right for the purpose of the page. You have the option of choosing from the following page templates (which use SharePoint content types):

» Page

» Error Page

» Information Page

» Multi-Area Page

» Web Page

Clicking a new page type in the New Document drop-down list brings up a page where you can specify the title of the new page, the web address, and the page layout. And in case that threw you for a loop, yes, you are using a SharePoint page to create a new SharePoint page. Experiment with a few pages and layouts to figure out how to use the different templates and what the different options mean.

The differences in the page templates are subtle. For example, you might wonder what the difference is between a Page template and a Web Page template. Microsoft makes an attempt to clarify differences by including a description next to each page template type, but it is still fairly unclear.

To understand the differences, you need to understand that these are actually SharePoint content types. A *content type* is a collection of fields. So the difference between a Page template and a Web Page template depends on the fields that are defined in each content type. If you click on the Library tab of the Pages app and click the Library Settings button, you see a section called Content Types. Notice that these are the same options from the New Document drop-down list. If you added a content type to this section, you would have another option on the New Document drop-down list.

You can click a content type to see the fields included in the content type. By clicking the Page content type and then clicking the Web Page content type, you can compare and contrast the differences. (Content types are covered in more detail in Chapter 8.)

Editing your pages

To edit any existing pages, browse to the Pages app and click a page. This displays your page in the browser. You can edit the page by clicking Page tab of the Ribbon and clicking the Edit button. You can then edit your page and add, modify, and remove content. The Contact Us page in Edit mode is shown in Figure 22-7.

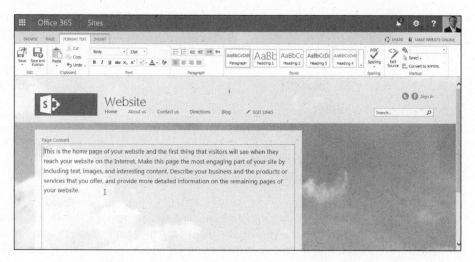

FIGURE 22-7:
Editing a Public Website page.

You see Page, Format Text, and Insert tabs of the Ribbon. Each Ribbon tab contains buttons that are familiar with any document editing tool, and they work exactly the same. You can format text and choose a different font, size, or color on the Format Text tab. You can insert content on the Insert tab. And you can preview, save, and publish the page on the Page tab.

Updating page properties

After you're done creating new pages, you may want to change some options for the site pages, such as the content type of the page or the contact for the page. These options are included on the Page Properties page, shown in Figure 22-8, that you can access by selecting the page in the Pages app and clicking the Edit Properties button on the Files tab of the Ribbon.

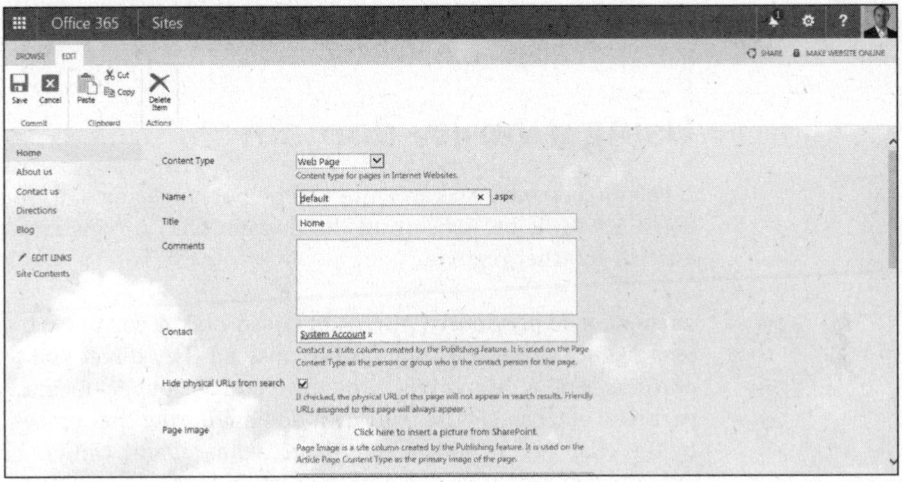

FIGURE 22-8:
Changing a page's properties.

TIP

If you don't have access to a page, then the Edit Properties button is disabled.

Changing the site's look and feel

An important and unique tab on the Ribbon of a public site is the Site tab, as shown in Figure 22-9. You see the Site tab when looking at any page in your public website (assuming you have permissions, of course).

The Site tab enables you to change the look of your site and edit important components such as the title, logo, menus, and Search text box. You can even edit the style sheet for the site in the Advanced section. If you're not familiar with style sheets, this option is best left unexplored. For you intrepid web developers out there, good luck!

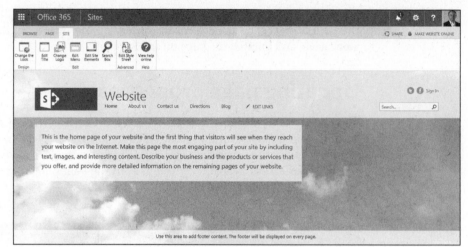

FIGURE 22-9:
The Site tab on
the Ribbon.

Using a vanity domain

If you already have a SharePoint Online public-facing site, you can use a custom domain with it by registering the domain with a registry such as GoDaddy or another Internet registrar.

TIP

As mentioned previously, Microsoft doesn't allow you to create new public-facing SharePoint Online sites any longer. Instead they direct you towards their select partners, GoDaddy and Wix. When you create a public-facing website using these partners, you can choose your own domain during that process (described earlier in the chapter). If you already have a SharePoint Online-based public-facing website, you can still add a custom domain to it.

You can change the domain name of your public-facing site, but you first have to register your domain name with Office 365. To do so, follow these steps:

1. **Browse to the Office 365 Admin page** (https://portal.office.com).

2. **On the left navigation, click the Domains link.**

   You see a page similar to Figure 22-10.

3. **Click the Add a Domain link.**

4. **Follow the wizard that walks you through adding a domain.**

5. **When you are finished with Step 4, go back to the SharePoint Online Administration Center (the SharePoint link in the Admin node from portal.office.com), select your existing public-facing website site collection, and click the Add Domain button in the Public Website portion of the Site Collections Ribbon.**

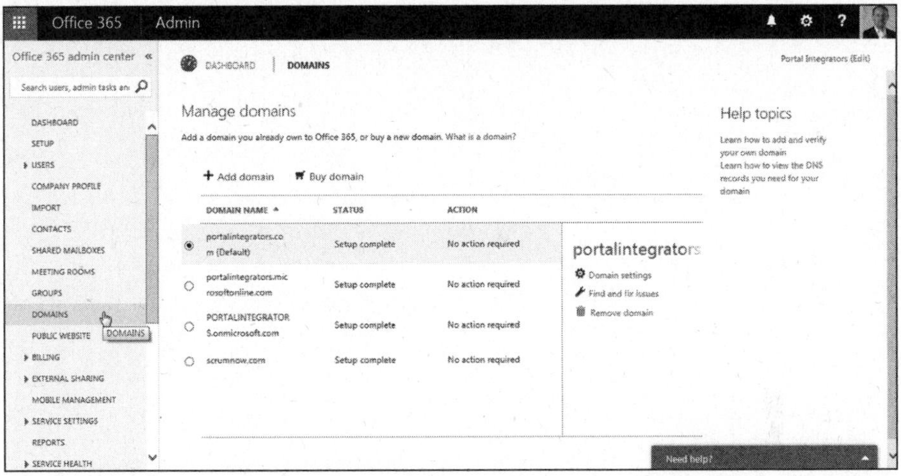

FIGURE 22-10:
Managing your
Office 365
domains.

6. **In the Select Your Domain dialog box, find your new domain name. Select it and click OK.**

TIP

If you do not see your new domain name yet, you may need to wait for DNS to switch your record from the previous location to Office 365. This usually happens within a day but can take up to 72 hours.

Chapter 23

Creating a Client Portal in SharePoint Online

Creating and using a SharePoint portal in SharePoint Online is easier than creating an entire environment from scratch (called SharePoint On–Premises). SharePoint Online takes away all of the difficulties in setting up the infrastructure (explored in Chapter 2), but you're still left with working with SharePoint itself. This means figuring out how to create your online users and what permissions to assign them in the SharePoint site.

In this chapter, you plan and implement a SharePoint portal using SharePoint Online. You add and manage users, as well as manage their permissions on the site.

Planning for Your Client Portal

Planning for SharePoint Online is similar to planning for a regular SharePoint installation in that you have to determine what the site will be used for and the types of activities that need to be supported in that environment. If you haven't yet read Chapter 2, you should take a look at that while doing your planning. However, a few items are worth noting when planning your Office 365 environment:

>> **The number of resources and the amount of storage space you have available in Office 365 is limited.** Storage is easy to understand, but resources are not on the surface. Basically, a number of physical and virtual resources on the hardware and operating system are monitored daily by SharePoint Online. The types of items measured include counts, seconds, numbers, CPU cycles, bytes, threads, and Windows handles. Each of these items has a hard upper limit based on the hardware that is handling the requests, and so you're granted a set number of resources per Office 365 subscription. You must allocate those resources based on what you think each site collection will need on a daily basis. You can change the allocation at any time, but remember that your total resource (and storage) allocations for your SharePoint subscription remain the same.

TIP

The SharePoint Online service administrator can set the storage limits for site collections and sites created by users. SharePoint storage limits depend on a number of different factors, but, in general, the storage is 1TB (terabyte) plus 0.5GB (gigabyte) per additional user. You can find all of the specifics by entering *SharePoint Online and OneDrive for Business software boundaries and limits* into your favorite search engine. Look for a link that is on office.com for official guidance. Also, keep in mind you can always buy more SharePoint storage if you need it.

REMEMBER

SharePoint Online is constantly being updated, and it's entirely possible that the limits will change. Make sure to check the Office 365 website for the latest limits and pricing information.

>> **You don't have control over some of the configuration items in SharePoint Online that you have for SharePoint On-Premises.** Most of the differences are at the farm administration level, but it's something to keep in mind. If you're dead set on particular functionality in SharePoint, then you want to make sure it's available in SharePoint Online.

SharePoint Online provides a number of advanced configuration options, but the way they're configured is different than SharePoint On-Premises. For example, SharePoint On-Premises uses the Central Administration tool. In SharePoint Online, you use the SharePoint Online Administrator Center, as shown in Figure 23-1.

Keep in mind that SharePoint Online is a product in motion. Microsoft is constantly updating and tweaking the user interface and location of components. The concepts are usually the same, but if you see something a little different than we describe, you might have to hunt around because you are likely seeing a new change Microsoft has made.

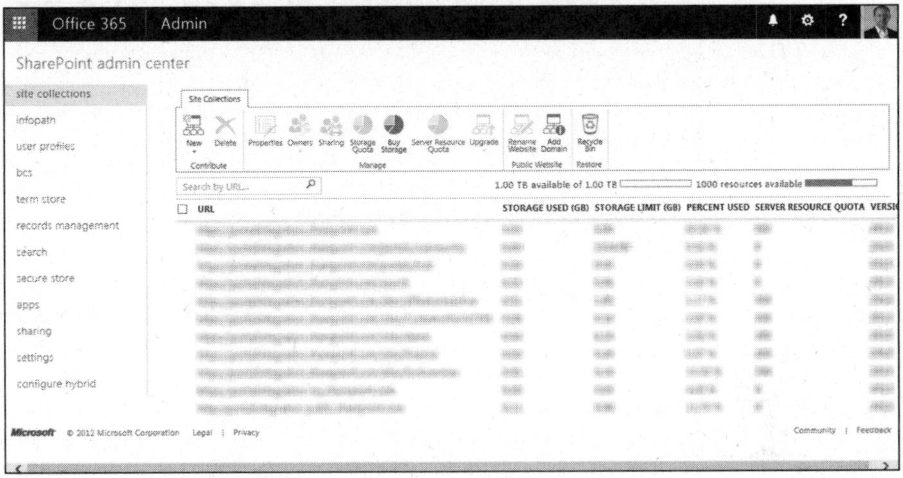

FIGURE 23-1:
The main
SharePoint
Online
Administration
page.

In addition, you should consider a number of things when planning out your SharePoint Online environment. These include

» Your DNS name, if you need to have a distinct URL to access your public-facing website. (For more information about configuring the DNS name, see Chapter 22.)

» Whether you will allow external users to browse to your SharePoint Online collaboration site. If you work with people outside your organization on an ongoing basis, and you need to share and collaborate with them, this is a useful option.

» Whether you will provide the My Sites capability for users and how much space they should be allocated in their quotas.

» How user profiles and roles will be assigned. From the User Profiles link in the administration center, you have the ability to configure many aspects of how users, audiences, permissions, and policies are configured, not to mention My Sites functionality if you decide to host this in the cloud. As shown in Figure 23-2, the options on this page are divided into People, Organizations, and My Site Settings. Although it's beyond the scope of this book to describe these settings in detail, you will probably need to manage and plan for at least some of these settings when you establish your SharePoint Online presence, especially if you're creating a collaboration space for more than a single organization.

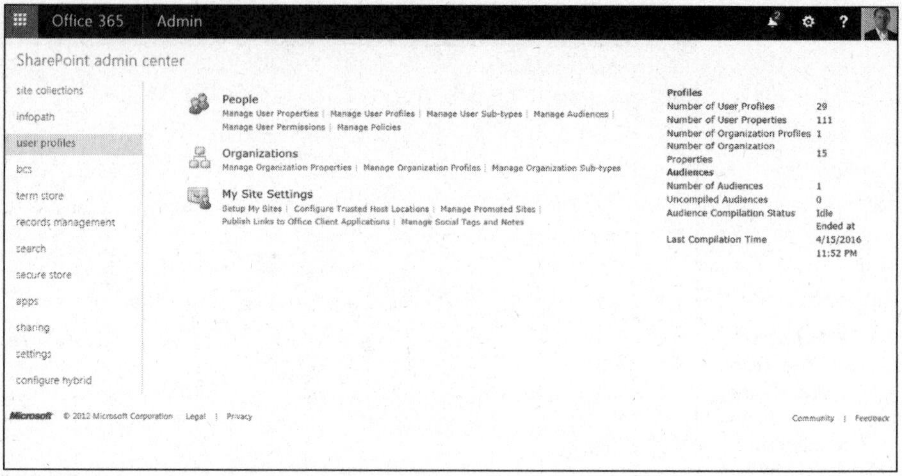

FIGURE 23-2: Configuring SharePoint Online user profiles.

Locking Down the Portal

The first thing that you want to do is determine who your site collection administrators are for each of your SharePoint Online site collections. This could be you or it could be someone else. After you determine who has these duties, assign them either the primary administrator or an additional administrator of the site collection by selecting the site and clicking the Owners button in the Ribbon. This displays the Manage Administrators dialog box, as shown in Figure 23-3.

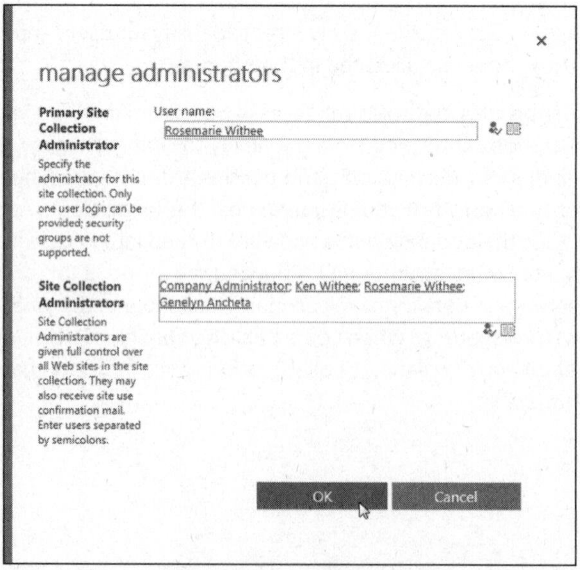

FIGURE 23-3: Assigning site collection administrators.

The biggest hurdle to locking down the portal is figuring out permissions. You need to determine which users have access and what they can do on the site. So you need to understand what SharePoint permissions are and how they are assigned, which is exactly what we cover in the next section. (You can also turn to Chapter 14 for more information on securing your site.)

Managing User Accounts

Depending on how your SharePoint Online/Office 365 environment is configured, you have three options for getting your users into the cloud:

>> You can set up users via Single Sign-On (SSO), which allows you to use all your current users' identities with their same corporate identities on Office 365 and SharePoint Online.

>> You can set up users via Active Directory synchronization, which goes hand-in-hand with SSO.

>> You can set up users with distinct credentials that are applicable only to Office 365/SharePoint Online. This is more burdensome on your users, but less burden on your IT staff. And if you're a small organization with plans to move to Office 365 and SharePoint Online exclusively, these credentials become your main credentials.

TIP

For external contacts (to Office 365), there is currently no limit to the number of people you can add. However, keep in mind that Microsoft sometimes changes limits (in the past, for example, the limit was 50 external users), so be sure to check in Office 365 to make sure.

After you decide on how your online user identities are going to be created, you'll manage them much in the same way you manage SharePoint On–Premises users, and the best way to do that is through the exclusive use of groups and group membership.

To access your users and groups, follow these steps:

1. **Click the Settings gear icon and choose Site Settings.**

TIP

If you don't see the Site Settings option, you don't have permission to administer the site collection. Check with your administrator to see if she can make you a site collection administrator on your portal.

2. **Click the People and Groups link in the Users and Permissions section of the Site Settings page.**

   The next page that comes up is usually the Members page, but this depends on the site template. The Members page is shown in Figure 23-4.

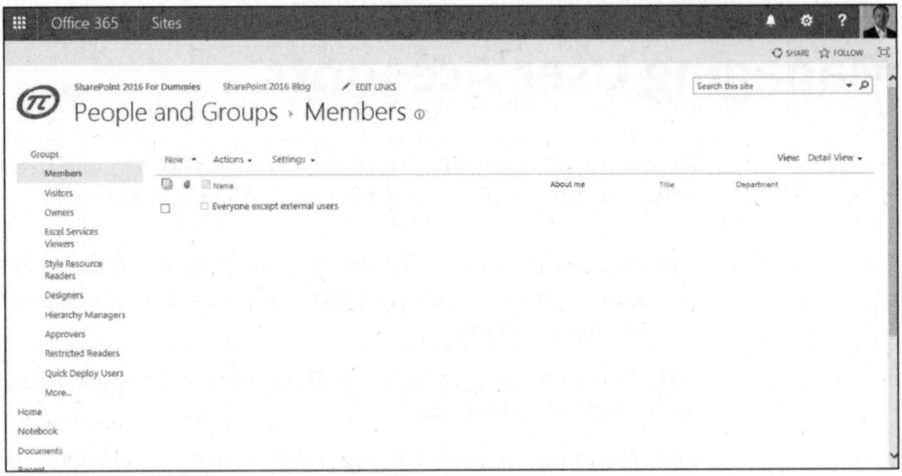

FIGURE 23-4:
Adding groups
and users to
groups from the
Members page.

   The Groups links in the left navigation are all the typical groups that are preinstalled with the Team Site template, such as Members, Viewers, Visitors, and Owners links. Each of these groups is assigned particular permissions. For example, visitors have the View Only permission level, which means they can only view information on the site but can't open and read documents unless the Office Web Applications are available. Site visitors, on the other hand, have the Read permission level and can download and read documents, as well as the other content on the site.

3. **Click the More link in the left navigation.**

   On the People and Groups page, you can see and edit the default groups and create and delete groups.

4. **From the New menu, click Group to create a new group.**

   As shown in Figure 23-5, there are many aspects to creating a new group, including the name, description, and owner of the group, as well as who can view and edit the group membership, where membership group requests are sent, and the permission level of the group. To understand more about permission levels, see Chapter 14.

FIGURE 23-5:
Creating a new
group in
SharePoint.

Working with users and groups in a SharePoint 2016 site is the same, regardless of whether you use SharePoint On-Premises or SharePoint Online. The main difference is in how users are created and managed outside of SharePoint. In other words, what you have to do to make users available to SharePoint. After users are available to SharePoint, the experience within a SharePoint site is identical.

After you realize how easy it is to create a new group, you may want to explore the types of permission levels you can assign to new groups. To edit these permission levels, click the Site Permissions link on the Site Settings page. Clicking the Site Permissions link takes you to a list of the permission levels that are the same as the groups, with the addition of the person who created the site.

To explore the different permissions, add a new permission level. To do this, follow these steps:

1. **Click the Settings gear icon and choose Site Settings.**

2. **Click the Site Permissions link in the Users and Permissions grouping.**

3. **Click the Permission Levels button in the Ribbon.**

4. **Click the Add a Permission Level button at the top of the page that lists all the built-in permission levels.**

   The Edit Permission Level page allows you to create a new permission level that can be assigned to your group. See Figure 23-6. The Add a Permission Level link only shows up if you are at the Site Collection level because that is where permission levels are located. We discussed permissions and SharePoint security in Chapter 14.

Office 365   Sites

⚙ ?

⟲ SHARE ☆ FOLLOW

S⊳

✎ EDIT LINKS

Permission Levels › Add a Permission Level

Home
PI Intranet
    Company Policies
    Documents
    Recommended Reading
    Knowledge Base
    Discussion Board
CustomerPoint
    Contacts
    Companies
    Touches
    Sales Pipeline
    Industry Reference
AssetPoint
    Assets
Recent
    Team Morale Event

Name and Description
Type a name and description for your permission level. The name is shown on the permissions page. The name and description are shown on the add users page.

Permissions
Choose which permissions to include in this permission level. Use the Select All check box to select or clear all permissions.

Name:

Description:

Select the permissions to include in this permission level.
☐ **Select All**

List Permissions
☐ Manage Lists · Create and delete lists, add or remove columns in a list, and add or remove public views of a list.

☐ Override List Behaviors · Discard or check in a document which is checked out to another user, and change or override settings which allow users to read/edit only their own items

☐ Add Items · Add items to lists and add documents to document libraries.

☐ Edit Items · Edit items in lists, edit documents in document libraries, and customize Web Part Pages in document libraries

FIGURE 23-6:
Creating a new permission level.

5. **Type a name and description in the Name and Description text boxes.**

6. **Select the check boxes for the permissions you want to assign to that level.**

7. **Click Submit.**

After you create a new permission level, you can use that level to assign your groups the correct permissions. After you do that, it's as easy as adding members to the particular group that gives them the appropriate access to your portal.

💡

TIP

In some cases, you simply need to assign one or two people special permissions to the site, and you won't want to create a new permission level and a new group for them, and that's okay. You don't want to burden yourself with the rule that all users should be managed via a group with the right permissions, but you do want to be able to manage users effectively with little ongoing maintenance. A well-planned group and permission level structure will help you in the end.

Launching Your Portal

The final question about your SharePoint Online portal is: When and how do you go about making it live? This may be a very easy question for you to answer, especially if this is your first foray into the SharePoint world. Or you may be wondering if you can ever actually launch your SharePoint Online portal because of the immense amount of pre-existing documents and information in your network drives or on your local computer.

Think of the new portal as a new lease on life for you and the people who use it. If you're starting fresh and are new to SharePoint, there's every reason to launch the portal as soon as you have your users configured and you've locked it down according to your company's policies and culture. If you're not starting fresh, you need to spend more time figuring how you're going to get people switched over to the new SharePoint Online environment. Here are a few approaches you can take:

>> **Have your users do the work.** This is a fairly low maintenance version of migrating content from one SharePoint environment to the next because you put the burden of content on the users' shoulders. The downside is that you run the risk of not getting everyone migrated at the same time, mainly because they won't see the benefit of moving to the new environment. This method requires some forceful tactics such as turning off the old, on-premises server.

>> **Help users devise a plan to migrate their content or at least identify content (and sites) that need to be migrated.** This approach takes a lot more time, but may be the most effective way to get users migrated completely and according to your timeline. It may also require some coercive tactics, such as the threat of turning off existing servers or making their content read-only, but at least it shouldn't be an outright scramble at the end.

>> **Invest in some third-party products that allow you to migrate your content from one site to the other.** The only thing you have to be aware of in this case is whether the product allows you to migrate to SharePoint Online. Some tools allow you to do this. Search the web for *SharePoint Online migration solutions* to get some idea of how these tools work and if they'll work for you.

After you have your users created, permissions assigned, and a plan in place to switch your users over, let them loose on your cloud-based portal.

7

The Part of Tens

Chapter 24

Ten Hot SharePoint 2016 Topics

Microsoft has a number of websites on which it posts all of its detailed product information. This chapter outlines some of these sites, including those geared for IT professionals, administrators, and end users of SharePoint.

Getting Up to Speed with SharePoint

Using SharePoint is fairly straightforward. At the base level, it's simply a website that users navigate to using their web browser. In this sense, SharePoint is no different than any other website. A number of resources go deeper into the intricacies of SharePoint from a user level.

Microsoft maintains an excellent resource for help at `https://support.office.com`. This site contains all sorts of help topics for Office apps, including SharePoint Online.

To find the SharePoint content, navigate to the site, click the More Apps link on the landing page to expand the list of icons (just below the main icons that say Excel, OneNote, and so on), and then click SharePoint. The SharePoint Online help center is displayed, as shown in Figure 24-1.

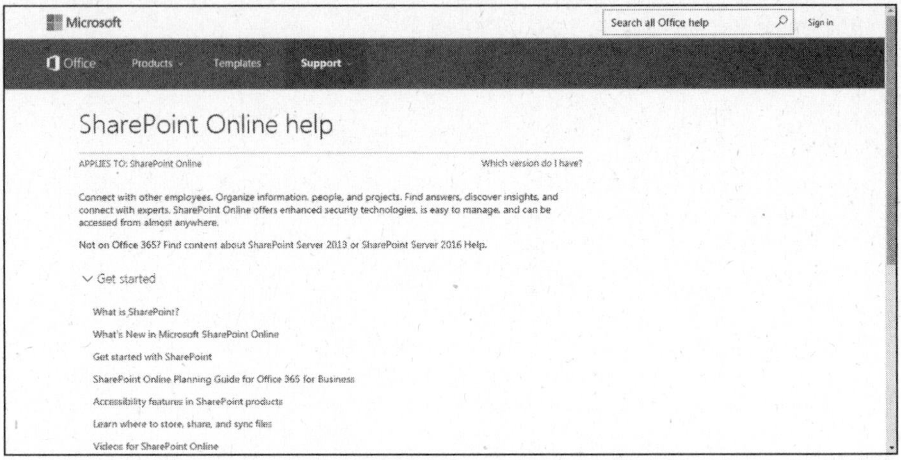

FIGURE 24-1:
The SharePoint
Online help
center.

What's New in SharePoint 2016 Video

```
https://channel9.msdn.com/Blogs/vladcatrinescu/Whats-new-in-
SharePoint-2016-for-IT-Pros
```

Channel 9 is a Microsoft-focused video-content site. In this episode, you learn about what is new with SharePoint 2016 for IT Pros.

Explore SharePoint 2016

```
https://technet.microsoft.com/en-us/library/cc261970(v=office.16).aspx
```

We have been working with SharePoint for years and years, and we still learn something new almost daily. SharePoint is a product with such depth that we doubt any one person can be a true expert on everything. Maybe a SharePoint master is out there somewhere who has explored every nook and cranny, but we have yet to meet that person.

When you're ready to dig deeper, the Explore SharePoint website excavates the SharePoint product in depth.

Plan for SharePoint

https://technet.microsoft.com/en-us/library/cc261834(v=office.16).aspx

One of the primary reasons an organization will hire a consulting firm to deploy SharePoint is because of their experience and expertise. Remember the old saying that hindsight is 20/20? Well, it couldn't be truer with SharePoint. We remember our first few implementations back in the mid-2000s. We cringe when we recall how painful those first few installations were. Having worked with SharePoint for years and years at hundreds of organizations, we have finally built up an expertise to get implementing SharePoint right the first time.

Not everyone has the time, or desire, to dedicate so much time to SharePoint. And not everyone wants to hire a consultant. Microsoft has captured much of the knowledge it takes to plan for a SharePoint implementation and posted it to the Plan for SharePoint section of TechNet.

If you are considering SharePoint Online, then you can find an excellent planning guide on the Office site at:

https://support.office.com/en-us/article/SharePoint-Online-Planning-Guide-for-Office-365-for-business-d5089cdf-3fd2-4230-acbd-20ecda2f9bb8

Install and Configure SharePoint

https://technet.microsoft.com/en-us/library/cc262957(v=office.16).aspx

Installing and configuring SharePoint is not for the faint of heart. We have seen implementations that cost up to seven figures (over $1 million!). Depending on the size of your organization and the resources at your disposal, you may decide it is better to choose SharePoint Online and let Microsoft handle the infrastructure. This choice frees you to focus on the business value SharePoint can provide. With that said, installing SharePoint On-Premises might be the right option for you so that your organization has total control over the product and can fit every nuance to your direct needs.

Microsoft does a great job explaining how the installation process of SharePoint works. TechNet includes articles for setting up the domain accounts and installing and configuring the operating systems, database, web server, and SharePoint itself.

TIP

SharePoint Online or SharePoint On-Premises does not have to be an either/or decision. There is also a hybrid approach, where you have an On-Premises installation that works in sync with Online. Our only warning with this approach is that you still have to take all the precautions you would with an On-Premises-only approach. The difference is that the On-Premises portion doesn't need to accommodate the entire organization, which reduces the footprint and the complexity of running SharePoint on your local premises.

Operate and Maintain

https://technet.microsoft.com/en-us/library/cc262289(v=office.16).aspx

Operating and maintaining SharePoint is extremely important and very complex. The SharePoint platform has a number of required technologies, and each of these needs to be operated and maintained as well (see Chapter 1 for an explanation of the technology SharePoint uses).

The TechNet site dedicated to the operation and maintenance of SharePoint includes a wealth of information about farm administration (such as managing services) and solution administration (such as administering site collections).

SharePoint Development

http://dev.office.com

When you need to bring in the developers, or if you are a developer yourself, then you will find the Office Dev Center as a great place to point your browser. The Dev Center provides resources for Office development of all types, including SharePoint development. Just look for the SharePoint icon under the list of Office applications on the main landing page, as shown in Figure 24-2.

TIP

The term *developer* has an ever-changing meaning. In the past, a developer was a hard-core computer programmer. A modern SharePoint developer may have never taken a single computer class. Just because you don't dream in code doesn't mean you won't find the Office Dev Center very useful.

FIGURE 24-2:
The Office
Dev Center.

SharePoint Workflow

https://technet.microsoft.com/en-us/library/jj227177(office.15)

Workflow is a critical business component to many organizations and Microsoft realized that stability is incredibly important to business process.

Within every organization is an amassment of processes. Processes are critical to every organization, whether you realize it or not. Maybe a new account has to be opened, or a new property has to be managed or transitioned: A process will be in place to help you get the job done. When you get down to it, the amount of processes that happen in and around any organization is staggering. We could produce a binder full of processes in a few hours.

In the SharePoint world, the orchestrator of processes is workflow. Using workflow, you can integrate not only technical processes, such as approving documents, but also human-based processes, such as giving a property tour.

In SharePoint 2016, Microsoft focused on increasing stability. To reduce the confusion around building and maintaining existing workflows, Microsoft chose to let workflow developers continue to use SharePoint Designer 2013 to build workflows in SharePoint 2016 and SharePoint Online.

Workflow is covered in Chapter 21, but to go further, you can visit the Getting Started page on TechNet to see how it all fits together.

You might also check out workflow development platforms from Nintex (www. intex.com/sharepoint) and K2 (www.k2.com/sharepoint).

Taking SharePoint for a Spin

```
https://www.microsoft.com/en-us/download/details.aspx?id=51493
```

If you are in the IT world and you want to check out SharePoint Server 2016, just download it for free and give it a spin.

```
https://products.office.com/en-us/sharepoint/sharepoint-online-
collaboration-software
```

On the other hand, if you would rather just use SharePoint, then you can sign up for a free trial account on Office 365 and see what SharePoint Online has to offer.

Staying Current: The SharePoint Blog

```
https://blogs.office.com/sharepoint
```

The SharePoint product team maintains a blog where they keep the community informed about what is coming and what is changing. If you want to stay current with SharePoint, be sure to add this blog to your list.

Chapter 25

Ten Ways to Maintain Control with Governance

*G*overnance has gotten kind of a bad rap, in part because of its association with the banking scandals of recent years. People hear the word and get all squirrely and anxious, especially when someone proposes governance that affects them. But a well-crafted website governance plan isn't about restricting people; in fact, it contains just enough detail to ensure a certain level of consistency and oversight. Website governance is about the people, policies, and processes that craft your site. *Your* governance helps you figure out how to apply all the best new SharePoint features you can read about in this book.

In this chapter, we show you ten things that influence how you think about your SharePoint governance.

Failure Is Not an Option (Neither Is Looking Away and Whistling)

One of Microsoft's key SharePoint product drivers was the goal to put more control and configuration in the hands of the users; SharePoint was designed to be The Platform of the People.

And people, as you've probably noticed, tend to be unpredictable. So SharePoint + Human Nature = Chaos. Sooner or later, an uncontrolled proliferation of sites and subsites, ways of doing things, ways of tagging and applying metadata, and ways of managing documents will produce a very unwieldy SharePoint installation indeed. Trying to identify and implement governance at that point can be an exercise in frustration.

This is a long way of saying that you'll have to address governance sooner or later. Take our advice: Make SharePoint governance a high priority and start now.

Getting Executive Buy-In and Support

Successful governance plans usually have a high-visibility advocate to support and communicate them. So find an executive to buy in. You won't have too hard a time making the case to leadership; they've already invested in a powerful SharePoint platform, and it's probably supporting functions that are crucial to the success of your organization. Line up executive support and enlist that support to drive the formation of and participation in governance committee activities.

Building an Effective Governance Group

IT commonly dominates governance committees; they have to manage server space, deal with security groups, and implement new functionality. These are ample motivation to formalize much of what they do with SharePoint. But a governance committee comprised entirely or even largely of IT resources won't get you where you need to be.

We recommend that in addition to your executive sponsor, your governance group represent a diverse mix:

>> **Include representatives from the business.** The information workers who use SharePoint all the time often are in the best position to produce realistic governance policies and to identify governance gaps, too.

>> **Include representatives from any compliance areas.** They can advocate for governance that promotes adherence to regulations that affect your business.

>> **Recruit folks from corporate communications and training.** These people are well placed not only to address governance in areas such as branding but also can help craft a plan to publicize governance decisions and provide organizational change management to support those decisions.

Finding the Right Level

Don't try to identify and address everything that someone might do with SharePoint; provide guardrails to steer your users in the appropriate things to do or to avoid. Those things vary by organization; there's no magic list of what to address. (Larger organizations tend to need more governance than smaller organizations.)

Over time, your governance group will uncover areas that need governance, and this will be helped along if you already have a clear process in place to propose, evaluate, and implement governance when and where the need arises.

Yours, Mine, Ours: Deciding Who Owns What

Kick-start a governance effort by thinking about who: Who can do what? Who owns what? For example, you might start with identifying who can provision top-level sites and who can provision subsites. Or who should determine where certain types of documents belong. Or who decides what merits a new content type (and who owns the changes to it).

If you have global navigation, identify who decides what goes there. And so on. The who will suggest the how, so you can consider that next.

One of our favorite governance exercises is to project the home page on the screen for your governance group. Then ask who has the authority to update the page. Because the home page usually links to so many other pages, it naturally leads the discussion into other areas of the portal that need ownership.

(Re)Visiting Social Networking Policies

If you have a social media governance plan in place, it may have been developed to govern external social networking tools; if this is the case, you need to revisit it in the context of SharePoint.

When social media, such as instant messaging, started to become pervasive, a lot of companies responded by locking Internet access to those applications out of fear about what employees would say and how much time they'd waste using them. Likewise, Internet discussion boards and wikis were treated with suspicion, and all kinds of corporate rules and regulations rose around them, making a lot of corporate intranets more like prisons. Over time, some companies evolved governance around when and how employees used external social networking on company time or using the company name. The goal was to keep everyone focused on documents and data and to minimize interpersonal exchanges.

Eventually, forward-thinking organizations recognized that actively facilitating informal interactions between individuals could benefit the organization by making the exchange of information more efficient, uncovering hidden pools of expertise, and (oh, by the way) recognizing that people are social creatures who need a certain degree of human contact to feel happy at work.

SharePoint 2016 includes components of the social media used in the real world into the workplace. And the ability for employees not only to connect with their peers but also use a corporate-sanctioned tool (SharePoint) to follow coworkers' activities (via live feeds and Twitter-like microblogging status updates), exchange opinions with peers (via social tagging and ratings), and pool information (wikis) represents a significant change from external social media. So if you have a specific governance policy around social media, revisit it in the context of internal communications. You'll probably find that you need a whole new strategy.

Design and Branding

Whether your SharePoint is an internal portal or a public-facing website, the interface should reflect your corporate image, present a certain level of design integrity, and provide users with a consistent navigation scheme that helps them find their way around.

Your governance plan should address look and feel and how things such as global navigation persist across your site. (To find out more about the look and feel capabilities of SharePoint, check out Chapter 13.)

Content Management

Metadata, content types, and taxonomies (oh my!) can help reduce the plague of redundant-but-slightly-different information.

To leverage the content management of your SharePoint installation, encourage consistency around metadata and how things are tagged. Content types are a great way to ensure that a core set of tags are consistently applied to similar content, making the content easier to find, easier to reuse, and easier to filter. So identify key metadata that needs to be formalized via content types and applied across SharePoint sites, and then develop governance around them.

Reusing Web Parts

One great feature of SharePoint is the fact that someone can create a really useful Web Part and then export and import it for use somewhere else. Plenty of third-party Web Parts are available for download on the web. Unfortunately, some Web Parts contain malicious code that can pose security problems or just simply don't work as advertised. Likewise, even some internally developed Web Parts can present problems if they allow users to configure them. When you're ready to use a third-party Web Part, make sure you look at a reputable company with plenty of SharePoint expertise.

Web Parts need to be subjected to controls before they're added to your SharePoint sites. Develop governance around how they're tested and approved, what the change control process looks like, and how they're released and made available.

Keeping Things Current: Web Operations Management

Web Operations Management is the care and feeding of your SharePoint sites. You may find it's easy to think about SharePoint sites as projects with defined beginnings, middles, and ends. But in reality, they're more organic than that. Websites are like living entities, which grow and change over time. Like decorative hedges, they require pruning and maintenance or they get out of control pretty fast.

The more traffic your site sees, the more important it is to stay on top of that maintenance. Web Operations Managers wield the pruning shears that shape SharePoint to reflect the strategic vision and technical goals of the company while ensuring that things like verifying that links still work or identifying and deleting irrelevant or outdated content get done. You need to designate someone with a green thumb to prune and water your SharePoint site.

Chapter 26

Ten Ways to Become a SharePoint Guru

As a SharePoint expert, you can add value to key SharePoint projects and your organization in general. By understanding the capabilities of SharePoint and understanding what is and isn't possible, you can steer a project and achieve efficiencies. By developing an encyclopedic knowledge of SharePoint, you avoid wasting the time of an army of people trying to figure out SharePoint for the first time. You will quickly become the go-to person for SharePoint in your organization. And because SharePoint is central to most processes, you will by default become a valuable asset. Don't believe us? Just put your resume up on a job board after you're a SharePoint expert and see how many organizations come calling.

In this chapter, we share with you some of the resources and approaches that we've used to master SharePoint. Even if your goal isn't mastery, these suggestions help you get up to speed and become a SharePoint expert in no time.

Getting Information from the Horse's Mouth

If you use SharePoint, then chances are you have used Microsoft's websites. In fact, you probably spend a lot of time on the support.office.com site because it comes up at the top of most search results.

If you're an IT professional, chances are you've used Microsoft's TechNet site, which is dedicated to the technical aspects of its products. On TechNet, you find technical libraries and administrator guides for IT administrators for SharePoint (and every other Microsoft product). The library includes loads of information on planning and deploying your SharePoint implementation. You also find dozens of worksheets you can use to assist in your planning. You can use TechNet to find all sorts of satiable information.

See Chapter 24 for the top ten greatest SharePoint content locations.

Microsoft's site dedicated to developers — the Microsoft Developer Network (MSDN) — features portals showcasing development-related articles and resources. You can find a Developer Center for SharePoint along with all the other Microsoft products. The home page for MSDN is `http://msdn.microsoft.com`. You can find the SharePoint Developer Center at `http://msdn.microsoft.com/en-us/sharepoint`.

TIP

Be sure to check out the latest edition of *MSDN Magazine*, the Microsoft Journal for Developers, while you're on MSDN. You'll find lots of detailed articles explaining how stuff works. Access *MSDN Magazine* at `http://msdn.microsoft.com/en-us/magazine`.

Software development kits (SDKs) are excellent resources for finding out how to develop custom SharePoint applications. Even if you never plan on writing one line of code, SDKs provide extensive documentation on product architecture. If you want to get your mind around what makes SharePoint work, poke your head into the SDK.

You can access the SharePoint SDKs online via the Developer Centers on MSDN. You can also find links that download the SDKs on the MSDN Developer Centers. When you download an SDK, it usually includes sample applications to demonstrate developer opportunities. The SharePoint Developer Center is located at `http://msdn.microsoft.com/en-us/sharepoint/aa905688.aspx`.

One of the best resources for accessing end-user documentation is Office Online. You'll find walkthroughs of all sorts of tasks and resources for use with SharePoint clients and servers. You can find Office Online at `https://office.microsoft.com/sharepoint`. Click the Products tab to see a list of all the products you can peruse on the site.

You can also find discussion groups for all the products in the Office 2016 suite, including SharePoint, at `www.microsoft.com/office/community/en-us/default.mspx`.

The Microsoft Download Center is an excellent resource for finding all sorts of downloads. By conducting an advanced search, you can choose SharePoint from a list of products to see all relevant downloads. Sort by release date to see the most recent downloads first. Visit the Download Center at `www.microsoft.com/downloads`.

TIP

Any time you download a file from Microsoft's website, be sure to scroll to the bottom of the page to see a list of related downloads.

Reading SharePoint Blogs

Now that SharePoint has been around for a while, you can easily find lots of good resources online. Plenty of websites are dedicated to SharePoint. And the blogosphere is chock-full of people blogging about SharePoint. Generally speaking, most of what you find about previous versions of SharePoint still applies to SharePoint 2016. However, we recommend avoiding content related to SharePoint 2003, 2007, and 2010. Most content for SharePoint 2013 is still relevant for SharePoint 2016.

Microsoft encourages its product teams and employees to blog about the products they're working on. These blogs give you an insider's track on announcements and tutorials that you can't get anywhere else:

>> **SharePoint Team Blog:** This is the official blog of Microsoft's SharePoint Product Group. You can find SharePoint-related announcements at `https://blogs.office.com/sharepoint`.

>> **Microsoft Cloud Blog:** Read everything you ever wanted to know about Office 365, including SharePoint Online, at `http://blogs.office.com/b/microsoft_office_365_blog`.

>> **Office Team Blogs:** This blog covers all of the latest Microsoft Office products. http://blogs.office.com.

>> **Searching MSDN Blogs:** Perhaps the best way to find good articles in blog posts from Microsoft employees is to search their blogosphere at http://blogs.msdn.com/search.

Finding Local User Groups

Most major cities have a user group (or two) dedicated to SharePoint. If your city or town doesn't, look for a .NET or Windows group and ask about SharePoint. User groups are a great place to connect with other SharePoint junkies (or newbies). Groups in larger towns often have SharePoint celebrities visit from time to time.

Many user groups also have an online presence. If you can't find a group in your immediate area, go online and find the one closest to you. These groups often use SharePoint and post articles and content from their meetings. Maybe they'd be willing to use Skype so you can connect online.

We also recommend keeping an eye on the Microsoft Events and Webcasts page (www.microsoft.com/events). You might find an event in your area or one worth traveling to.

Building a Virtual Lab

Sometimes, you just need a place to play. That's the role of a virtual lab. (And not the role of your personal My Site, we might add.) Running a virtual lab is easier than you think.

TIP

Another option is to set up a Site Collection in your Office 365 tenant that you use as a playground. Then you can log into the site from anywhere and work with SharePoint. This is great for end users learning SharePoint and exploring Share-Point Online. If you are looking to learn more about SharePoint On-Premises, then you can leverage some of the other options we outline in this section.

In the old days, you had to use dedicated hardware to run a lab. Now, you can use software in a virtual machine — a kind of machine inside a machine. We use a dedicated server to host lots of virtual machines, but we also run virtual machines on our laptops all the time.

Popular virtualization platforms include Microsoft's Hyper-V, VMWare's Workstation, and Oracle Virtual Box. If you use virtual machines on your own hardware, it takes some time to get up to speed.

If you want to have a company host your virtual machine in the cloud, you can check out Microsoft's Azure services and Amazon's Web Services. Lately, we have been using the Azure service and have been very happy.

You don't even have to build your own virtual machine. Microsoft has made available a prebuilt virtual machine in Azure so all you have to do to create a new virtul machine is log into Azure and choose the SharePoint 2016 template.

This has really saved strain on our backs because we no longer have to lug around a beefy laptop with all our virtual machines stored on external drives. We carry a light laptop and connect to our virtual machines (hosted in Azure) over the Internet.

Starting with a Good Foundation

If you really want to master SharePoint, you need a good foundation. SharePoint is built on the .NET Framework, which is a good starting place, but it also helps to know these skills:

>> Web developer skills, such as XHTML, CSS, and JavaScript for creating visually interesting user experiences

>> XML, XSLT, and XPath for manipulating content into the format you need to drive great user experiences

>> ASP.NET for understanding how to get the most out of the SharePoint toolkit

>> HTML and .NET development for creating next-generation visual presentation of content and building desktop SharePoint applications

Depending on what you're trying to master in SharePoint, you may need other domain-specific foundations.

Borrowing from Others

The code-sharing site CodePlex and GitHub are great places to find utilities and add-ons that help you get the most out of SharePoint. Not only can you find useful tools, but you can also download the source code. Even if you aren't a coder, sometimes just reading through the help text and the code can give you insights as to how things work in SharePoint.

You can find CodePlex online at `www.codeplex.com` and GitHub at `https://github.com`.

Getting Certified

Microsoft offers certifications for their products. You can find specifics at

`https://www.microsoft.com/en-us/learning`

Pursuing certification is a great way to really dig into any technology; it forces you to get familiar with all the dark corners of the software that you might otherwise ignore.

Taking a Peek under the Covers

One way to really get acquainted with SharePoint is to review the source of the web pages rendered by SharePoint. We like to use Chrome and Firefox because they both color-code the text. You can look at different kinds of pages — publishing pages and Web Part pages — to see the differences. Or you can create a new Web Part page using SharePoint Designer 2013 and then review the code after you methodically add and remove things from the page. Watching the source code change in the browser, you start to see the naming conventions and figure out how things work.

We also like to use a tool such as Firebug with Firefox to view the hierarchical structure of the page. This tool gives you lots of good information about whatever site you're viewing.

Digging Deeper under the Covers

When we're trying to figure out how to do something in SharePoint, we always ask: How did the Microsoft developers do it? All the site templates, pages, and Web Parts that come with SharePoint can be reviewed to see how they're implemented.

All these elements are stored in the 15 Hive, which is located at `C:\Program Files\Common Files\microsoft shared\Web Server Extensions\<version number>`. Most of what you want to review is in the Templates folder. This is where you find everything from the Publishing Portal template to the templates used to display menus on the web page.

WARNING

This is a look-but-don't-touch exercise. Don't change these files because they're used by the system. If you want to open them and check them out, make sure to copy them to a location such as your desktop or Documents folder. Never edit the files SharePoint is actually using.

Deconstructing a SharePoint Site

Visual Studio also provides some great new tools for deconstructing SharePoint sites. With Visual Studio, you can explore a site and copy items, such as columns and content types, for reuse. One of our favorite features is the ability to import a site template into Visual Studio. That means you can create a site with the browser, save it as a site template, and then import the template into Visual Studio. Then you can see the underlying XML that SharePoint uses to define the site.

Index

Symbols and Numerics

Approve permission
level, 187

approvers, identifying, 257

Approvers option, 175,
299–300

approving
about, 237
items, 302–303

apps
about, 31, 75–76
accessing, 77
Ad Hoc views, 121–122
adding columns, 93–100
adding to Quick
Launch, 168
adding to sites, 76–77
Calculated columns,
103–105
checking status of
workflows in, 304
choosing display styles,
119–120
configuring General
Settings, 80–90
creating, 91–107
creating Calendar view,
122–123
displaying tasks in Gantt
view, 123
downloading from
SharePoint Store,
106–107
editing data, 117–119
filtering with views,
115–116
getting documents into,
239–246
importing spreadsheets as,
101–103
included in default site, 313
Lookup columns, 103,
105–106

managing data in
Datasheet view, 120–121
planning, 92
removing from Quick
Launch, 168
reusing columns in, 96
security of, 177–183
settings, 78–80
Title column, 100–101
using folders in, 244
validating data entry,
98–100
viewing data in, 109–126

Apps category, 67

archiving
about, 275
Content Organizer,
281–283
creating information
management policies,
276–280
managing records, 283–284
placing records on litigation
hold, 284–285
setting up Records Centers,
280–281
terminology, 276

Arial, 162

ASP.NET, 149

assigning
permissions, 171–172, 328
user profiles/roles, 323
users as site collection
administrators, 185

asterisk (*), 261–262

asynchronous behaviors, 70

Audience Targeting option
(General Settings), 81,
89–90

auditing policy, 277

authorization model, 185

Automatically Declare Items
as Records When They
Are Added to This List
option, 283

B

background color, 163

backup, 27

barcodes policy, 277

Basic Table style option, 119

BCS (Business Connectivity
Services), 16

Blog category, 67

blogs, 199–200, 209–211,
347–348

Boolean operators, 262–263

Boxed, No Labels style
option, 119

Boxed style option, 119

branding, 16, 50, 343

browsers
SharePoint and, 8
viewing documents in,
251–252
viewing team sites in, 43–45

business applications,
SharePoint for, 9

Business Connectivity
Services (BCS), 16

Business Data category, 67

business intelligence
defined, 16–17
SharePoint for, 8–9

buy-in/support,
executive, 340

C

Calculated columns, 97, 103,
104–105

Calendar app, 49

content types, 276

Content Types option (Advanced Settings), 84

Content Types section, 79–80

contextual commands, 52, 76

contextual navigation. *See* current navigation

Contribute permission level, 187

creating

Ad Hoc views, 122

alerts, 224–225

apps, 91–107

blogs, 209–211

Calculated columns, 104–105

Calendar view, 122–123

client portals in SharePoint Online, 321–329

discussion board apps, 215

documents in OneDrive, 195–196

folders within apps, 244

information management policies, 276–280

List workflows for Documents app, 293–294

permissions for apps/documents, 179–180

permissions for subsites, 177–178

profiles, 202–203

public websites, 309–319

SharePoint sites, 39–41

Standard view, 112–120

views for small screens, 230–231

Web Part pages, 60–61

wiki apps, 212

Wiki Content pages, 55–60

workflows, 292–295

credentials, 325

CRM (Customer Relationship Management) system, 288

Currency column, 97

current navigation

about, 142

configuring, 145–146

custom apps. *See* apps

Custom List app, 31

Custom Send to Destination option (Advanced Settings), 85

Custom View, 111

Customer Relationship Management (CRM) system, 288

D

data, viewing in apps, 109–126

data center, 26–27

data entry, validating, 98–100

Datasheet view, 111, 120–121

Date and Time column, 97

deconstructing SharePoint sites, 351

default view settings, 125

deleting

groups, 178

permissions, 178

Web Parts, 71–72

deprecated, 208

description, changing, 81

design, 343

Design Manager link (Look and Feel section), 138

Design permission level, 187

Designers group, 175

developer, 336

device channels, 231

Device Channels link (Look and Feel section), 138

Dialogs option (Advanced Settings), 85

disabling

content approval, 258

features, 152–154

Quick Launch, 168–169

Discard Check Out button, 250

discussion boards

about, 214

creating apps, 215

posting to, 215–216

replying to, 215–216

Discussion Groups (website), 347

displaying

RSS feeds, 221–223

tasks in Gantt view, 123

views via Web Parts, 125–126

Windows Media Player, 68

displays, choosing styles for, 119–120

DNS name, 323

document sets, 276

Document Sets category, 67

Document Template option (Advanced Settings), 84

document workflow, 238

document/item administrators, 184

documents

archiving. *See* archiving

checking in/out, 248–250

creating in OneDrive, 195–196

editing properties, 247–248

following from other sites, 197–198

getting into apps, 239–246

moving, 243

recovering deleted, 252–254

restoring from Recycle Bin, 253

security of, 177–183

sending links to, 250–251

sending via email, 240

sharing, 238

updating properties using Quick Edit view, 242–243

uploading, 48, 239–246

viewing in browsers, 251–252

working with, 246–252

Documents link (Quick Launch), 167

Documents section, 48

domain names, 318–319

downloading apps from SharePoint Store, 106–107

dual authentication, 45

Due Date for All Tasks option, 300

Dummies (website), 4

Duration Per Task option, 300

Duration Units option, 300

E

ECM. *See* Enterprise Content Management (ECM)

Edge, 43

eDiscovery, 17

Edit Links button, 166

Edit option, 114

Edit permission level, 187

Edit the Current View options, 69–70

editing

app data with Quick Edit, 117–119

document properties, 247–248

pages, 316–317

Web Part properties, 70–71

wiki pages, 213–214

ellipsis, 246–247, 249

email, sending documents via, 240

EMail a Link button (Share & Track group), 207

embedding YouTube videos, 57

Enable Content Approval option, 300

enabling

content approval, 255–256

features, 152–154

RSS feeds, 219

End on Document Change option, 300

End on First Rejection option, 300

Enterprise Content Management (ECM)

defined, 20

SharePoint for, 8

Enterprise Keywords, compared with social tags, 60

Enterprise-class software, 21

equality operators, 116

Everyone feed, 217

Everyone group, 175

Excel Services Viewers group, 175

excluding terms in searches, 262

executable files, 242

executive buy-in/ support, 340

Expand Groups option, 300

expert, becoming an, 345–351

Explore SharePoint (website), 334

extending SharePoint with features, 154–155

Extensible Stylesheet Language Transformations (XSLT) template, 223

External Data column, 98

external users, 323

extranet, 42–43

F

failure, 340

farm, 132

farm administrator, 132

FAST, 19, 260

favorite sites, tracking, 200–202

features

about, 151–152

disabling, 152–154

enabling, 152–154

exploring, 154

extending SharePoint with, 154–155

feeds, 216–218

fields, 92

15 Hive, 351

files, executable, 242

filling in profiles, 203–204

filtering apps with views, 115–116

Filters category, 67

finding

local user groups, 348

Site Settings, 130–131

terms in proximity, 263–264

public websites *(continued)*
   existing, 312–319
   Go Daddy, 310–311
   Wix, 312
Publishing HTML, 98
publishing page, 32–33
publishing sites, 55, 314
pushing content to
      smartphones, 231–232

Q

query rule, 267
Query Rules link (Search
      section), 136
query string, 67
Quick Deploy Users
      group, 175
Quick Edit
   editing app data with,
      117–119
   option (Advanced
      Settings), 85
Quick Edit view, updating
      document properties
      using, 242–243
Quick Launch
   link (Look and Feel
      section), 137
   using, 167–169
quotation marks, searching
      for strings using,
      260–261

R

Rackspace (website), 23
Rating option (General
      Settings), 80, 89
Read permission level, 187
reading RSS feeds with
      Outlook, 220–221
records

archiving. *See* archiving
managing, 283–284
placing on litigation hold,
      284–285
Records Center, setting up,
      280–281
records management,
      18–19
records management site
      template, 276
recovering deleted
      documents, 252–254
Recycle Bin, 253
redundancy, 27
refining search results,
      265–266
Remember icon, 4
removing
   apps from Quick
      Launch, 168
   content from search
      results, 271–272
   permissions, 178–179
   tabs in Top Link bar, 166
renaming Title column, 100
replying to discussion
      boards, 215–216
requesting SharePoint sites,
      41–43
resources, for SharePoint,
      333–334
resources, Internet. *See also*
      public websites
   Cheat Sheet, 4
   CodePlex, 350
   defined, 13
   Discussion Groups, 347
   Dummies, 4
   Explore SharePoint, 334
   Fpweb.net, 23
   GitHub, 350
   Microsoft, 348

Microsoft certification, 350
Microsoft Cloud Blog, 347
Microsoft Developer
      Network (MSDN), 346
Microsoft Download
      Center, 291, 347
Microsoft Office
      Online, 347
MSDN Magazine, 346
Nintex, 188, 289, 337
Office Team Blog, 348
OneDrive, 194
Pinterest, 207
Rackspace, 23
SharePoint 2016
      video, 334
SharePoint Developer
      Center, 346
SharePoint Online, 45
SharePoint Server
      2016, 338
SharePoint Team Blog, 347
TechNet, 24, 58
Wikipedia, 209
restoring
   documents from Recycle
      Bin, 253
   Web Parts, 72
Restricted Interfaces for
      Translation permission
      level, 187
Restricted Read permission
      level, 187
Restricted Readers
      group, 175
restricting access to folders,
      245–246
Result Sources link (Search
      section), 135
Result Types link (Search
      section), 135
retention policy, 277

SharePoint 2016 *(continued)*
  installing, 335–336
  maintaining, 336
  operating, 336
  page sections for, 44
  planning for, 335
  power user role, 12
  requesting sites, 41–43
  resources for, 333–334
  technical administrator
    user role, 12
  terminology for, 15–20
  tools, 35
  user role, 12
  video for, 334
  viewing on mobile
    devices, 230
  visitor role, 11
  web browser and, 8
  web pages, 52–55
  workflow in, 289–291
SharePoint Designer
  about, 291
  connecting to sites, 292
  creating workflows,
    292–295
  Custom View, 111
  managing access to, 188
SharePoint Developer Center
  (website), 346
SharePoint farm, 60
SharePoint groups, 42
SharePoint Online
  about, 9, 10, 21–23, 132
  benefits of, 25–27
  compared with SharePoint
    On-Premises, 24–25,
    322, 336
  creating client portals in,
    321–329
  feature matrix, 24

  navigational elements in,
    164
  popularity of, 23
  sharing documents
    with, 179
  website, 45
SharePoint On-Premises,
  compared with
  SharePoint Online,
  24–25, 322, 336
SharePoint Server 2016
  about, 9
  website, 338
SharePoint Server Enterprise
  Site features, 154
SharePoint Server Publishing
  Infrastructure feature,
  152, 164
SharePoint Server Standard
  Site features, 154
SharePoint Store,
  downloading apps from,
  106–107
SharePoint Team Blog
  (website), 347
SharePoint team site
  about, 47–48
  changing style and
    brand, 50
  collaborating, 50
  organizing, 49–50
  sharing your, 49
  syncing, 50
  uploading documents, 48
sharing
  about, 237
  documents, 238
  SharePoint team site, 49
Silverlight Web Part, 68
Single Line of Text column, 97
single sign-on, 45
Single Sign-On (SSO), 325

Site Actions section (Site
  Settings), 139
Site Administration section
  (Site Settings), 134–135
site administrators, 184
Site App Permissions link
  (Users and Permissions
  section), 132
Site Assets Library option
  (Advanced Settings), 85
Site Collection
  about, 41
  administrators, 184
  security, 176–177
  settings, 184–185
Site Collection
  Administration section
  (Site Settings), 139–140
Site Collection
  Administrators link
  (Users and Permissions
  section), 131
Site Columns link (Web
  Designer Galleries
  section), 133
Site Content and Structure
  tool, 303–305
Site Content Types link
  (Web Designer Galleries
  section), 133
Site Contents link (Quick
  Launch), 167
site icon, changing, 158–160
site mailbox, 50
Site Members, 172
site name, 42
Site Owners, 172
Site Pages, 53
Site Pages library, 56
Site permission type, 185
Site Permissions link (Users
  and Permissions
  section), 131

third-party companies, 154–155

third-party products, 329

third-party Web Part, 70

Times New Roman, 162

Tip icon, 3

Title, Description, and Logo link (Look and Feel section), 137

Title column, working with, 100–101

Title property, 114, 248

titles, changing, 81

toggling views, 110

Toolbar Type section, 70

tools, SharePoint 2016, 35

Top Link bar, 142, 165–167

Top Link Bar link (Look and Feel section), 137

top-level site, 172

tracking
favorite sites, 200–202
locations, 232

transaction app, 105

Translation Managers group, 175

Tree View, 168–169

Tree View link (Look and Feel section), 137

Twitter, 217–218

U

updating
document properties using Quick Edit view, 242–243
page properties, 317
web pages, 313

uploading documents, 48, 239–246

URL, 42, 251

usability, 163

user accounts, managing, 325–328

user groups, local, 348

user profiles/roles, 323

users
about, 10–12
accessing, 325–326
adding to groups, 173–174
assigning as site collection administrators, 185
checking permissions, 182–183
external, 323
types of, 42

Users and Permissions section (Site Settings), 131–132

V

validating data entry, 98–100

validation, 88

Validation option (General Settings), 80, 88–89

vanity domains, 318–319

Verdana, 162

verifying
documents in/out, 248–250
status of workflows, 304–305
status of workflows in apps, 304
user permissions, 182–183

Version column, 115

version histories, 238

Versioning option (General Settings), 80, 81–84

Versioning Settings page, 249

video
inserting, 57
for SharePoint 2016, 334

View Only permission level, 187

View tab (Ribbon), 248

viewing
data in apps, 109–126
document properties using Ribbon, 248
documents in browsers, 251–252
group permissions, 181–182
listings of features, 153
Office documents on mobile devices, 232–233
RSS feeds, 218–220
search results, 265–266
SharePoint on mobile devices, 230
site permissions, 185–187
team sites in browsers, 43–45

views
Access, 111
Ad Hoc, 121–122
All Documents, 109–110
All Items, 109–110
apps, 109–111
Calendar, 111, 122–123
Classic, 230
Contemporary, 230
creating for small screens, 230–231
Custom, 111
Datasheet, 111, 120–121
displaying via Web Parts, 125–126
filtering apps with, 115–116
formats of, 111–112
Full Screen, 230
Gantt, 111, 123
managing, 124–125

About the Author

Rosemarie Withee is president of Portal Integrators (www.portalintegrators.com) and founder of Scrum Now (www.scrumnow.org), the first Philippine-based Scrum organization with locations in Seattle, Washington and Laguna, Philippines. Portal Integrators is a Scrum-based software and services firm. She is the lead author of *Office 365 For Dummies* (Wiley, 2016), *SharePoint 2016 For Dummies* (Wiley, 2016), and *Office 365 Apps For Dummies* (Wiley, 2016).

Rosemarie earned a Master of Science degree in Economics at San Francisco State University. In addition, Rosemarie also studied Marketing at UC Berkeley-Extension and holds a Bachelor of Arts degree in Economics and a Bachelor of Science degree in Marketing from De La Salle University, Philippines.

Ken Withee is founder of Portal Integrators (www.portalintegrators.com), a Scrum-based software and services firm. He lives with his wife Rosemarie in Seattle, Washington. He is the author and coauthor of a number of books on Microsoft technologies and currently writes TechNet articles on Office Server products for Microsoft.

Ken earned a Master of Science degree in Computer Science at San Francisco State University. He has more than 14 years of professional computer and management experience working with a vast range of technologies. He is a Microsoft Certified Technology Specialist and is certified in SharePoint, SQL Server, and .NET.

Author's Acknowledgments

We would like to acknowledge our families in both the U.S. and Philippines. An extraordinary amount of special thanks to Katie Mohr, Christopher Morris, and the rest of the For Dummies team for providing more support than we ever thought possible. It is truly amazing how much work goes into a single book. We would also like to send a special acknowledgment to Genelyn "Gen" Ancheta, who is an amazing person and developer. She has saved the day so often that we think of her as a superhero.

We would also like to thank the Portal Integrators team in Laguna, Philippines for their hard work, dedication, and late nights. They are truly an extraordinary team and we are very lucky to work with them. A little about them below, in alphabetical order:

Ace Cyrille Gatcion earned a degree of Bachelor of Science in Computer Science from Laguna College, and has been a web developer at Portal Integrators for two years. He specializes in programming with JavaScript and PHP and has also been a Microsoft Certified Professional and Specialist in HTML5 with JavaScript and CSS3 since May 2014. Ace has also just recently finished leading a SharePoint-based project, which has been one of the biggest challenges he has faced and conquered. When he's not working, he de-stresses by playing with his beloved Siamese cat, and working on his photo-editing skills.

Genelyn "Gen" Ancheta holds a Bachelor of Science degree in Computer Engineering from Colegio de San Juan de Letran. She is a tireless seeker of knowledge, a thinker, and incidentally, also a web developer with Portal Integrators. Gen has more than 10 years of web, mobile, and database development experience. She is a Microsoft Certified Solutions Developer specializing in SharePoint applications. She loves listening to music, and when she is not busy debugging code, she indulges in watching movies and TV series.

Jeff Michael De Las Alas is a developer with Portal Integrators who finished his Bachelor's degree in Computer Science from Laguna College. Before being with Portal Integrators, he worked as an intern in a cable TV company from his hometown. Jeff's excellence in his chosen field was shown when he received several awards from his college, including the Best in Thesis, Excellence in Programming, and Leadership awards. Achievements aside, Jeff is just a regular guy who likes watching anime in his free time.

Mariel Pamulaklakin is a developer at Portal Integrators. She graduated from the University of the Philippines – Los Baños with a Bachelor's degree in Computer Science. She has been with Portal Integrators for over two years, continuously honing her skills in web and mobile development in the company. She is also a Microsoft Certified Professional and a Specialist in programming in HTML5 with JavaScript and CSS3. Outside of work, Mariel is a church choir member, a dog lover, and a self-confessed nerd who dreams of traveling the world in the near future.

Marriel Bondad holds a Bachelor of Science degree in Information Technology graduate from Laguna College. She is a developer with Portal Integrators, and has worked as an intern in a local government office. She can be described as a responsible and diligent person when it comes to her career, which was proven by her achievements as a Best in Programming and Leadership awardee, and a scholarship grantee. Marriel also served as President of the Junior Philippine Computer Society – Laguna College Chapter. Outside her professional life, she is a semi-introvert and an aspiring photographer who enjoys the adventurous side of life, discovering new places, and working on achieving her dreams.

Dedication

We would like to dedicate this book to our families. Both in the Philippines and here in the United States.

Publisher's Acknowledgments

Executive Editor: Katie Mohr

Project Editor: Tamilmani Varadharaj

Copy Editor: Christopher Morris

Technical Editor: Genelyn Ancheta

Editorial Assistant: Kayla Hoffman

Sr. Editorial Assistant: Cherie Case

Cover Image: ©agsandrew/Shutterstock